D1158247

MILES

ON MILES

INTERVIEWS AND ENCOUNTERS
WITH MILES DAVIS

MILES

ON MILES

INTERVIEWS AND ENCOUNTERS
WITH MILES DAVIS

Edited by Paul Maher Jr. and Michael K. Dorr

Lawrence Hill Books

Library of Congress Cataloging-in-Publication Data

Miles on Miles : interviews and encounters with Miles Davis / edited by Paul
Maher Jr. and Michael K. Dorr. — 1st ed.
    p. cm.
    Includes bibliographical references and index.
    ISBN-13: 978-1-55652-706-7
    ISBN-10: 1-55652-706-3
    1. Davis, Miles—Interviews. 2. Jazz musicians—United States—Interviews.
I. Maher, Paul, 1963– II. Dorr, Michael K. III. Title.

    ML419.D39A5 2008
    788.9'2165092—dc22

                                        2008014067

Interior design: Visible Logic

Copyright © 2009 by Paul Maher Jr. and Michael K. Dorr
All rights reserved
First edition
Published by Lawrence Hill Books
An imprint of Chicago Review Press, Incorporated
814 North Franklin Street
Chicago, Illinois 60610
ISBN 978-1-55652-706-7
Printed in the United States of America
5 4 3 2 1

To David Amram
Master musician, true friend, and inspiration
  —PAUL MAHER JR.

To Samuel Menashe
Poet and friend

For all the right reasons
  —MICHAEL K. DORR

CONTENTS

INTRODUCTION

Some called him the "Prince of Darkness" or the "Picasso of Invisible Art." He was the consummate rebel, exuding the daunting aura of the "Prince of Silence" or even Mr. "Don't Call Me Cool." All of these monikers, however, contradict the man who brightens these pages with canny insights and droll humor as he expounds his philosophy about the skewed social order of his world. There is the mediocrity and the genius of his musical peers, his hatred of racism, his insistence that the word "jazz" is nothing more than a pejorative term for "niggers": "Jazz is a nigger word," he states to an unsuspecting interviewer. As if what Miles thinks about the word "jazz" is sheer nonsense, the interviewer goes on using the word anyway for lack of a better way to classify Davis's music. And for certain, much of what Miles did accomplish is unclassifiable—much like the man himself.

Most times, Miles comes across as anything but the "Prince of Darkness": he's bright, comical, brutally honest, intelligent, in control, and entirely at ease even in the most trying or inauspicious occasion. He is honest to the extreme, so much so that at times he becomes graphic about things like sex, his copious heroin use, his short period playing the pimp. Then there's his constant vernacular mainstay—"motherfucker." "He plays like a motherfucker," "my band is a bunch of motherfuckers," "those guys are dirty motherfuckers," "my legs hurt like a motherfucker during that tour," "she's fine as a motherfucker." His language is colorful, leaving intact the vocabulary of a Midwestern black man from East St. Louis, raised in a middle-class household. He studied for a while at Juilliard, but absorbed the bulk of what he learned from the city streets, within the din of smoky Harlem clubs, or from watching on the sidelines the true masters of the form: Charlie "Bird" Parker, Thelonious Monk, Bud Powell, and Dizzy Gillespie.

After a tour of duty with Parker, Miles was ready to leap forward confidently, a flashy zeal in his tailor-cut Italian suit, from under Duke Ellington's elongated shadow. Ultimately, and conscientiously, by not "Uncle Tomming" to his audience, by not grinning like Louis Armstrong or performing upon a shoeshine box, he swore musical fidelity to self-respect, not only for what he was accomplishing but also because he, too, was a valid card-carrying member of the United States of America. He shone a whole new light upon his race. If Adam Clayton Powell was dazzling at the pulpit, then Miles Davis dominated the stage. He played with authenticity, with feeling, always challenging the audience not to underestimate just what he was doing when his back was turned away from them under his lonesome spotlight. He didn't have to be poor and play his horn from the broken stairs of a southern chicken-shack to play the blues. His contribution was just as valid as those Mississippi Delta bluesmen who had forged the genre decades earlier.

Being a musician, oftentimes he wanted to discuss anything *but* music, because his music said everything he wanted to say by virtue of its existence. He hated discussing his past and despised detailing his guiding aesthetic. Most times he directed the topic toward his band members, as in "Herbie plays like a motherfucker." This presents an undeniable challenge for the interviewer: either face the likely prospect of disdain for pursuing the role of an intrusive journalist or charge determinedly into the dark abyss hoping to emerge from the other side unscathed (and with enough material to complete the assigned article). When this doesn't work, writers instead describe Miles's surroundings or mannerisms or strive to capture his quick, deft sketching on a drawing pad. More banal is the avid attention the interviewers sometimes devote to how he eats, orders his food, or even how he *breathes*. In all of these things there lurks a distinct personality. Davis, for all of his quirks and foibles, comes across as a genius of music—but not of life.

A constant searing theme of these pages is racism in all its insidious incarnations. America—from the year of Miles Davis's birth in 1926 until his death in 1991 (and beyond)—still judged people on the basis of their skin color rather than on "the content of their character." Although government laws and constitutional amendments—dating from shortly after the Civil War—assured civil rights on paper, the pernicious air of racial prejudice still permeated America's streets. It wasn't going away anytime soon, if ever, and Miles knew it. His love for Ferraris and women (*white* women) made certain that his most envious detractors, enraged by his constant affronts to white entitlement, would cause the trumpeter incessant hassles.

When he was a boy, a white man calling him "nigger" chased him down the street. It was a hateful memory that echoed through the years, always resurrecting in an instant that harsh realization and harsher reality. Although critics, fans, and fellow musicians viewed him as an important and groundbreaking composer/bandleader/performer, whites waiting for Miles to "entertain" them still thought of him (as related in many of the following interviews) as just a "nigger." The bitter diatribes Miles unleashed concerning racism succeed more in revealing the depths of his sensitivity than in labeling him as a ranting anti-white bigot. David Amram, who knew Miles as an acquaintance from 1956 until his death in 1991, remembers well that sensitivity. One rainy night in 1956 Miles entered the Café Bohemia. Amram decided to play it cool and not bother the man who'd successfully captured everyone's attention and brought the bustling nightclub to a standstill. As he walked by, Amram caught a glimpse of Davis looking toward him from the corner of his red-rimmed eye, carefully considering him from behind his trademark impenetrable sunglasses. What Amram saw wasn't contempt but a steely gaze of hurt.

For all of his contributions to music and visual arts (he took up drawing and painting during the 1980s), Miles still wanted to be accepted and remembered most by people of his own race, by black youth. He was never content to be thought of as merely a "jazz" musician, a label he came to disdain. By not looking back, he learned, he could pave a road into the future. He claimed he never read what the critics wrote, but the fact that he knew they were dismissing his latest offerings made him strive all the more to be less accepted.

In the 1970s his music became denser, cacophonous, dissonant, as if daring the listener to cut through the thicket, to slice through the vines, in order to absorb Miles's intentions. Was he purposely alienating his audience? Was he catering to the audiences of the future? Since the critics couldn't peg his personality, they tried to peg his music.

"What do you want us to call it, Miles?" they asked.

"Call it music" was his simple but right-on response.

What they *could* "get" was 1980s-era pop songs. This time they could deci-mate the musical deity that was Miles by calling his latter-day output purely sentimental drivel. Miles was really selling out, instead of changing the face of music like they'd been expecting him to do with each new album. He'd done so for roughly forty years, morphing his signature phrasing through all the vari-ants that he made possible: bebop to the *Birth of the Cool* to *Kind of Blue* to *Bitches Brew* to *On the Corner* to *Tutu*. Each didn't signal a musical compromise, but rather a daring musical direction.

What the critics said, we now know, was irrelevant. Miles, in the end, would have the last word—or the last note. These pages are but myriad mirrors to his life, reflecting not only Miles but also how the world understood and treated him. Because we love his music, we love the man despite his foibles, peccadil-loes, addictions, quirks, indifference, violent outbursts, and even his percussive slap of downright rudeness. These are things we endure in order to have what we most want—our fix. Miles was especially adamant about the prospects of selling out. He told Les Tompkins in one of the interviews in this book: "I mean, I wouldn't do it, for no money, or for no place in the white man's world. Not just to make money, because then you don't have anything. You don't have as much money as whoever you're trying to ape; that's making money by being commercial. Then you don't have anything to give the world; so you're not important. You might as well be dead."

The third millennium broadens our scope of what Miles Davis achieved in his lifetime. Columbia Records continues to open its vaults and unleash on an unsuspecting public a voluminous quantity of work of surprisingly consistent quality, music that his vigorous energy and voracious creativity made possible. We have jazz (for lack of a better word), bebop, funk, soul, and syncopated fusion. He tossed all he wanted into its cacophonous fray. One has to pine for how he would've addressed these post-9/11 years, what elegy would've exuded from the vibrating brass of his horn. But we still have what is perfect already—a dauntless musical legacy of emotion and, yes, integrity. In the view of the edi-tors of this volume, his songs of rage, love, passion, fire, and bliss, as well as his wavering sound of profound sadness, are not felt elsewhere in music. He hangs it out there vulnerably and leaves it there. We hope this volume of interviews and encounters with Miles Davis succeeds in the best manner possible—by sending the reader back to those unparalleled records and transforming him or her into a listener again.

The final selection was compiled with the help of numerous Miles Davis collectors in the United States and Europe. Since Miles Davis's death in 1991 and throughout his career, an underground trading circle passed these gems from hand to hand, many surfacing from actual audiotape, some so far removed from their original sources that it becomes difficult to hear the interviewer himself.

These pieces dispel the myth that Miles Davis was a recluse and misanthrope, or that he refused interviews and remained in the public's eye as a taciturn personality. Nothing could be further from the truth; Davis was open to discussing anything but was intolerant of those interviewers who didn't do their homework. He kept at arm's length those who wanted to explore "his music," or sought to talk about it as if the music itself didn't do all the talking already. Although he would talk about his jazz contemporaries or composers as unlikely as Stockhausen and Stravinsky, he was often reluctant to discuss his own music. This poses a consistent roadblock to meeting the reader's expectation of some kind of "certain" insight into Davis's creative vision, process, and accomplishments. More often than not, what he chooses not to say tells us more about his personal desires and demons, the same demons that often created the music in the first place.

As one listens to the interview tapes, the growls and vernacular become easier to decipher, and one senses beneath Miles's rough exterior a tender, sensitive heart open to embracing the world, but always ready to shrink back into his recalcitrance. This is usually when the subject becomes caustic, crude, sometimes just plain insensitive. But these are the things that make Miles Davis interviews a revealing, interesting, invaluable read.

As editors in an ideal world, we would have liked to include *Playboy*'s September 1962 interview, its first, with Miles Davis, conducted by Alex Haley, but the magazine denied our dogged efforts to obtain permission to reprint it. Racial tensions in America at the start of the 1960s were still bristling and violent. They contributed to a surge of African American art and culture as well as to a stifling of them. The forces at large stuck in Davis's craw. He had considered himself an accomplished man of his own making as well as the product of a hardworking family. Davis took advantage of *Playboy* magazine's broad platform (it aimed its pages at a white male demographic) to voice his hatred for racial prejudice and the constant demands, underscored by racial overtones, by the press to justify his actions.

For this reason the interview is valuable, but certainly not *in*valuable to a collection of this nature for two reasons. First, the interview is widely available in earlier and recent *Playboy* collections, as well as in *Playboy Cover to Cover: The '50s* and online.

More importantly, despite its reputation as a revealing dialogue with Miles, the interview suffers from the defects of its interviewer. Alex Haley, author of the bestselling, award-winning *Roots* (which Stanley Crouch calls "one of the biggest con jobs in U.S. literary history"), was a plagiarist and fabricator, who settled a lawsuit out of court for $650,000 and whose genealogical claims have been roundly disproved. As Philip Nobile, the investigative journalist who helped expose the *Roots* hoax, only to realize that integrity often has no place in the consciousness of people who continue to profit enormously from the book and subsequent miniseries, has noted: "[Haley] did not begin stealing in *Roots* in 1976. Haley's habit went as far back as 1962 in his legendary *Playboy* interview with Miles Davis. Unable to record the uncooperative Davis on tape, Haley faked parts of the Q&A by appropriating quotes from other writers."

We would have also wanted to include one of the interviews from *DownBeat*, a great jazz magazine that followed Davis's career with care and clarity, but unfortunately its publisher was unnecessarily proprietary with reprint rights in order to assure the exclusivity of the magazine's own published collection, the majority of which are record and concert reviews and news features rather than interviews. That volume and this one are more complementary than competitive.

The one interview that we seriously regret being unable to include is *60 Minutes*'s interview with Miles. Simon & Schuster had paid a hefty advance for Davis's autobiography (cowritten with journalist Quincy Troupe) and aptly titled *Miles*. Writing a reasonably accurate account of any legendary figure's life, particularly one as long and complex as Davis's, within a few hundred pages is a daunting and monumental task. In the case of *Miles*, the pioneering trumpeter's visceral disdain for the past and his shredded memory, along with Simon & Schuster's tight deadline, exacerbated the inherent challenges. In the end, as has been well documented, Miles's autobiography relied heavily, sometimes word for word, on the work of three biographers: Eric Nisenson, Ian Carr, and Jack Chambers (especially the latter) and credited none of them. See the introduction to Chambers's 1998 single-volume paperback edition of *Milestones* for a full, fascinating discussion of this issue.

One of Simon & Schuster's conditions was that Davis must promote his autobiography. Out of this came his interview with *60 Minutes*'s Harry Reasoner. The ever-sharp Miles proved to be exceptionally irascible, thwarting with devious, mischievous pleasure Reasoner's often inane questions ("Do black musicians hurt more?" and "Do you feel young?") and his decidedly nonjournalistic judgments ("You did a lot of bad things"). Needless to say, ole Harry was neither amused nor pleased. But it makes for great reading. Unfortunately, according to CBS News Archives, "due to a restriction on this *60 Minutes* episode we cannot give you permission to reprint the transcript of the November 12, 1989, interview with Miles Davis." Despite further inquiry, no further illumination was provided as to the nature and cause of this "restriction."

But in the plethora of excellent interviews and profiles that follow, we see a man struggling with his own personality, when it's easier to evoke the poison within through the brass of his trumpet than to rely on the dubious nature of words. It's easy to sympathize with the interviewer, just trying to do his or her job. But so is Miles and it is he who earns the most sympathy.

—PAUL MAHER JR.
Fitchburg, Massachusetts

—MICHAEL K. DORR
Brooklyn, New York

SELF-PORTRAIT BY MILES DAVIS

Interviewer: George Avakian
Columbia Records Publicity, November 26, 1957

George Avakian was the man to see if one wanted to record for the prestigious Columbia record label. Since 1953, Miles had approached Avakian on several occasions seeking to break free from Prestige's jazz label. Avakian was fully aware that Davis's contract with Prestige didn't expire until 1955, and he maintained a reluctance to show even a slight interest in taking on the ambitious and able trumpeter. In July 1955 Miles's blazing performance on "'Round About Midnight" at the Newport Jazz Festival (the music press labeled it Miles's "comeback," to which Davis retorted, "What's all the fuss? I always play that way") caught the attention of Avakian and his photographer brother, Aram, who encouraged George to sign Miles as soon as possible. After haggling with Columbia executives over Davis's request of a four-thousand-dollar advance against royalties (they thought a "known junkie" would be dead before he could ever earn them back the money), the trumpeter was formally signed to Columbia's thinning jazz roster. Davis maintained a solid, historic relationship with the label until 1986, when he jumped ship to Warner Brothers.

You want me to tell you where I was born—that old story? It was in good old Alton, Illinois. In 1926. And I had to call my mother a week before my last birthday and ask her how old I would be.

I started playing trumpet in grade school. Once a week we would hold notes. Wednesdays at 2:30. Everybody would fight to play best. Lucky for me, I learned to play the chromatic scale right away. A friend of my father's brought me a book one night and showed me how to do it so I wouldn't have to sit there and hold that note all the time.

My mother wanted to give me a violin for my birthday, but my father gave me a trumpet—because he loved my mother so much!

There was a very good instructor in town. He was having some dental work done by my father. He was the one that made my father get me the trumpet. He used to tell us all about jam sessions on the Showboat, about trumpet players like Bobby Hackett and Hal Baker. "Play without any vibrato," he used to tell us. "You're gonna get old anyway and start shaking," he used to say, "no vibrato!" That's how I tried to play. Fast and light—and no vibrato.

By the time I was sixteen I was playing in a band—the Blue Devils—in East St. Louis. Sonny Stitt came to town with a band and heard us play one night. He told me, "You look like a man named Charlie Parker and you play like him too. C'mon with us."

The fellows in his band had their hair slicked down, they wore tuxedos, and they offered me sixty whole dollars a week to play with them. I went home and asked my mother if I could go with them. She said no, I had to finish my last year of high school. I didn't talk to her for two weeks. And I didn't go with the band either.

I knew about Charlie Parker in St. Louis, I even played with him there, while I was still in high school. We always used to try to play like Diz and Charlie Parker. When we heard that they were coming to town, my friend and I were the first people in the hall, me with a trumpet under my arm. Diz walked up to me and said, "Kid, do you have a union card?" I said, "Sure." So I sat in with the band that night. I couldn't read a thing from listening to Diz and Bird. Then the third trumpet man got sick. I knew the book because I loved the music so much I knew the third part by heart. So I played with the band for a couple of weeks. I had to go to New York then.

My mother wanted me to go to Fisk University. I looked in the *Esquire* book and I asked her, "Where's all of this?" Then I asked my father. He said I didn't have to go to Fisk, I could go to big New York City. In September I was in New York City. A friend of mine was studying at Juilliard, so I decided to go there too. I spent my first week in New York and my first month's allowance looking for Charlie Parker.

I roomed with Charlie Parker for a year. I used to follow him around, down to 52nd Street, where he used to play. Then he used to get me to play. "Don't be afraid," he used to tell me. "Go ahead and play." Every night I'd write down chords I heard on matchbook covers. Everybody helped me. Next day I'd play those chords all day in the practice room at Juilliard, instead of going to classes.

I didn't start writing music until I met Gil Evans. He told me to write something and send it to him. I did. It was what I played on the piano. Later I found out I could do better without the piano. (I took some piano lessons at Juilliard, but not enough.) If you don't play it good enough, you'll be there for hours and hours.

If you can hear a note, you can play it. The note I hit that sounds high, that's the only one I can play right then, the only note I can think of to play that would fit. You don't learn to play the blues. You just play. I don't even think about harmony. It just comes. You learn where to put notes so they'll sound right. You just don't do it because it's a funny chord. I used to change things because I wanted to hear them—substitute progressions and things. Now I have better taste.

Do I like composing better than playing? I can't answer that. There's a certain feeling you get from playing that you can't get from composing. And when you play, it's like a composition anyway. You make the outline. What do I like to play? I like "'Round About Midnight." In fact, I like most any ballad. If I feel like playing it.

What do I think of my own playing? I don't keep any of my records. I can't stand to hear them after I've made them. The only ones I really like are the ones I just made with Gil Evans (*Miles Ahead*), the one I made with J. J. (Johnson) on my Blue Note date about four years ago, and a date I did with Charlie Parker.

People ask me if I respond to the audience. I wouldn't like to sit up there and play without anybody liking it. If it's a large audience, I'm very pleased because they are there anyway. If it's a small audience, sometimes it doesn't matter. I enjoy playing with my own rhythm section and listening to them. I'm studying and experimenting all the time.

I know people have some rhythm and they feel things when they're good. A person has to be an invalid not to show some sign—a tap of the finger even. You don't have to applaud. I never look for applause. In Europe, they like everything you do. The mistakes and everything. That's a little bit too much.

If you play good for eight bars, it's enough. For yourself. And I don't tell anybody.

AN AFTERNOON WITH MILES DAVIS

Interviewer: Nat Hentoff
The Jazz Review, December 1958

In 1958 Miles Davis's reputation as a formidable jazz musician in his own right was affirmed by both his fiery concert performances with his great quintet of John Coltrane (tenor saxophone), Red Garland (piano), Paul Chambers (double bass), and Philly Joe Jones (drums) and by its transformation into a sextet when he included Julian "Cannonball" Adderley (alto saxophone) in the band. The long-playing records of *Milestones*, *'Round About Midnight*, and the Gil Evans collaboration of *Miles Ahead* placed the young trumpeter within the American jazz pantheon. Nat Hentoff was a jazz critic with a reputation both within his profession and among jazz musicians. He was, along with Leonard Feather, one of the only critics for whom Davis expressed any respect and admiration.

Miles lives in a relatively new building on Tenth Avenue near 57th Street. The largest area in his apartment is the living room. Like the other rooms, it is uncluttered. The furnishings have been carefully selected and are spare. Miles has a particular liking for "good wood" and explains thereby why his *DownBeat* plaques—and even his Four Roses Award from the Randall's Island "festival"—are all displayed. He has a good piano and an adequate non-stereo record player.

The idea of the afternoon—the first of a series of observations by Miles to be printed at regular intervals *[Editors: It would be the first and the last due to financial restraints.]* in this monthly—was to play a variety of recordings for him and transcribe his reactions. This was not a blindfold test, for while I find those adventures in skeet shooting entertaining, I doubt if they serve much purpose except transitory titillation.

First was Billie Holiday's 1937 *I Must Have That Man* with Wilson, Clayton, Goodman, Young, Green, Page and Jo Jones. "I love the way Billie sings," Miles began. "She sings like Lester Young and Louis Armstrong play, but I don't like all that's going on behind her. All she needed was Lester and the rhythm. The piano was ad-libbing while she was singing, which leads to conflict, and the guitar was too loud and had too much accent on every beat."

Miles was asked whether he agreed with most of the writers on jazz that the Billie of twenty years ago was the "best" Billie and that she is now in decline. "I'd rather hear her now. She's become much more mature. Sometimes you can sing words every night for five years, and all of a sudden it dawns on you what the song means. I played 'My Funny Valentine' for a long time—and didn't like it—and all of a sudden it meant something. So with Billie, you know she's not thinking now what she was in 1937, and she's probably learned more about different things. And she still has control, probably more control now than then. No, I don't think she's in decline.

"What I like about Billie is that she sings it just the way she hears it and that's usually the way best suited for her. She has more feeling than Ella and more experience in living a certain way than Ella. Billie's pretty wild, you know.

"She sings way behind the beat and then she brings it up—hitting right on the beat. You can play behind the beat, but every once in a while you have to cut into the rhythm section on the beat and that keeps everybody together. Sinatra does it by accenting a word. A lot of singers try to sing like Billie, but just the act of playing behind the beat doesn't make it sound soulful.

"I don't think that guys like Buck Clayton are the best possible accompanists for her. I'd rather hear her with Bobby Tucker, the pianist she used to have. She doesn't need any horns. She sounds like one anyway."

Miles' reaction to Clifford Brown's "Joy Spring" as played by the Oscar Peterson Trio on *The Modern Jazz Quartet and The Oscar Peterson Trio at the Opera House* (Verve MG-V 8269) was intensely negative. "Oscar makes me sick because he copies everybody. He even had to *learn* how to play the blues. Everybody knows that if you flat a third, you're going to get a blues sound. He learned that and runs it into the ground worse than Billy Taylor. You don't have to do that.

"Now take the way he plays the song. That's not what Clifford meant. He passes right over what can be done with the chords," and here Miles demonstrated on the piano, as he did frequently during the afternoon. "It's much prettier if you get into it and hear the chord weaving in and out like Bill Evans and Red Garland could do—instead of being so heavy. Oscar is jazzy; he jazzes up the tune. And he sure has devices, like certain scale patterns, that he plays all the time.

"Does he swing hard like some people say? I don't know what they mean when they say 'swing hard' anyway. Nearly everything he plays, he plays with the same degree of force. He leaves no holes for the rhythm section. The only thing I ever heard him play that I liked was his first record of *Tenderly*.

"I love Ray Brown. As for Herb Ellis, I don't like that kind of thing with guitar on every beat—unless you play it like Freddie Green does now. You listen and you'll hear how much Green has lightened his sound through the years. If you want to see how it feels with a heavy guitar, get up to play sometimes with one of them behind you. He'll drive you nuts.

"Back to Oscar. He plays pretty good when he plays in an Art Tatum form of ballad approach. And I heard him play some blues once at a medium tempo that sounded pretty good. But for playing like that with a guitar, I prefer Nat Cole. I feel though that it's a waste to use a guitar this way. If you take the guitar and have him play lines—lines like George Russell, Gil Evans or John Lewis could make—then a trio can sound wonderful."

The next record was a track from *Kenny Clarke Plays André Hodeir* (Epic LN3376). It was Miles' own *Swing Spring* and these are Hodeir's notes on the arrangement: "*Swing Spring* is also treated as a canon, after an introduction featuring an elaboration of the main element of the theme, the scale. Martial Solal's brilliant solo is followed by a paraphrase with integrated drum improvisations. Both Armand Migiani (baritone sax) and Roger Guerin (trumpet) take a short solo."

Miles hadn't looked carefully at the liner notes and was puzzled for the first few bars. "That's my tune, isn't it? I forgot all about that tune. Goddamn! Kenny Clarke can swing, can't he? That boy Solal can play, but the pianist I like in Europe is Bengt Hallberg. Damn! You know, I forgot I wrote that. That's the

16

wrong middle—in the piano solo—why does he do that? Because it's easier, I suppose. The arrangement is terrible. It was never meant to be like that. It sounds like a tired modern painting—with skeletons in it. He writes pretty good in spots, but he overcrowds it. Kenny and Solal save it. I think I'll make another record of this tune. It was meant to be just like an exercise almost." Miles went to the piano and played the theme softly. "It was based on that scale there and when you blow, you play in that scale and you get an altogether different sound. I got that from Bud Powell; he used to play it all the time."

Miles started to talk about his strong preference for writing that isn't over-crowded, especially overcrowded with chords. He found some acetates of his forthcoming Columbia *Porgy and Bess* LP which Gil Evans had arranged but for the scoring of which Miles had made a number of suggestions. He put *I Loves You Porgy* on the machine.

"Hear that passage. We only used two chords for all of that. And in *Summertime*, there is a long space where we don't change the chord at all. It just doesn't have to be cluttered up."

From the same Verve Opera House LP, I played the Modern Jazz Quartet's version of *Now's the Time*. "If I were John," Miles began, "I'd let Milt play more—things he'd like to get loose on—and then play these things. It would be all the more effective by contrast. You can do a lot by setting up for contrast. Sometimes I'll start a set with a ballad. You'll be surprised at what an effect that is."

The conversation turned on pianists. "Boy, I've sure learned a lot from Bill Evans. He plays the piano the way it should be played. He plays all kinds of scales; can play in 5/4; and all kinds of fantastic things. There's such a difference between him and Red Garland whom I also like a lot. Red carries the rhythm, but Bill underplays, and I like that better."

Miles was at the piano again, indulging one of his primary pleasures—hearing what can be done with voicings, by changing a note, spreading out the chord, reshaping it. "You know, you can play chords on every note in the scale. Some people don't seem to realize that. People like Bill, Gil Evans and George Russell know what can be done, what the possibilities are."

Miles returned to the MJQ recording. "John taught all of them, Milt couldn't read at all, and Percy hardly. All John has to do is let Milt play with just a sketch of an arrangement. That's what we do all the time. I never have anybody write up anything too difficult for us, because then musicians tighten up.

"I love the way John plays. I've got to get that record where he plays by himself. I usually don't buy jazz records. They make me tired and depressed. I'll buy Ahmad Jamal, John Lewis, Sonny Rollins. Coltrane I hear every night. And I like to hear the things that Max Roach writes himself. A drummer makes a very good writer. He has a sense of space and knows what it feels like to be playing around an arrangement. Philly Joe plays tenor and piano, and he's starting to write."

The talk came to Coltrane. "He's been working on those arpeggios and playing chords that lead into chords, playing them fifty different ways and playing them all at once. He's beginning to leave more space except when he gets nervous. There's one frantic tenor in Philadelphia, by the way, Jimmy Oliver."

Then came Louis Armstrong's *Potato Head Blues* of 1927 with Lil Armstrong, Kid Ory, Johnny Dodds, Johnny St. Cyr, Baby Dodds, and Pete Briggs on tuba. "Louis has been through all kinds of styles," Miles began. "That's good tuba, by the way . . . You know you can't play anything on a horn that Louis hasn't played—I mean even modern. I love his approach to the trumpet; he never sounds bad. He plays on the beat and you can't miss when you play on the beat—with feeling. That's another phrase for swing. I also love the way he sings. He and Billie never made a record, did they?" Miles was informed they had, but the material was poor (c.f. Billie's *The Blues Are Brewin'*, Decca DL 8707).

"There's form there, and you take some of those early forms, play it today, and they'd sound good. I also like all those little stops in his solo. We stop, but we often let the drums lay out altogether. If I had this record, I'd play it."

Before four bars of Ahmad Jamal's *But Not for Me* on Argo LP 628, Miles said happily, "That's the way to play the piano. If I could play like Ahmad and Bill Evans combined with one hand, they could take the other off. Jamal once told me he's been playing in night clubs since he was eleven. Listen to how he slips into the other key. You can hardly tell it's happening. He doesn't throw his technique around like Oscar Peterson. Things flow into and out of each other. Another reason I like Red Garland and Bill Evans is that when they play a chord, they play a *sound* more than a chord.

"Listen to the way Jamal uses space. He lets it go so that you can feel the rhythm section and the rhythm section can feel you. It's not crowded. Paul Chambers, incidentally, has started to play a new way whereby he can solo and accompany himself at the same time—by using space well.

"Ahmad is one of my favorites. I live until he makes another record. I gave Gil Evans a couple of his albums, and he didn't give them back. Red Garland knew I liked Ahmad and at times I used to ask him to play like that. Red was at his best when he did. Bill plays a little like that but he sounds wild when he does—all those little scales."

Miles by now was back at the piano, talking with gathering intensity about the need for more space and less chord-cluttering in jazz. "When Gil wrote the arrangement of *I Loves You, Porgy*, he only wrote a scale for me to play. No chords. And that other passage with just two chords gives you a lot more freedom and space to hear things. I've been listening to Khachaturian carefully for six months now and the thing that intrigues me are all those different scales he uses. Bill Evans knows too what can be done with scales. All chords, after all, are relative to scales and certain chords make certain scales. I wrote a tune recently that's more a scale than a line. And I was going to write a ballad for Coltrane with just two chords.

"When you go this way, you can go on forever. You don't have to worry about changes and you can do more with the line. It becomes a challenge to see how melodically inventive you are. When you're based on chords, you know at the end of 32 bars that the chords have run out and there's nothing to do but repeat what you've just done—with variations.

"I think a movement in jazz is beginning away from the conventional string of chords, and a return to emphasis on melodic rather than harmonic variation. There will be fewer chords but infinite possibilities as to what to do with them. Classical composers—some of them—have been writing this way for years, but jazz musicians seldom have.

"When I want J. J. Johnson to hear something or he wants me to, we phone each other and just play the music on the phone. I did that the other day with some of the Khachaturian scales; they're different from the usual Western scales. Then we got to talking about letting the melodies and scales carry the tune. J. J. told me, 'I'm not going to write any more chords.' And look at George Russell. His writing is mostly scales. After all, you can feel the changes.

"The music has gotten thick. Guys give me tunes and they're full of chords. I can't play them. You know, we play *My Funny Valentine* like with a scale all the way through."

The next record was *Ruby, My Dear* with Thelonious Monk, Coleman Hawkins, Wilbur Ware and Art Blakey (from *Monk's Music*, Riverside RLP 12-242).

"I learned how to play ballads from Coleman Hawkins. He plays all the chords and you can still hear the ballad. Who's playing bass? He doesn't know that tune. As for the performance as a whole, the tune wasn't meant to be played that way. I guess Hawkins figured that with young cats, he should play 'young.' It's a very pretty ballad and should be played just even. This way you can't hear it the way it is; I'd play it more flowing. Monk writes such pretty melodies and then screws them up.

"You have to go down to hear him to really appreciate what he's doing. I'd like to make an album of his tunes if I can ever get him up here.

"Monk has really helped me. When I came to New York, he taught me chords and his tunes. A main influence he has been through the years has to do with giving musicians more freedom. They feel that if Monk can do what he does, they can. Monk has been using space for a long time.

"The thing that Monk must realize is that he can't get everybody to play his songs right. Coltrane, Milt Jackson and maybe Lucky Thompson are the only ones I know that can get that feeling out of his songs that he can. And he needs drummers like Denzil Best, Blakey, Shadow, Roy Haynes, and Philly.

"I love the way Monk plays and writes, but I can't stand him behind me. He doesn't give you any support."

The final record was Bessie Smith's *Young Woman's Blues*, 1926, with Fletcher Henderson, Joe Smith and Buster Bailey.

"Listen to Joe Smith's tone. He's got some feeling to it." Miles laughed while listening to the lyrics. "They're pretty hip. This is the first time I've heard this record. I haven't heard much from Bessie, but I like her everytime I hear her. She affects me like Leadbelly did, the way some of Paul Laurence Dunbar's poetry did. I read him once and almost cried. The Negro southern speech.

"As for those lyrics, I know what she means about not being a high yellow and being a 3/4 brown or something like that. In those days high yellow was as close to white as you could get. It's getting more and more mixed though and pretty soon when you call somebody an m.f., you won't know what kind to call them. You might have to call them a green m.f.

"I'd love to have a little boy some day with red hair, green eyes and a black face—who plays piano like Ahmad Jamal."

MILES DAVIS:
WINNER TAKE ALL

Interviewer: Lionel Olay
Cavalier, August 1964

By 1964 Miles Davis was still trying to find a tenor saxophonist for his second quintet, a formidable task since the departure of John Coltrane in 1960. The year saw able and challenging saxophonists like George Coleman and Sam Rivers enter and exit Davis's lineup, none of whom entirely suited Miles. Ultimately filling the bill was Wayne Shorter, a favorite of Davis's who couldn't join earlier for contractual reasons. (Shorter had been playing with Art Blakey's Jazz Messengers.) Shorter joined Herbie Hancock (piano), Tony Williams (drums), and Ron Carter (bass); together they recorded their first official album, *E.S.P.*, in January 1965.

Labeled the "Ultimate Free Lancer" by none other than journalist Hunter S. Thompson in his 1967 obituary of Lionel Olay, Olay contributed a number of articles to *Cavalier*, a premier (for the time) men's magazine. In 1967 he went to Cuba to fight beside Fidel Castro on the Isle of Pines. He was killed among a group of American volunteers.

The problem of the hero in our time—in all times, let's say—is that the more we know about them the less heroic they become. In these days, though, with the Goldfish Bowl as the major reward of achievement, it has taken on a new dimension. Distance lends enchantment, and the converse works, too, and nowhere does this hold more true than in the case of our jazz heroes.

Since jazz is our own contribution to the world pot, instead of apple pie, which is moot—a more apt phrase for jingoists would be "as American as jazz"—our jazz heroes can only emulate themselves. De Gaulle is inconceivable without his awareness of Napoleon. Castro, without Bolivar, unthinkable; Hitler, without Frederick the Great, a loser. The *idea* of a spiritual predecessor can be a great source of comfort when you decide to climb out there into the high and dizzy places.

In the case of our jazz heroes, however (and we've spawned only a few), each of them has to start again from Go, since nothing in the harum-scarum lives of King Oliver, Bix Beiderbecke, or even Louis Armstrong can be any source of illumination to a Thelonious Monk, a Sonny Rollins, or a John Coltrane, to mention three of the New Crop of adulated figures, or even to a Miles Davis, perhaps the most authentic heroic figure the jazz scene has yet produced.

This is so, leaving aside Miles' musical contribution, which is considerable. We will speak of that aspect later, but for now we are concerned with his extramusical "statement," that which takes him out of the common mold and stamps him Hero of the People. (In the folk world, the same process is now happening to Bobby Dylan, a beardless youth of 22, who walked out of Minnesota determined to be Woody Guthrie, got captured by the hero-makers, and now can't let go of that high-voltage wire called Popularity.)

Jazz heroes, folk heroes, let's call them all pop-music heroes and include the early Sinatra—who evolved from hero into politician, a lesser role but easier to sustain—and the current Belafonte, whose sights are set on some far-off horizon of achievement that inhibits his holding still for the full hero treatment. None of them will be happy at being grouped together, but the simple truth is that, talent aside, there is a great deal of similarity in what are the significant aspects of their personalities. And none of them characterizes and epitomizes the breed—*Kitsch* hero, mock angry lover, seemingly disdainful of the prerequisites of power—more than Miles Davis, trumpet player and self-dedicated *bon vivant*.

My assignment was to get him to talk; a toughie, I knew, from mutual acquaintances who had only guarded good words to bring to any discussion of him. (I did not bother with opinions from those sycophants who live on his by-products, since their judgments have long ago atrophied into a steady drone of superlatives for winners and a sneering whine for losers.)

Miles, a clear winner by all but the most abstruse standards, has a reputation for cool indifference with everyone except a few friends from the old days, and I knew that no *some of my best friends are Negroes* or *I just love jazz* approaches would make it.

However, a meet was set up on California's Monterey Peninsula. Miles, according to my Hollywood liaison man, who claimed they were tight like that, had only grunted when the idea was broached, but I was assured the grunt did not mean a flat no and that anything above a flat no from Miles was like ten yesses from Eddie Fisher. I was in, it seemed.

So I set off with what I figured was about a 70-30 chance of seeing him, with the odds against it, especially since I am afflicted with a strange personality quirk that makes me want to steer clear of people who don't want to see me.

Let me here and now cop out in words of one syllable: When I need a trumpet player I go not to Miles but to the completely delightful Dizzy Gillespie, the Archie Moore of jazzdom, ageless, getting better all the time, an entertainer of the first rank as well as a pioneer musician from whose rib Miles sprang three-quarters formed. Diz, bless him, is always *muy vivo*, where Miles seems always wrestling with some private woe with which I make no contact.

Anyway, I met Miles, as arranged, late on a Friday afternoon. And the first thing I learned was that my Hollywood connection proved to be a kiss of death where Miles was concerned, and it took all my earnestness to persuade him to disassociate us in his mind. "You guys always ask the wrong questions" were the first words he rasped to me, remembering apparently some other clown who'd been sicced on him by Mr. Tightlikethat.

I've been peripheral on the jazz scene most of my life; my closest friend for a long while was (and is) a first-rank arranger-composer, and I'd even done some time as the husband of a jazz singer who, although remarried, still burnishes my name, so I didn't think I had any wrong questions for Miles, like what's your favorite song or what do you think of Louis Armstrong.

Besides, I'd been listening to Miles for a long time and had also watched him metamorphize. The son of a dentist, he grew up in Alton, Illinois, and then perfected his original embouchure in St. Louis, where his first hero was Roy Eldridge. When Billy Eckstine came through with his big band that included both Charlie Parker and Dizzy Gillespie, Miles persuaded Diz to let him blow with the section. (From the beginning—and this, too, is a common thread running through hero candidates—Miles had not a moment of doubt as to who and where he wanted to be.)

At 19, making the only sound move available, he came to New York and enrolled at Juilliard to shore up his knowledge of harmony and counterpoint.

Dizzy suggested he study piano so he could learn more precisely the nature of the variant chords and how best a soloist could or, depending upon the musical circumstances, could not play above such harmonies.

This kind of technical knowledgeability, seemingly wasted on the layman who can't tell a flatted fifth from an air-raid siren, is that subliminal part of music that makes some of it soar and the rest just lay there. Rules are best violated by those for whom they have become second nature.

So, while Juilliard was not without value for him, Miles' real mecca was Harlem, and especially Minton's where Dizzy and Bird were holding court. Negroes dominated the complex musical picture that was emerging in a postwar reaction to the saccharine music that always seems to accompany collective violence. Negroes will always dominate jazz, but in those days of be-bop, as it was called, such gifted ofays as Red Rodney, Allen Eager, and Stan Getz proved as good as the best and better than most, color to the side. (Only Stan Getz, incidentally, who was dealt a new hand when Bossa Nova crazed in, has survived professionally.)

Miles, during this time, was emulating Dizzy, and it was Thelonious Monk, with his Old Man Moses kind of wisdom, who told him that if he ever wanted the brass ring he'd have to learn to sing in his own voice.

Thelonious, of course, remains Exhibit A for the validity of his dictum. For years he was scorned by all, regarded as a flat-out nut with a fraudulent gift. But he persisted until he prevailed, so that he's got it his own way now and is a fully ordained Hero of the People himself, as is Miles, who took his advice. (Was it Yeats who said that every true and original artist must himself create the taste by which he will be relished?)

Miles' own voice, which was a far cry from the exuberant essentially life-positive one with which Dizzy greeted the world, was a long time in evolving. A master of his horn and a swinger of the first water, it wasn't until he joined the small Charlie Parker combo that he really began to come out with what *he* felt.

Bird was the real goods, a genius who took the material at hand and transformed it into a personal vision. His place in jazz is roughly similar to Picasso's in art in that he established a school of seemingly infinite variations and a colossal indifference to the dichotomy between what is considered "pretty" and "ugly." It was from Bird, probably, that Miles became emboldened enough to tell his own story and bust out from under Dizzy's considerable shadow, where it was clear he didn't fit. There was an added advantage, too, in that Bird, playing alto, could make finger-popping sheets of notes that were outside the limitations of Miles' horn, so that any kind of direct influence was impossible.

Those were the days of Miles' birth: Birdland, Nola Recording Studios with one off-label gig after another, and endless jamming in Harlem at all hours. Coming up, though, were those other requisites for Hero status: death and resurrection.

Charlie Parker, a genius, was a martyr, not a hero. The difference also can best be illustrated in art. Picasso (in this case unlike Parker), for example, is a hero; Van Gogh was a martyr. (Martyr, according to Oxford: One who voluntarily undergoes the penalty of death for refusing to renounce the faith. "I want to live to be 172," Miles told me.)

Bird liked what heroin did to his consciousness, but the penalty was death, and he paid it. Miles, Stan Getz, Art Pepper, several others tried it and passed the cup. There was a period, though, in the early '50s, when the opiates were shaping the content of jazz a lot more than just a little. It was the Birth of the Cool, as some imaginative liner writer phrased it. But for those unstampedeable types who grew up and on with Basie, Lester, et al., those tortured mewlings never sounded like anything more than what they were: disoriented junk dreams articulated about one-eighth as brilliantly as their authors conceived them. (Like the drunk who thinks he's being witty, junk dreams are less, not more, than what they seem.)

During these years, Miles went into eclipse. "Illness forced Miles into a physical and musical decline," wrote George Avakian, one of the New Critics in the rapidly growing Jazz Establishment. Whatever the reasons for his bow-out, Miles' second coming took place at the 1955 Newport Jazz Festival.

Using one of Thelonious' most haunting melodies, '*Round About Midnight*, to showcase himself, he showed the kind of hard-core guy he is. For the new Miles, *Midnight*'s reflective changes were the best possible vehicle—a lonely, agonized, yearning, highly charged statement that was not without beauty. Miles, the hero, came into being that year, and since then he has encompassed an ever-widening audience.

Jazz buffs, like all buffs, would rather be right than left behind, and The Word has been out on Miles for years now, so that even when he blows a bunch of nothing—which is often—that, too, acquires meaning and food for further exegesis. Barring an overt act of violence, Miles is enshrined now and could even make it to the barn with just half the lip he has left. There are at least twenty trumpet players that come immediately to mind who can outblow him technically.

Now, from this, a reader might conclude that Mr. Davis is no great favorite of mine, musically, and he'd be right. A little Miles lasts me a long time. (I was going to say there are Miles that make me happy, and there are Miles that make me kinda blue. But I am determined to keep this on a high plane.)

In any case, what I do want to say is that for years this prejudice disturbed me, since I don't like to think of myself as the hip nay sayer. I point to my record of liking Barbra Streisand, Dave Brubeck, Sarah Vaughan, to mention only a few overpraised artists whom it has become fashionable to list as having no talent whatever.

That Miles is overpraised as a musician I have no doubts. As a hero, though, he is authentic, and we're going to be zeroing in on that aspect of him. But, first, let's make it clear that he is distinctly antiperformance: refusing (1) to announce the titles of his selections and (2) to take cognizance of his audience to the point where he often blows with his back to them and leaves the stand when his part is finished; and (3) greets all applause with a blank stare which, to put it as kindly as possible, barely masks his contempt and hostility for his fans. Ironically, the worse he behaves the more intriguing the buffs find him, since what is being perfected is not a musician but an image, and the image is that of the abused and aloof Master saying, "It's too late to apologize, throw money!" (And they do, to the tune of $5,000 a week. It's a seller's market in the hero business.)

Since I have made clear my less than enchanted evaluation of Miles as a performer, let's look at what he does have. Foremost, and it's so big a foremost that it nearly negates all the above, Miles can make sounds as few men can, and on occasion he does. His tone is soft and rich and exquisitely intimate; he's more wired into his horn than even Dizzy, who always has to be playing it, ever was. Miles, at his best, *becomes* his horn so that he might well be singing, so effortless does it become. And his playing, characterized by the nervous jagged lines that came out of the bop school and overlaid with the pensive relaxation of the cool or junk period that followed, coupled with his loss of lip, produces that curious inner tension that never satisfies, yet cannot be ignored. This outwardly relaxed style that barely masks the seething interior is precisely Miles' statement, both musically and extra-musically, and therein lies his appeal as a hero and his deficiencies—for my dough—as a jazz great.

Friday night Miles was performing, so naturally he was inaccessible. Nothing to do but watch him from the wings. By common consensus, it was an off-night for Miles, and he walked through his gig in such a way that one of the managers said in disgust, "He could have mailed it in."

Still, the crowd, loaded on high spirits and whatever else, loved him anyway, and he came off to heavy mitts. It was gala, it was swell, but I had to set up a place to talk to Miles, and, with that end in mind, I bellied up to the bar where he was belting them pretty good, doubles.

"Miles," I said, "when can we talk?"

"What about?"

Well, he had me there. First question, and it was all wrong. "Cabbages and kings," I tried, and got a snort for my effort. Okay, no more charm, we'd try self-interest. I could see that he was weighing me for a yo-yo and that two more strikes and the ref would stop it.

"Here's what it is I want to say," I said, throwing one from the floor. "Someone once asked Sonny Liston what he's found different about what's expected of him now that he's famous, and he said, 'Nothin', except now I'm supposed to laugh when nothin's funny.' What do you think of that?"

Miles dropped another weight on the balance, weighed it, drank his drink. "Yeah, and a lotta people tell me the sky is blue. Come over to the hotel Sunday morning, but *not too early*."

He turned and moved away, a short, well set up little rooster who walks like a fighter, mainly because he is a fighter. He's justifiably proud of his boxing skills, works out regularly, and I'm sure that in his heart of hearts he's certain he could have been Sugar Ray had the cards been dealt differently.

So I had my chat with the Miles of Davis. Miles, I learned, distrusts talk. It's not his turf, and he's skittish on it. Which does not mean that he is not one formidable cookie, any way you bite into him. He could have retired yesterday on the rentals from the apartment buildings he owns, and when talk doesn't make it he goes other ways.

The scene: A lily-white, Anglo-Saxon, hilltop inn overlooking the Pacific Ocean, the high-line place to stay in the area; Sunday morning, noonish, with a bright clear sun. Poolside, Miles in swim shorts and his wife, Frances, in a bikini, both trim, lithe, esthetically pleasing, pretty people. With them was Miles' manager, Benny Shapiro, a fellow from Los Angeles I've known slightly but for a long time.

Around us, carefully shielded by large umbrellas, were The Folks, taking their lunch. They wore white ventilated shoes, funny sport shirts, pleated pants—old Dodsworth and the missus brought up to date.

Miles was keeping the white-coated Filipino waiter jumping with his steady reorders of fresh orange juice with a side of Jamaica rum. Below glistened the blue Pacific, and, off on the horizon, little specks that were steamships seemed fixed like rivets on its skin.

The pool looked inviting, but I hadn't thought to bring a suit, so I had to settle for the orange juice and rum. What follows is what I could get off the tape that made any sense.

OLAY: Lenny Bruce once said that trumpet players made Miles Davis because the people don't know what's good until they're told what to like. The other trumpet players get together and say, "That's The Man. Spread it," and it then filters down to the herd, and that's how it's done. You think that's true?

DAVIS: Hell no. I don't. I think people are smarter than what musicians give them credit for.

OLAY: Musically?

DAVIS: They *got* to be, man.

OLAY: Maybe your appeal is not really a musical appeal, maybe it's something else. . . .

DAVIS: I ain't got nothing else. You know, I always believed, ever since I was a child, that people are smarter than what musicians say they are today. You know, all that music in Chicago and Kansas City, they couldn't be that dumb, man. I mean, not to notice when music is good and when it's bad. Nobody's that dumb. They might ignore it, but they know it's good.

OLAY: Have you ever speculated about your own appeal as a musical personality, about it growing outside the range of being merely a musician?

DAVIS: Nah.

OLAY: You never speculated about it . . . ?

DAVIS: No, man. I don't even know what you're talkin' about, man.

OLAY: Really and truly?

DAVIS: Sure. I don't know what you're talking about.

OLAY: Yeah. Well. Maybe it's my hang-up to speculate about things, to wonder. Like Bird, who was just a saxophone player. I remember seeing him on 42nd Street, coming out of those all-night movies, eating candy bars, and hanging on to his old lady like she was his seeing-eye dog. And since that time he's become a legend, which is a bunch of nonsense. Or is it?

DAVIS: Nobody thought like Bird. Nobody played like that. It's the truth, not a legend. It's the truth. What he did on his own was his own business. A lot of people do the same thing but don't nobody say nothing. *I* do the same thing.

OLAY: You mean the self-destructive aspects of a public figure's life are his own business and shouldn't be gone into; that that's not what he's selling?

DAVIS: Self-destructive? Man, I don't believe I can buy that.

OLAY: You don't like that term?

DAVIS: No. Because he was having himself a ball, man, in everything he did. Hell, he was enjoying himself. I do the same thing. I try to please myself wherever I can, as much as I can, and I dig it. If I want to get drunk, I get drunk.

OLAY: Okay, I see what you mean. The term self-destructive is a white term anyway. It really doesn't hold all that much water, because in the end even breathing is self-destructive, moving you that one pace nearer the little black door. Laying in the sun is going to take a few minutes off at the other end, drinking a glass of booze. . . .

DAVIS: And talking nonsense.

OLAY: Right.

DAVIS: I'll tell you one thing; I sure as hell don't wanna die kneelin' down praying. If you can't do what you feel like doin' without hurting anybody . . . you know you can't play, man. Listen, man. I like to enjoy myself, period.

OLAY: Well, that's not so simple an achievement as it sounds. I know so many who feel guilty about enjoyment.

DAVIS: Listen, I know 'em, too. I went by boat first class to France, and those people don't know how to enjoy themselves.

OLAY: How do you mean?

DAVIS: That boat, man, was sadder'n a bitch. They enjoyed *that*. They enjoy what you give 'em. Goddam, if that's freedom, don't let me free. Let me stay the way I am.

(Then Shapiro dominated a rather recondite discussion about the question of guilt. It concluded as follows:)

OLAY: The Jews suffer from guilt more than anybody I know. Negro guilt is a very rare thing.

SHAPIRO: Lenny Bruce says it's related back to killing Christ.

DAVIS: Only thing makes me feel bad is to know I can't live to be 172.

OLAY: The racial scene doesn't bug you?

DAVIS: Yeah, it bugs me. I was in London, in an Indian restaurant. There was a drunk Dutchman in there sittin' across from me, puttin' rice all over his face. And I had some *nice* food, and he was starin' at me before I even had a chance to enjoy it. I told him if he didn't put some words with that look I was gonna knock him out. 'Cause I didn't feel like sittin' there eating my food watching him watch me.

OLAY: Well, he was drunk.

DAVIS: Yeah. I told his friend to tell him what I said, and his friend says, "Well, you know, he's drunk, and he's funny." So I said, "Well, I'm funny, too." I am. If I go into a restaurant, I don't think about do they know who I am or if I'm a Negro. I'm not ugly and I'm figuring I'm as good as any man. So I'm thinking about is the food gonna be good and not what everybody else is thinking. And my wife, she thinks the same way. She's never ducking and all that. I don't like them duckers, man. If you duck, you get hit. I don't speak for the American Negro, I speak for myself.

SHAPIRO: But you happen to be an American Negro, so therefore it. . . .

DAVIS: Yes, I'm very lucky.

SHAPIRO: You're proud of your heritage. . . .

DAVIS: I sure am, man. It knocks me out to be me. It really kills me.

OLAY: You had a good childhood. Enjoyed yourself?

DAVIS: I always enjoy myself. I feel sorry for somebody that's jim crowing. It's a shame. I can't explain to you how it makes me feel to read about somebody getting bombed. It just makes me sick, man. And the only way to get rid of that stuff is not by picketing and praying, but you got to hit the sonofabitch that hits you. You *gotta* hit him, man. You don't turn the other cheek, you try and knock him on his ass if you can.

OLAY: Lay down in front of the train and if it runs over you. . . . You know *that* won't work. So the next time you blow the bridge.

DAVIS: That's where it's at. You do whatever works. If somebody killed my kid like that, I'd have to go kill one of theirs. I'd just do it, man, and I wouldn't feel bad, I'd go home and go to sleep. I'm trying to live as long as I can and I don't want to be living with a knot in my stomach. If you hit me, man, and I didn't hit you back and I could, it would make me sick for about ten years. If a guy gives me a ticket I'll drop it on somebody else. If the ticket was for $15, and I'm supposed to get $100, I'll ask for $115. I'm satisfied. That way I don't get ulcers.

OLAY: You'd be good if everybody else was, but somebody else has to start it.

DAVIS: What do you mean, start it?

OLAY: Start being good. If somebody beats you out of, say, three grand, you're not going to say, "Well, I'm going to start being good from here on in. I won't try and get that back. . . ."

DAVIS: No. I'm not gonna pray. I'm gonna get it back.

OLAY: And then the one you got it from is gonna get it back from somebody else.

DAVIS: I don't know if they're that slick about it.

(Here Shapiro, who has become a self-styled moralist after a highly checkered career, tried to interject something about such an attitude not working very well. If everyone thought that way, etc.)

OLAY: What Miles is trying to say is that the Maserattis aren't come by through prayer, and he digs his Maseratti.

DAVIS: You wanna know something? I get the same kick driving my Maseratti as I would walking from here to Big Sur. It would knock me out. Walk or ride, either way.

OLAY: Right. Life is good.

DAVIS: And I'm trying to make it better.

OLAY: And that strikes me as a very Christian attitude. You're trying to make the world better by one. A noble effort, right?

DAVIS: Left. That's enough, I feel like a swim.

So Miles swam, and I swilled, and my visit closed with an incident that had Miles written all over it: The pool itself was empty, with the few poolsiders obviously in swimwear for sunning only. So Miles had the pool to himself. Coming up for air at my side, he leaned over conspiratorially to whisper, "You see what it is being a Negro. Nobody wants to swim with you." And for the first time he cracked his impassivity and gave me a big wink.

I DON'T HAVE TO HOLD THE AUDIENCE'S HAND

Interviewer: Arthur Taylor, January 22, 1968
From *Notes and Tones: Musician-to-Musician Interviews*
(Expanded Edition, Da Capo Press, 1993)

One of the great jazz drummers and bandleaders, Arthur Taylor drummed with Coleman Hawkins, Bud Powell, Sonny Rollins, Charlie Parker, Dexter Gordon, John Coltrane, Thelonious Monk, and, of course, Miles. In the 1990s Taylor engendered a new incarnation of Taylor's Wailers, which caused him to enjoy an all-too-brief resurgence prior to his unexpected death in 1995. During his long career he also interviewed these and other renowned jazz performers (many of them friends). These frank dialogues between musicians were collected most recently in the 1993 edition of the classic *Notes and Tones*, praised as "a bible for anyone who considers himself serious about jazz" (*International Herald Tribune*). In this excerpt from his introduction Taylor describes what led up to his recorded conversation with Miles, which follows, and in which they discuss boxing, drumming, Gil Evans, Dr. Dolittle, white movies, and getting your money first.

In 1968 *[Editors: He probably meant 1967.]* I was living in Paris and the Miles Davis Quintet came for a concert. Naturally, I was planning to go; but when I got there I couldn't buy a ticket, and couldn't get backstage either. I was pacing back and forth in front of the concert hall, and who came along but Miles himself. So I walked in with him. And that night's concert was one of the calmest that I'd seen backstage in Paris. There were no newspaper people, no photographers, no fans, no nothing. It was especially nice for me—I was the only one backstage except for the band and the people who were working. So I had the opportunity to talk with the musicians.

Months later I was visiting New York. Whenever I would visit, there were two people I would go to see immediately—Miles and Clifford Jordan. Talking with these two men, I'd get to feeling the mood of the city immediately. This time Miles said to me, "Come on and go to the gym with me. I'm going to work out and after I work out, we'll go downtown and get something to eat." So we got into his Ferrari or Lamborghini or whatever it was at 79th Street—from that moment I knew I would never ride in a car with him again—and we got out at 125th Street. I was really happy to get out of that car. I sat and watched Miles work out, when who walked in but Jimmy Cobb, the drummer. During my conversation with him, I spoke about how Miles had allowed no photographers, no newspaper people backstage while he was playing—about how quiet it was there. I said to Jimmy, "I should interview Miles." He said, "Yeah, you should. Why not?" So when Miles got dressed and we were walking out to go downtown and have lunch, I said, "I want to do an interview with you." He looked at me like I was crazy. But he agreed. The next afternoon I was at his house. He put on the tape recorder . . .

———

Do you have a list of things you want to ask me?

No, I would like to ad-lib.
Hello, hello, hello, hello my ding. Look out, look out, my duke. What do you want to talk about, Arthur?

Why do you go to the gymnasium so often, Miles?
I go to the gym to keep my body in shape, so I can hold notes longer, so my stomach will be flat and so I'll look handsome.

How long have you been doing this?
Let's see . . . ever since I can remember. The reason I started doing it was to make my legs stronger.

Do you think boxing is comparable to music?
I think it is. You have to have rhythm and good time to do both. Timing has to be good on both of them. Doing exercise makes you think clear and your blood circulate. It makes you think stronger, feel stronger, and you can play whatever instrument you play with greater strength, whether it's wrong or right.

What about drums? Do you remember we were talking about drums the other day?
Drums? Drums? Oh, yeah! I think all musicians should have some kind of
knowledge of drums and piano; not necessarily the bass, but at least piano and
drums. Because drummers scare a lot of musicians. Like Tony [Williams]—a lot
of musicians can't play with him because they're used to playing on the first
beat and he accents on the second and third beats if you're in 4/4 time. Sometimes he might accent on any beat. And he might play 5/4 time for a while,
and you've got to have that. You've got to know about rhythms and the feel of
different rhythms in order to play with him, because he might haul off and do
anything rhythmically. If you don't have any knowledge of time and different
time changes, he'll lose you. You have to have it when you first start out, so it'll
be back in your head, so it'll be natural.

How do you go about picking a drummer for your band?
First I look at my ding! When I look at a drummer, it's just like when I look at a
fighter. I watch his reactions to different things, his quickness, whether he's on
time and whether he can clean up, you know what I mean?

Would you be more explicit about that?
Say a guy makes a phrase and the phrase isn't exactly what he wants it to be;
well, the drummer is supposed to be hip enough to sorta add to the finished
phrase. If you know your drummer is capable of doing that, then you won't feel
funny if you miss a certain phrase you're thinking of. It might be one of those
off-beat phrases, or out of time.

The first thing I listen for in a drummer is if he can roll. You know, a lot of
drummers can't roll. When you end a song, a roll is the most natural way for
it to die off, and you can cut off. I also watch to see how fast his hands move. I
look at a drummer's hands to make sure he does not play with his arms but with
his wrists and to see how his wrists are. If they are nice and fast, then he can be
cultivated and you just let him go. I listen to check if he has good time and he
doesn't play the bass drum too loud. The bass drum has to be played even. And I
listen to the top cymbal to hear whether he plays it even or not. He may not play
it like I want him to play it, but he can be taught how to play it if he plays even.
I changed Joe's [Philly Joe Jones] top cymbal beat. He was kind of reluctant at
first, but I changed it so it could sound more ad-lib than just straight dang-di-di-

dang-di-di-dang: I changed it to dang-di-di-dang-di-di-di-di-dang, and you can play off that with your snare drum.

But you sometimes get a drummer who plays with his arms or else his foot is too heavy . . . it may be heavier than the group he's playing with or lighter than the group . . . well, it's best to be lighter, because you can always come up. Right? I made Tony play his bass drum, because he didn't play it at all. And he didn't play his sock cymbals, so I started him on the sock cymbals. I made him play the bass drum even, and all the rest he had. I suggested he cut all his phrases off on the fourth beat, so it wouldn't sound like you're starting in a chorus every time. Like 1-2-3-4, you say 1-2-3 . . . 1, accent on the fourth beat. Erroll Garner accents on the fourth beat. A lot of people don't know that. And let's see who else? Baby Laurence. It's like a pickup. Or else you can leave it. It's hipper to leave it. I also told Tony not to stop his roll but just to let it die out and keep the tempo.

Where did you get the idea of using a guitar for the record Miles in the Sky?
I got it from my head. I wanted to hear a bass line a little stronger. If you can hear a bass line, then any note in a sound that you play can be heard, because you have the bottom. We change the bass line quite a bit on all the songs we play. It varies. So I figured if I wrote a bass line, we could vary it so that it would have a sound a little larger than a five-piece group. By using the electric piano and having Herbie [Hancock] play the bass line and the chords with the guitar and Ron [Carter] also playing with him in the same register, I thought that it would sound good. It came out all right. It was a nice sound.

Did you compose all the music?
Well, Herbie, Wayne [Shorter] or Tony will write something, then I'll take it and spread it out or space it, or add some more chords, or change a couple of phrases, or write a bass line to it, or change the tempo of it, and that's the way we record. If it's in 4/4 time, I might change it to 3/4, 6/8 or 5/4.

Is there anything you want to add?
How about my ding? I want to add my ding.

I know you wanted to get that in. What interests you besides music and boxing?

Nothing other than music and girls. Let's see, what else? Drummers, bass players, money, slaves, white folks.

Do you have any particular hobbies?
Making fun of white folks on television. That's my main hobby. That's about it. Driving my Ferrari. I like driving a Ferrari. I don't like to drive anything else. That's a good, fast car.

You can't drive a car like that too fast in the city.
I drive that fast in this block. Whenever you can, you do it. You try not to hurt anybody. Those are about my only hobbies.

Do you go to sporting events often?
I only go to the fights. I like to see nice slick fighters, or else good entertainers like Sammy Davis, Jr., but the rest of that shit ain't nothing.

Has New York changed much since the early days when you were on Fifty-second Street?
They don't have anyplace to experiment for young guys who start playing and who play their own stuff. It's because of all those records they make nowadays . . . you know, the guys copy off the records, so they don't have anything original. You can't find a musician who plays anything different. They all copy off each other. If I were starting out again, I wouldn't listen to records. I very seldom listen to jazz records, because they all do the same thing. I only listen to guys that are original, like Ahmad Jamal and Duke Ellington, guys like Dizzy Gillespie, Sonny Rollins and Coltrane.

Can we start again, Miles?
What? Sock it to me! Come on out with it!

What kind of music interests you besides jazz?
Yesterday I listened to an album of music from Poland: Penderecki's *Threnody for the Victims of Hiroshima.* I have *Dr. Doolittle* here, which Columbia sent me, and *Camelot.*

Of all the music that's been sent to you through the years, how much have you used?
It's all stacked up there. Most of the songs are so weak that you have to rebuild them, so it's like composing yourself.

Is it better for you to compose your own music?
It's better because you can put what you want in it. Gil [Evans] and I looked over most of this music, and it's kind of weak.

Have you and Gil recorded anything that hasn't been released?
We've been working on something for about three years. I don't know how it's going to turn out, though.

Do you think it will culminate soon?
It has to, because we've been working on it for so long.

When you say working on it, what exactly do you mean?
You see these little sketches here at the piano? [He plays] Little things like this . . . trial and error. We write, and then we take out everything we don't like, and what's left is what we record. We try different combinations of instruments, different voices.

Three years seems like quite a long time to be working on one piece of music.
We do it off and on. Gil has to work, and he doesn't work that much. He has to do albums to get money to live on. So we just work on the side.

What about this piece of music on the piano?
Dr. Doolittle has about three songs in it that are worth something, but the rest have to be rebuilt.

Is Dr. Doolittle *playing on Broadway?*
No, they made a movie out of it.

Do you go to the movies often?
I haven't seen any I liked. Let's see, I saw *The Graduate*. That was pretty good. But I can't stand those white movies about white problems. I'd like to see a

movie dealing with Negroes as human beings with emotions, not just a black maid or a doctor. I'd like to see one in everyday life . . . like an executive, or the head of a company. One who falls in love and out of love; one who drives a sports car; and one who acts like me or like you; who has girls, white girls, colored girls, Chinese and Hawaiian and German and French, you know? They don't have that in the movies, so I don't go. Every time I go I feel like I'm giving my money away. Some money! I'd rather shoot tigers or something. I have a funny feeling all day after I've seen a movie with the same white problems. You know, full of girls with long hair and where everybody's having a lot of fun, and we don't have any fun. You don't see any Negroes. It makes me feel funny. It makes me feel like I just gave my money away. If I'm going to give my money away I can give it to something. It's a form of Jim Crow when you have white people dancing and having a good time, and they don't show any Negroes or what Negro feelings are, or any Chinese people, just white girls dancing, with their hair going and going. It's tiresome to me. I want to see somebody acting and living like I do or like you do. Not just white. I saw a movie last night on television. It was just all white all the way through. I figure if the white people keep on showing us their problems on television like they're doing, then we will be able to tell their problems by their facial expressions pretty soon, 'cause they're running out. I was telling Herbie the other day: "We're not going to play the blues anymore. Let the white folks have the blues. They got 'em, so they can keep 'em. Play something else."

Do you like traveling for your work?
It doesn't bother me as long as the band sounds good.

Do you get enjoyment from touring the world with your band?
No, because I'm bringing the pleasure, and whenever I go someplace, I'm going there to please somebody else. So I don't get any kick out of a foreign country unless I go there not to play but on a vacation.

Do you find traveling a strain?
It doesn't bother me, because I don't drink. I stopped drinking.

Do you feel better?

I feel better; a lot better. I don't tire myself out so quickly. When you do one-nighters, like we did in Europe, and you drink every time you eat, you wind up feeling real tied before a concert. You get up early in the morning . . . you might have a hangover and it carries on, and you won't be able to think right. I don't mind traveling, but it just bothers me when guys like George Wein did what he did in Spain and blamed it on me.

What was that?
He tried to slip two extra concerts in and told me he'd pay my room rent, which made me mad, so I left. At the plane I told him I wasn't going to make it. It's all right. He pays enough money and everything, but if he's going to put another concert in and have television, and get paid for it . . . I went along with it, but when it gets you so you feel like you're being taken advantage of, it's best to leave, because he's not treating you like a man. I don't think the fact he married a colored girl changes anything. It doesn't matter to me who he married. He married her, not me. I take him for the way he treats me. But he gets real common after a while. He's all right except when he tries to get like one of the boys; then he gets sickening, because nobody's interested in that. All I want to do is play the concert and get the money. He said I stranded my band. They had already been paid, they had their transportation, you know, the tickets.

He wanted everybody to think he was my manager in Europe. I didn't say anything, but that's kind of disrespectful to a musician. And then he would ask me about how I live. It's none of his business. I told him so. I said: "George, you can't live like me because you don't make that much money." He asked me once, "What do you do with your money?" I told him to shut up and don't say nothing 'cause I'd break his neck. If I play a concert, Arthur, I like to play the concert and leave. You don't have to be nice to me or nothing. Let me play the concert and leave me alone. I'll play the music. Pay me off, and that's it. But don't come around to me trying to be a nice guy or a big shot, with some bitches or something, because it doesn't have any effect on me.

The only thing I asked George was, "Wherever we go, try to find a gymnasium in the town so I'll have something to do." He didn't do it. I figured he'd take care of it himself, but he had those in-between guys, the middlemen, who didn't think it was important. But to me it was important. I guess they thought it was a joke. I had a nice time in Europe, because the band played good. That was the only reason. The band plays pretty good sometimes. Oh yeah, George stopped a check because I didn't play in Spain. I was there for two days. So now I'm suing him for what he said. For always dropping all the weight on me. Well, promoters always do this, anyway.

Do you see any solution to problems like that?
Yeah, get your money first. That's what I do. I mean it was all right . . . I called him and said: "George, if we're doing an extra concert, give me some more money." And guess what he said: "Man, like I don't have no bread." So how you going to talk business like that? He tries to use slang and be hip, and: "I don't have no bread, man." I said: "If you don't have no bread, get somebody else, 'cause I'm leaving." So I left.

Do you think it's easier for someone like myself to interview you?
I think it's much easier, if you have something that you want to ask me about music. Because you think the same way, on the same line I think on. Most guys want to know about . . . well, they say I'm rude, and that I turn my back on the audience, and that I don't like white people. And that I don't like the audience. But the thing is, I never think about an audience. I just think about the band. And if the band is all right, I know the audience is pleased. I don't have to hold the audience's hand. I think audiences are hipper than musicians think they are. They wouldn't be there if they didn't want to hear some music, so you don't have to con them into believing that this music is great. I figure they can judge for themselves, and those who don't like it don't have to like it, and those who like it will have a nice time listening. If I go to a concert, I take it like that.

THE MILES DAVIS: A SEMI-AFFECTIONATE REMINISCENCE

Interviewer: John Palcewski
Cavalier, May 1969

John Palcewski has enjoyed an eclectic career as a publishing house copywriter, wire service photojournalist, magazine editor, music/drama critic, literary novelist, and fine arts photographer. He interviewed Miles in fall 1968. The interview was originally commissioned by John Berendt at *Esquire*, but Palcewski thinks they turned it down because it wasn't "snide" or "cutting" enough. "Miles made it clear to me he did not want to talk about anything related to his former drug use, and in the course of several interviews I came to believe that particular topic had little relevance to the simple fact that as a musician he was unique, a true genius." By this time, Miles Davis's second great quintet had virtually dissolved, while Davis was in the process of experimenting with electronic instruments in his music. The quintet's last officially recorded music consisted of some tracks recorded in June 1968 for *Filles de Kilimanjaro*. Shortly thereafter, Ron Carter and Herbie Hancock left to pursue other avenues of musical interest, though Hancock would return for Miles's recording sessions through the early 1970s. Tony Williams and Wayne Shorter hung around long enough to contribute to the first inklings of Miles's electronic musical expressions, first on the September sessions for *Filles de Kilimanjaro*, and later for the December set Palcewski witnessed at Boston's Jazz Workshop, where Dave Holland replaced Carter, and Chick Corea and Wynton Kelly, both on electric keyboards, replaced Herbie Hancock.

Miles sits behind his piano, sounding random chords with delicate, bony fingers; his head is bent over the keyboard with an expression that looks like a cross between defensive arrogance and sadness. He knows he can't be pinned down by any journalist. He knows he's unapproachable—that's his style. He senses your uncomfortableness and ponders briefly on whether he should get up and leave the room or stay and largely ignore you. Or maybe say something in a quiet whisper so you have to say, "What was that Miles?"

His brow wrinkles with dissatisfaction and irritation. He repeats the sentence, striking a strong diminished seventh. "I said, when you gonna start the interview?"

Buddy Gist, a close friend, is there and he interjects that the interview has already started. "Yeah, Miles. He's taking all this down in his head."

I nod my head and say nothing. Miles doesn't like to listen to a lot of chatter. He doesn't like to be questioned. "If you want to do an article on Miles," Buddy Gist had said, "just sit there and let him do all the talking."

Miles continues with his piano abstractions, and I look around the room. It resembles something out of Hugh Hefner's *Playboy* mansion. The left wall is made up of a console that looks like Mission Control at Houston. Two Ampex 800 tape decks, Lafayette AM-FM tuner, Garrard turntable, banks of control buttons. Beyond where Miles is sitting is a circular couch which takes up nearly half the room. On the floor is a huge lion skin and head from Tanzania. On a far wall is a collection of porcelain masks.

A pretty Negro girl comes into the room and leans over and whispers something in Miles' ear. He grunts, keeping his eyes on the keyboard. She asks Buddy and me if we'd like something to drink. We tell her Canadian Club and Scotch on ice—no water. As she leaves the room, Miles speaks.

"Bitches are all the same," he says. His voice is hardly a whisper. Just a low, rasping sound that's difficult to read. Miles once had an operation to remove nodes on his vocal chords. The operation was to have restored his voice eventually, but he got into an argument with a nightclub manager and he shouted himself into what may be permanent hoarseness. "Yeah, they're all the same," he continues. "Nothin' different about any of them. They all say to you, 'You don't love me anymore.' A cat has to go 'round sayin' 'I love you' over and over again."

Buddy leans back in the couch and half grins. "Thass right, Miles. You got it."

Miles stops playing and gets up. He slowly walks toward the kitchen, and slowly walks back with a can of Fresca. He takes a few swallows and carefully sets the can down. He says something.

"What was that?" I ask.

He repeats. "How much they paying you for an article on me?" For the first time he looks me directly in the eye.

I tell him I don't know. Things like that are always open, always speculation. Who knows, maybe the magazine won't even publish it.

"Whatever you get, you give me half," he says.

I say yes, I'll give you half. Why not? Miles once got seventeen hundred from a magazine that wanted a story. Miles Davis is supposed to be hot copy. He doesn't grant interviews unless something tells him it's time for his name to appear in print. Sometimes he gets whimsical and says okay, you can write about me. The rest of the time he tells magazines and their writers to go to hell. Once a reporter from *Time* called him up and said they wanted to put him on the cover with a couple of other people for a big "Jazz" story. Miles asked him, "What the fuck is it, Nigger Week up there?" The man stuttered as Miles slammed down the phone.

Buddy Gist on Miles Davis: "Miles doesn't need the money. He's a millionaire. He owns five music publishing houses, all kinds of stock and two real estate agencies. This apartment building? He owns the whole damn thing. Used to be a Greek Orthodox Church. Miles had it torn down and completely rebuilt according to his own specifications." (The building is on the west side of New York, on 70th Street, and from the outside it looks like any other brownstone.)

"Sometimes when I call him up," Buddy had continued, "I ask him what he's doing. 'Counting my money,' he says. He's got money coming in from *everywhere*. He got the rights to every single piece of music he's ever written. Sometimes the checks that come in the mail stack up about a foot high."

The pretty Negro girl comes back and hands Buddy and me our drinks. "Here's your poison," she says, and we nod our thanks. Miles thumbs through a stack of records. Buddy gets up and inspects one of the porcelain masks. I sit and watch Miles.

He makes a selection and places it on the turntable. Hiss, scratch, pop. Then the sound of his horn fills the room. He grins. "Ain't even been released yet," he says.

Back to the piano to accompany himself. The thing is perfectly in tune. You can hear the strings vibrate with multiple harmonics. Miles leans back with his eyes closed and a thin film of sweat forms on his forehead, even though the apartment is air-conditioned. The music is Miles Davis all right. Like the soft whisper of a sad woman. Melancholy. Intense, sensitive.

We sit quietly all the way through, then Miles switches off the machine. Miles starts walking back toward the kitchen, stops suddenly and goes into a boxer's stance. He punches the air swiftly and rapidly and dances lightly around, grunting softly with the effort. "Ahhhhhhhhh, shit!" he says with a final swing—his knock-out punch—and regards an imaginary opponent lying on the floor. He goes to the kitchen entrance and disappears.

Buddy talks about Miles with enthusiasm. "Miles just don't like to have people get close to him, that's all." He explains that deep inside, Miles is tender and sensitive. Anybody who doesn't really know Miles comes to the conclusion that he's just a black sonofabitch who just doesn't give a shit. He's rude and insulting. Crude as hell. He's out for number one, and to hell with the rest of the world.

I believe everything Buddy says. The first thing Miles said, in fact, when we got into the apartment was, "What the fuck do *you* want?"

"This guy wants to do an article on you," Buddy had said.

One would naturally want to say, "Not *that* much, man. It's not really so important if you're going to be such a bastard about it."

But if one reads his former mistress's account . . . "Miles is a gentle imposter playing that vicious game called life. Nobody in the world can play music as beautifully as he does and not be a beautiful person inside. It is this haunting beauty that betrays this extreme defense mechanism. He has built that transparent wall around him and doesn't know that written on the outside in big bold letters is a sign saying 'I have to keep you away from me because I can be easily hurt if I let you get too close.'" . . . why not just wait and see? Maybe the guy isn't so bad after all.

Miles comes back into the room with a plate bearing a huge steak. He cuts out a chunk and sticks it with his fork. He shoves it toward me. "Want a bite?"

What's this, anyway. Does he want to see if Whitey can stand to eat from a nigger's plate? No, that's not the look in his eyes. Take the fork, taste the steak. Medium-rare, excellent.

"This is good. You cook it yourself?"

"Yeah."

Buddy leans over. "Tell him why you cook, Miles."

Miles grins. "I started to cook when I found out that bitches never do it right." He eats slowly. Buddy and I keep sipping from our drinks. Finally he puts the plate down. He's getting into a good mood.

"Hey," he breathes.

"What?"

"You got one of those notebooks writers carry around?"

"Sure."

"Well, put *this* in that article. I got the whole solution." He pauses, pleased with himself.

"The solution to what, Miles," I say, getting out a pen and the book.

"To all this Vietnam shit. What we gotta do is draft all the bitches under twenty-five and send them over there. All kinds of tough-lookin' *white* bitches, with all that clean, white skin and blonde hair and big tits. When these cats read in the paper that a hundred of them get killed by the Viet Cong, the whole thing will be over in a day."

Buddy and I laugh, and I write it down. Miles grins. "Now you be sure to put that in, you hear?"

"Sure, Miles."

He gets up and stretches and yawns. Buddy reads it as a signal for us to leave. We go down the steps, and Miles speaks again. "Hey."

I look up.

"I'm playing in Boston in a couple of days. Come on up."

"I'll be there."

When we're out in Buddy's car, he says, "You motherfucker. He likes you."

Miles Dewey Davis III was born in Alton, Illinois, in 1926. His father, Miles II, gave him a trumpet when he was thirteen years old. Of him, his father has said, "By genetics and breeding, Miles is always going to be ahead of his time. Historically way back to slavery days, the Davises have been musicians and performed classical works in the homes of plantation owners."

Miles' childhood was hard, in spite of the family's financial stability. Miles' father was a dental surgeon and one of the first Negroes to graduate from Northwestern University Dental School. It was the stigma of being black in a white society, the accounts read, particularly for a sensitive and perceptive young man like Miles, that left permanent emotional scars.

Although Miles had told me that "white people are a bitch," I found that essentially he has developed a tolerance or an indifference to the present racial situation. One of Miles' closest friends, music arranger Gil Evans, is white and Miles has said that "Gil and I think on the same wavelength." Buddy commented that it doesn't make any difference to Miles whether a man is white or black "or even green." His criteria, it's said, is whether a man is honest or not and can relate to him on personal values and merits.

But prejudice has confronted Miles, sometimes in brutal ways. He related an incident in front of Birdland when he was arrested for assault on a policeman. Miles said he was taking a break and had escorted a white girl to a taxi. A cop approached him and told him to move on. Miles said he explained he was *the* Miles Davis and was working in Birdland. The officer raised his club, and Miles, fearing that his hands or his lips would be injured, struggled with him. A nearby detective came into the fracas, and Miles received a blow on the head. A tape recorder, owned by a person living in an apartment immediately above the scene, produces the following dialogue:

"Take him to the precinct—that black c—s—. Don't let him get away free. Get that f— out of here."

"I'll punch him right in the nose, so help me."

"Why don't we all go to the precinct. I saw what happened."

"That m—f— ain't no police. He ain't no police."

The result of the incident was five stitches in Miles' head, a charge of assault on a policeman and, after being acquitted, Miles threatened a lawsuit against the city of New York which he eventually dropped.

When Miles related the incident to me, he spoke with what appeared to be boredom. Later, when I checked on the details, I found that he added nothing to the published accounts. One would expect to hear bitterness or anger, but the way Miles told it, it might have happened to someone else.

Miles' first idol was Roy Eldridge. When Billy Eckstine's band came through St. Louis, where Miles' family moved when he was a boy, he met Charlie Parker and Dizzy Gillespie, who let him sit in with the band. At nineteen, he got permission from his father to go to New York to study at Juilliard. As soon as he got to New York though, Miles spent his first month's allowance trying to find Charlie Parker. He eventually moved in with him and subsequently made his first recording with Parker.

Writer Nat Hentoff relates that Miles' close association with Parker was vital to him musically. "He learned to play by listening to Bird, almost never by hearing him discourse on theory." Today Miles consistently hesitates to talk about music, or much about anything else. Ralph Gleason writes, "Miles says don't talk about the music . . . it speaks for itself."

Boston. The Jazz Workshop. I got there just a few minutes before Miles was scheduled to go on. The drummer was setting up his equipment and the club's manager was testing the microphone and adjusting the lights. The place was about three-quarters full of well-dressed people who sat and talked quietly. I found a seat near the stage and ordered a Scotch.

Next to me was a man drinking double vodkas who mumbled under his breath. He turned to me and said, "This Miles Davis is a punk. If it weren't for Charlie Parker, he'd be nowhere." He drunkenly mumbled on loudly until another man told him to shut up or he'd have him thrown out on his ass. The man returned to his vodka and was quiet.

Miles appeared from a side door and slowly walked on stage. He had a distant, aloof look on his face. Ignoring the applause, he put the horn to his lips and started playing. He seemed to be in his own private world, not recognizing anything but the sound of the music. The start of the set was spontaneous. He made no sign to any of the members of the quartet. Miles kept the horn steady in front of the microphone, tilted toward the floor. His playing was incredibly intricate, but he gave the impression that he expended no effort. The only sign of tension or pressure was on his forehead. It was completely covered with gleaming sweat in spite of the club's air-conditioning.

At the finish of the solo he quietly turned away and walked to the side of the stage while the sax took over. He lit a cigarette and sat in a chair with his arms on his knees, taking deep drags and slowly blowing the smoke to the floor.

His apparent indifference and detachment while performing can be misleading. Buddy told me, "When Miles walks off the stage it looks like he doesn't pay any attention to what his group is playing. But he hears every note. Miles has fantastic hearing. He can walk all the way across the room and get a drink of water or something, but he knows exactly what's going on."

Miles put the cigarette in the ash tray and slowly walked back on stage. At the precise moment when he put his horn to his lips and joined the sax player, the audience collectively gasped. His entry was perfection—musically the sound of the horn picked up a theme at precisely the right moment. His timing was incredible.

I looked at the crowd around me. They sat motionless and silent. There was a young man wearing glasses sitting at a table not two yards from Miles. He looked like a college student, wearing a striped tie and tweed jacket. His head was bowed and he was smiling with his eyes closed, nodding with the rhythms of the music. I thought for a moment he was drunk. But when the set was over, he looked up with a satisfied look on his face—much as if he had just gotten a tremendous high from some good pot. He was completely sober. The vodka drinker sitting next to me said nothing. He kept shaking his head.

Later in the evening I went up next to the stage and sat down at Miles' table. When he finished a set he came over and lit another cigarette. He said nothing for five minutes, then he tilted his head toward me and asked, "What the fuck are you doing up here?"

"Watching you," I said.

He grunted, then was silent for another five minutes. Then he said, "My lip's hurting."

"It looks split," I offered. A bit of blood trickled down on his chin. He dabbed it with his handkerchief.

"It's split, all right."

"Are you going to put something on it?"

"Yeah, this trumpet, what else?" he said.

Polcari's restaurant, Boston. We left the cab and Miles handed the driver a dollar. The cabbie gave Miles a mean look because the fare was ninety-five cents and he expected a large tip. During the ride over, he recognized Miles and he figured he was going to make a bit of extra money. "Thanks," he said.

Miles turned away from him. "Fuck you," he breathed.

We entered the restaurant and took off our coats. With us was Miles' boxing trainer, Bobby, who had just finished a work out with Miles at the New Garden Gym. Miles likes to keep in good physical shape. Miles told Bobby to call up a boxer named Gerry and tell him to join us for dinner.

The place was ornate, complete with a huge mirrored bar, scarlet carpets and waiters wearing full-dress tuxedos. We were escorted to a table. Miles and I sat down and the waiter brought a large red tablecloth and spread it in front of us. There was a small stain on the corner. Miles looked sharply at the waiter and said, "Why are you putting a dirty tablecloth in front of me?"

The man looked surprised, then nervously laughed. I think he was kind of wondering who the nigger thought he was, talking that way. He said, "It's not really that dirty."

"This place looks like a whorehouse," Miles said. He turned to me. "It really gets me when a place tries to be first-class when they really aren't." He motioned to a pile of coats on a table across the room. "See that?" he said. "A really good restaurant wouldn't have that around."

Bobby came back to the table and said that Gerry was on his way. Miles grunted and sipped his water. He was in an expansive mood. "Water," he said.

"Yeah," Bobby said. "One thing about water. You can't get rid of it. There's more water in the world than anything."

Miles grinned. "No, man. That isn't it."

Bobby looked up expectantly.

"There's more *bullshit* than water. That's what the world's full of."

When Gerry showed up, we placed our order. The waiter said they had some really good soup and that he recommended that we start with that. Miles nodded. When the soup came, Miles took a couple of spoonfuls, then called the waiter. "Bring the goddamn cook over here," he said.

The cook approached the table. "Did you cook this soup?" Miles asked.

"Yes," the man replied nervously. "You like it, no?" He spoke with an Italian accent.

"It tastes like you look," Miles hissed.

The cook looked offended. "It is not good?"

Bobby interrupted. "Yeah, it's good. Miles has just been bragging on it." Miles grinned, then called the waiter back and ordered a broiled swordfish filet and a bean salad. Bobby ordered the same and Gerry got a rare filet mignon. I asked for spaghetti and meatballs and a half bottle of Chianti. Miles said nothing while Bobby and Gerry discussed boxing. He sat and ate his salad with quick movements.

"Man," Miles said. "Sometimes I get so hungry I can't stop. I'm going to eat everything they bring me."

I had a cigarette burning in the ash tray in front of me and Miles said, "Say, why don't you put that cigarette in your fucking salad?"

When we finished the meal the waiter came up and said, "You people look familiar. Are you with Jimmie Brown's band?"

Miles looked up. "Sheee-it," he said roughly. "This here's a trainer," he said, pointing to Bobby, "this is a boxer, this is a writer, and *ah'm* Miles Davis."

"Oh, yeah," the man said. "I've heard of you. You're that famous trumpet player."

"You're goddamn right," Miles said.

TALKING TO LES TOMPKINS

Interviewer: Les Tompkins
Crescendo, 1969

In this interview Miles Davis talks about his humble beginnings as a fledgling trumpeter, his technique, and his new band. Les Tompkins was a veteran jazz critic and historian well respected by practitioners in the field. During his tenure Tompkins conducted hundreds of interviews with many of the jazz elite. He possessed a gift, making his subjects open up about their jazz aesthetic, their past experiences, their present situations, and what their plans were for the future. Miles Davis was no exception. He had it in his heart that day to reveal to Les who he was, where he came from, and where he thought he might be going with his new musical direction.

You want to know how I started playing trumpet? My father bought me one, and I studied the trumpet. And everybody I heard that I liked, I picked up things from.

It was when the Billy Eckstine band came to St. Louis that you first got together with Bird and Diz, wasn't it?
I'd heard 'em on records. But I was playing like that, anyway. You got to understand, man. See white folks always think that you have to have a label on everything—you know what I mean?

Well, I don't, necessarily.

That's how you're spelling everything—when you say: "You heard Diz." But two guys can do the same thing, and still won't see each other. So it was *happening*, like I say. It actually happened in Kansas City. If you listen to Charlie Parker, he sounds like Ben Webster, you know. Dizzy doesn't sound like Charlie Parker; they're two different people. Right?

Yes. But Dizzy's playing underwent certain changes. Or perhaps evolution is a better word. He doesn't play now the same way he played in his earlier years. Why?

Well, on some of the early records he sounded something like Roy Eldridge. Then the critics were wrong, man.

But you couldn't hear the things that developed later in his playing at that time. Maybe there was nothing to develop. Right?

At a certain point his playing sort of found a new direction, I suppose. I don't hold it against Dizzy, you know, but if a guy wants to play a certain way, you work towards that. If he *stops*—he's full of crap, you know. I mean, *I* wouldn't do it, for no money, or for no place in the white man's world. Not just to make money, because then you don't have *anything*. You don't have as much money as whoever you're trying to ape; that's making money by being commercial. Then you don't have anything to give the world; so you're not important. You might as well be *dead*.

That's the way it goes. I mean, guys should keep on doing it right, no matter what it is. If you sacrifice your art because of some woman, or some man, or for some colour, or for some wealth, you can't be trusted.

I mean that goes for anybody. I'm not putting Dizzy down or anybody else, you know. But I think they should just keep *on*, no matter what happens.

You've always believed in playing exactly the way you wanted to at all times? Course. I want to see if I can do it.

There was the period when you seemed to be using the mute quite a lot.
I use it if I want to play something, here and there. Not because some people said to me: "Miles, you sound good with a mute." I know it sounds good, else I wouldn't pick it up.

On a lot of the records that were very successful, tracks like "All of You" and "Bye Bye Blackbird," when you played with the mute close to the mike, you had what came to be known as the Miles Davis sound.
I got it from Dizzy.

I don't remember hearing that sound from Dizzy.
Listen to "Ko Ko." But, you see, all my ideas of a tone come from listening to trumpet players who play *round*—with no tag on the end of the tone. I would never try and play like Harry James, because I don't like his tone—for me.

It's too sort of creamy, I suppose.
What you call creamy and what I call creamy may be two different things. It's just white. You know what I mean? He has what we black trumpet players call a white sound. But it's for white music.

Do all white players have a white sound?
Well, no—there's still something that isn't there, you know. I can tell a white trumpet player, just listening to a record. There'll be something he'll do that'll let me know that he's white.

It's like listening to somebody's accent, is it?
Right. I can hear a gray singer that's trying to sing coloured—I don't mean black, I mean coloured—and all of a sudden, like, he'll say "mother" and his "-er" won't get that true sound. Tom Jones is funny to me, man. I mean, he really tries to ape Ray Charles and Sammy Davis, you know.

Yes—but he's making a success of it.
Well, see, he's nice-looking; he looks good doing it. I mean, if I was him, I'd do the same thing. If I was only thinking about making money.

What did you think of Chet Baker?

I liked Chet. But white guys play a certain way, man. They *lean* on notes, you know, when they set a rhythm. I used to enjoy all the white bands when I was a kid listening to the radio.

But the record companies, they take music and label it—like, they say "rock." Because the white singers can't sound like James Brown, they call him "soul." They've been doing that for *years*. That's the prejudice crap. So you get rock groups that are white, that are actually prejudiced. They say "freedom," but they only mean freedom for *themselves*.

And I see all those white producers—trying to make young films. But they don't understand that scene. They mess them white kids up; the kids don't know whether to f— or ride. Or get high. I see 'em getting high most of the time.

When white people get high, they say: "It's all right for *me*." There's a lot of guys in jail, man, for ten years, that had two sticks of reefer, you know—because they're black, and with a white girl or something. Now you get a white kid with two sticks of reefer, they'll throw it away—and let him off.

I mean, it's those producers and record companies the way they *sell* things helps with a lot of prejudice. It builds a white image.

Like, jazz is an Uncle Tom word. They should stop *using* that word for selling. I told George Wein the other day that he should stop using it.

But is there any substitute word?

Just *music*, man. We might play *anything* out there. It gets back to you asking me how I learned how to play a trumpet. I mean, you hear correct fingering and all that crap. But when you sell one side. . . . White people can handle a horn and other white people want to see 'em, with their long hair and all that—okay. But also sell the black man, so he can appreciate his black brothers.

Look at John Wayne. He's a sad so-and-so outside movies. You know—the way he thinks. You can get somebody other than Sidney [Poitier] building up the spade guys and groovin' them girls. All the white men want to make love to all them pretty black girls. You know—they're always *looking*.

I mean, you can have it in movies so the guys can see the girls and the girls can see the guys, so they can like their own people—since it's such a sin to make love to a white. But that's the way they sell it, the record companies and the movies.

Nevertheless, though, some of the record producers do have a certain amount of integrity and try to promote the best in music.
A guy might start out with good intentions, you know, and when he comes to selling it, he goes to somebody else. The sales department sells that stuff.

The beautiful albums you did with Gil Evans—there's an artistic endeavor.
Everybody knows that.

Whoever was responsible for the production was doing something worthwhile.
The first time it came out, it had a white woman with a little boy on the cover.

It didn't get that sleeve in Britain.
The reason you didn't was because I told 'em to take it *off.* There's some sad things happen, man. I'm 43 and before I die I want to see *somebody* get something. I can make all the money I'm never going to need. That's not important; I was doing that when I was ten, selling papers. I mean, that's easy—just to make money. But the other part needs straightening out.

I mean, Gil and I might do something, you and I might do something, but when it gets to the sales department, they say: "The young white kids have the most money," which isn't necessarily true. So they say the white kids buy dope because they have too much money. Well, how come there's so many Spanish people and Negroes in jail for dope? It doesn't balance, man, no matter what you say.

I have to play the way I want to play, because that's the only way I can *feel* like something, you know. I feel like crap, man, out there. If I would go to a war or something, I don't have anything at home. If I go out, I might have to fight. I got shot at six times—I mean, that's all on account of a white man, even if indirectly, trying to make a Negro have as much money as he has. He shoots at me—a black man, you know. But it doesn't do any good, because you can't change no white man. I'd rather die than to be so *sad.*

In America, the home of jazz, it seems to be treated with contempt, almost.
As I said, we don't even use that word jazz. It's an Uncle Tom expression.

But initially it was just a way of describing improvisation.
Americans don't like *any* form of art, man. All they like to do is *make money.*

They don't like me, Sammy Davis, or anybody else. They don't like nothing. They just like Sammy because he can make 'em a lot of money.

Well, they like to go out and be entertained by you and Sammy.
I mean, it makes me sick when I see a white man sitting there smiling at me being entertaining, man. When I know what he's gonna do after he gets through. You know, when you see that thing on their face—like: "Entertain me." You know what I mean? Even the black guy that's trying to be white—even he can have that crap on his face.

I'm there because I know how to play music better than most musicians. I mean, my conception is considered by musicians to be top, you know. And I know it; that's the reason I'm there. Those people should know that, that I'm not out there grinning, Tomming. I'm out there doing the best that I can. My lip is cut and I'm still playing. I'm not trying to be cute. I know how I look. I'm not messing around with nobody's woman. If I want a woman, I go get her—you know what I mean? So I'm just there performing. I'm straight. Actually, I think, old-fashioned, you know. I'm just straight.

But at least a proportion of the audience is as sincere as you are.
People who like music, man, they seem to like all types. And they don't care whether you're black or white—you know, the real music-lover. But those people sitting over there, *they* care.

I can let Dave [Holland] play sometimes—you hear loud applause; that's all from white people. I *know* they're gonna do it. It's like it's a boxing match.

But me and the guys I grew up with, we used to sit and listen to music, and we didn't care who was playing or what colour you were. I heard Buddy Rich—damn, he could play! Gene Krupa, you know. All them musicians came down and jammed with us. If they couldn't *play*, whether they were white or coloured, man, made no difference.

It was either good or bad. Well, that should be the only criterion.
That's the way you judge a car, man, when you start it up. It's just the same thing. I mean, I drive a Ferrari—not to be cute, but because I dig it. I'd rather drive a ten-year-old Ferrari than one of them new things—they don't go.

The movement for playing complete freedom—is this part of a reaction against these attitudes?
No, it's just something that happens, man. We started doing that when we started leaving the piano out. Remember when we'd take the piano out and you could never tell where anything was? You could just kinda fool around. Now piano players are just getting so they can kind of feel you, you know. But your reflexes and ears have to be with it, to take you through. No matter what tempo it is, you have to just feel it right.

But there has to be a lot of sympathy between the musicians to bring it off.
Of course. Sometimes it doesn't happen, because maybe a guy's wife'll come in, you know, and his ego will catch him. If everybody's completely just straight—without any old ladies over here, a fourth of whiskey over there; if it's balanced right, it'll come off. It *has* to be. But when you get egos involved with playing free, you can't do it.

However free you get, though, it's based on a given form, isn't it?
Oh, you have some kind of form. You have to start *somewhere*. I mean, other-wise we'd all be living outdoors. You have walls and stuff, but you still come in a room and act kinda free. There's a framework, but it's just—we don't want to overdo it, you know. It's hard to balance. Sometimes you don't even know if people like it or not.

Can't you gauge it from the audience reaction you get?
Well, I never really *listen* to that, you know.

You might wonder whether they're genuine, or just applauding because they think this is "the thing."
No, I only look at writers like that. The writers that say it was out of sight, and I know it *wasn't*. But audiences—they like colour, you know. I can go out there wearing a red suit, man, and they'll say I'm out of sight.

But you've got to give 'em some credit, too. You *must*. I mean, look at Duke, man; he drops some things on 'em. I think they should be educated; you should always drop something on an audience. And friends should educate you, you know. Or else they shouldn't be around—if they're just gonna drain you.

When you get in front of an audience, you should try to give 'em something. After all, they're there looking at you like *this*. You can't go out and give 'em *nothing*.

You see, women usually make the men satisfied and contented. Bitches like to feel good, have their back rubbed at the same time, look good in the latest clothes, have their man where they want him. You know, they like the *comfort*. Then, when you come on the stage they want that same thing. They don't want to have to think, or follow you. If they don't like you right away by the way you look, or something, they won't go for you.

Guys should stay away from women—that comfort thing. There's too much crap going on in the world that you're supposed to be comfortable. You've got to be on your toes. You can't just stand—because they're fighting somewhere, man, and it's pretty messy.

You've really got to challenge yourself, and also the people who are listening to you.
If I go to hear someone, I'm at their mercy. I'm listening, you know, but I don't go there and say: "*Do* something." I'm trying to get whatever they put out. But I don't *demand* it, because things don't *come* like that. You know what I mean? I mean, we might visit London once in two years, and it might be an *off night*. But you can't say I'm a sad so-and-so, because I've got too many points.

This is something that people don't always take into account—that musicians are human.
Right. If I go to hear Dizzy, I hear what I want to hear in him, you know. I don't hear what they *see*. I hear little things that he does, that make me say: "Yeah, okay"—and the rest of the jive, I just don't listen. Or look.

Do you go out and listen a great deal to other music?
All the time.

To classical music some of the time?
Yeah, but not to be comfortable. I want to *hear* something. I'm 43, man—I've heard Ravel. The only way I'll play Ravel is, if I want to refer to his kind of impressionism in some way. 'Cause this is 1970, man.

Some of Gil's writing on the albums had the feel of the romantic composers. Then you got the Spanish sound.

If you want to sound Spanish, you can do it; but you have to *lean* to each note. That's the trick right there. To get one of those scores—we used to do 'em together, you know. A lot of people don't know that.

You worked on them together? You would suggest something and he would put it down?

Then I would write something and give it to him. I'd say: "Put this on this note." You know, we have a big-band sound now, that's really out of sight, man. We did that last year. If you'd hear it, you'd say: "Wow!"

A large orchestra?

Yes, but it's not that *bull*— you hear. Because we have a different set of instruments. First of all we have our whitey guitar (John McLaughlin); we have tuba, French horn, double bass, clarinet, bassoon—all sounds like that, you know. Flute, piccolo, harp, mandolin, two electric pianos. But you should hear that *sound*. I mean, that other big-band sound is *over*. It's *been* over for quite some time.

If it's dead, there's a lot of people who won't let it lie down.

They should get away from four saxophones, four trumpets, four trombones. Trombones don't serve any purpose at *all*. The sound *we* have—it's out of sight. Then you can write into it, so that a certain part's written and other parts will be *ad lib*, and you can't even *tell* it.

On my last date, I used a regular bass and electric bass, two electric pianos, one organ and four drummers. And a bass clarinet. You ought to hear *that*. Conga drums, and the other drums just played different sounds. And a guitar.

Interweaving with one another?

Right. A lot of the kind of thing that just falls. Then sometimes a bass line and it swings, just like a pulse. There's a lot of color. A lot of times I told the bass clarinet to play with other instruments.

I used John McLaughlin on guitar, but I had a bass playing with him—and me, too. Some lines were written and some lines were just played together, you know.

Charlie Parker and I used to do that. He'd play on top, I'd play on the bottom, and I would never clash with him. But never play the same thing—you know what I mean?

Complementing one another.
Right. You can do that with all sorts of things.

So long as you've got the musicians with the ability to do it.
That's the trick—getting the musicians. You get a good musician, and tell him what to do. And what you tell 'em to do has to be what they *want* to do, anyway. I mean, you can't tell 'em something they don't want to *do*. It won't come out. This last album we made was really *something*.

Was Dave Holland on that? Playing normal bass and electric, was he?
Yeah, I think he might have been playing guitar, too, and electric bass. I mean, if you can get a sound that's supposed to come in and all your feelings go to make that little sound. . . . It might be bells; it might be a little flute with the bells.

I know I wrote one thing on just a rhythm pattern. Like, pap-pap-pap, pap-pap-pap—like that, and it kept repeating it. You can't even tell when it stops. But you keep adding chords to it, and sounds, you know. Not building, so much as what's in between, that makes it sound different every time you hit it. You keep on doing it, but the inside is different. You can just keep it going all night, man.

It's like listening to a train a lot of times; you know, sometimes it's the same and other times it changes. Yes, you can hear different things all the time against it.

But watch those people who want to be comfortable, man—they'll turn you in. Who wants to be comfortable?

You heard Dave originally in Ronnie Scott's club, didn't you?
He doesn't play like that now.

He doesn't play the way he was playing then?
Mm-mm. What—over a year ago?

This is because he's been influenced by the whole group, or by you particularly?
Well, Dave plays the way he wants to play. And it's usually what's needed. You know, Dave is such a deep thinker. You can't tell him too much, else it might spoil his spirit, you know. Then when you tell a guy something, you get to thinking—well, who are you to tell him anything, anyway? Let him do what he does; maybe you'll be *gaining* something.

But you heard enough in him to know he'd be able to grow in the group?
I know whatever he does, it won't be any bull—. That's enough right there. I've had guys say: "Man, why don't you get a brother to play the bass?" I say: "Can he play like *that*?" I don't give a damn *who* it is, what *colour* he is. Miroslav [Vitous] was playing most of it, too.

Oh yes, he was over here with Stan Getz.
Ah, but you couldn't hear it. You can't hear him with *Stan*.

It seemed, somehow, that the rhythm section were pulling one way, while Stan was pulling the other.
I can't understand why Stan can't play that other way, you know.

He's too deeply immersed in what he's doing.
That's hard to say. He's a good player; but it's that *ego* there again, you know.

As you say, he doesn't want to do anything that's not natural to him.
Oh no—it's back to being comfortable again. You know what I mean? He's just *comfortable* where he is.

He's not trying to find new fields.
Feels—not fields! Because you have to. Your point of balance should change, you know. You can't do everything flat-footed. In boxing I learned that; I mean, a lot of times you throw a punch from the upper body, and you might want to throw it lower down. Then you have to do it from the hips. See, a lot of boxers don't know that stuff—like, how to swivel. That's what a player has to do.

You see Chick [Corea] do funny kinds of things—because the beat is all messed up. He might play an eleven-note phrase. *That* isn't comfortable, either. I mean, the beat might be here, and he might be playing way up on top of it. You have to fix yourself sort of a point of balance—anywhere. That's what I mean by not being comfortable.

This is perhaps a big pitfall with many musicians. They get to a certain point, feel that they're established and it is comfortable for them to stay with it.
You should never be comfortable, man. Being comfortable fouled up a lot of musicians.

By the same token, some musicians, by trying too hard to break away completely from their roots, or their past, might have got on to a plane that was unnatural to them.
Well—if you're going to be in that field among a lot of those guys, it shouldn't be unnatural. If you're trying to be hip, be hip.

Like, Coleman Hawkins had been playing in an established swing way for many years, and then he got with other schools of musicians.
You take Coleman, if he had changed instruments, maybe his balance point would have changed. If he'd played, maybe, an alto or a soprano sax, his balance right here (holding hips) would have gone somewhere else.

I told Chico to switch—what's his name, that died; he used to play with Coltrane—I told Chico to switch him off of alto. Eric Dolphy. See, when he got on the bass clarinet, he sounded different. You can take a guy off a trumpet, put him on a bass trumpet, and he plays different. Take a guitar player that you think is bad, and put him on electric bass—that does the trick.

You got yourself a good interview. About the first in the last three years.

MILES OF MUSIC

Interviewer: Hubert Saal
Newsweek, March 23, 1970

By 1970, Miles had taken another new direction—this time his decisive turn into experimenting with electronic music. *In a Silent Way* had now blossomed into the terrible beauty of *Bitches Brew*, a double album rich with random exploration, complex polyrhythms, and the urgent soloing of Miles's trumpet and Wayne Shorter's soprano saxophone; this rich amalgam of musical expression had transformed the face of jazz once again. By using state-of-the-art recording studio technology, the music evoked psychedelic experimental forays already explored in recent years by Jimi Hendrix and the Beatles. *Bitches Brew* was recorded shortly after the Woodstock Festival; by discarding traditional forms of jazz, Miles favored a more dissonant approach to improvisatory music. The extensive postproduction with Teo Macero gave the music its edge, causing a new breakthrough in not only jazz but also in rock music, fusing the two together with stunningly effective results. The bestselling album, which garnered Miles his first gold record, was—in the words of most jazz critics—a commercial "sellout" recorded solely to attract those white hippie audiences flocking to rock festivals. At this time Davis had begun performing at rock clubs like the Fillmore East and Fillmore West, often opening for bands like the Grateful Dead and the Steve Miller Band.

At 43, Miles Davis is a legend, larger than life both as man and musician. He lives in a New York house that is more like a castle in Spain. When he leaves it, dressed in trousers made from snakeskin and in boots of Spanish leather, he climbs into a $17,000 red Ferrari and speeds uptown to the gym where he trains as assiduously as any contender. Likely as not one of the beautiful girls he attracts will be on hand to watch him. He and his third wife, Betty, were recently divorced. They remain close friends. Says Miles, "We just didn't want to be bound by any piece of paper."

As a musician, Davis has been in the forefront of jazz since he was 19 and joined the great Charlie Parker just after World War II. In the last two decades he has kept his role in the vanguard from bebop to cool, from cool to progressive. Out of his combo, usually a quintet, have come the late John Coltrane, drummers Philly Joe Jones and Tony Williams, pianists such as Herbie Hancock and Bill Evans. As trumpeter and group leader, Davis dominated the jazz polls of the '60s, of critics and fans alike.

The Fillmore East, where Davis recently finished an engagement, would appear to be an unusual setting for his group. As the home of rock music in the East, its audiences are tuned into and turned on by volume and beat. But Davis and his distinguished sidemen—electric pianist Chick Corea, saxophonist Wayne Shorter, drummer Jack DeJohnette, bassist David Holland and percussionist Airto Moreira—were not intimidated by the under-20 crowd. "We don't play to be seen," says Davis. "I'm addicted to music, not audiences."

Still, Davis produced some surprises. The piano and bass were electrified and everyone heavily miked. What was substantially different during the uninterrupted 50-minute set was the music. Absent was the traditional announcement of theme, the usual round robin of solos, with each man extending himself as if on a merry-go-round for the brass ring, and Davis blowing that mournful, thoughtful, melodic horn, ending in a nice soft landing together.

Frenetic: Instead, take-offs and landings were instantaneous and without seat belts. Melodic and rhythmic lines were fractured into dissonant bits and pieces. The group improvised at a dizzying frenetic pace, pitting rhythm against rhythm, chords against chords, minor against major, in round after round of challenge and response. It was an extraordinary display of abandoned but coherent spontaneity at reckless speed, too fast for thought, mostly pure feeling.

Davis led and personified this fresh sound. He looked the same—slender, muscular, knees bent as he reached for a note, cocking his head to the side from time to time like a marksman aiming his rifle. He made all kinds of sounds. Occasionally there were brief passages of the familiar Davis, melodic, spare, pensive, tentative. But for the most part he blew a bugle sound, lean and hard, exploding into a flurry of notes, or else a single note followed after a long interval by another. And sometimes he appeared to be echoing Brazilian Moreira in producing a barking, coughing staccato, an aggressive sound that hunted down the outlandish notes he sought. In his spare, economical style, he evoked images of Webern and Stravinsky.

In other respects Davis was his usual self. He didn't announce titles. "Why announce it?" he says. "It's only a feeling." He refused to acknowledge applause. When not playing he prowled gracefully around and off the stage. Of course he played no encores. "The only reason I played Fillmore," he said last week, "was because Clive Davis, president of Columbia Records, asked me to. He bends backward for me. All I have to do at Columbia is produce and they try and sell me like they would a white idol with a head of blond hair. That means the next black man that comes up will get the same treatment."

Label: As for the incongruence of jazz at the Fillmore, Davis rejects the term "jazz" as a white man's word. "It's all just music, man. It's just being out there. André Watts plays a good piano; so does Herbie Hancock; and Bill Evans. Puccini is great and Jimi Hendrix. Everyone who's out there is connected, not pigeonholed according to some label."

Davis learned to play trumpet in St. Louis where he grew up. "In St. Louis we don't shake the notes, we bend them," he says. "That's why I have no vibrato. Vibrato is white men." By 1948, he had left Charlie Parker and formed a group of nine musicians including Gil Evans, John Lewis and Gerry Mulligan, whose Capitol recordings, now called "Birth of the Cool," ushered in a new jazz era. He has never looked back, leading the way through understatement into progressive jazz, and bringing back to jazz in the '60s a new emphasis on melody that was both thoughtful and feeling in its mournful muted style.

Gil Evans, who orchestrated many of the big-band experiments Davis made, says: "I don't want to make a hit parade but I would place him number one. Everything connected with his music has beauty, fire, vitality and grace. His tone on the trumpet is the first change since Louis Armstrong. His rhythm makes the group come together, like a magnet."

Obstacles: Just how much Miles composes and how much is improvised remains his secret. "It's part of the pleasure you get from listening," he says. "Anyway, everyone adds, everyone responds. Sometimes you subtract, take away the rhythm and leave just the high sound. Or take out what you know belongs to someone else and keep the feeling. I write for my group, for something I know Jack can do, or Chick. Or would want to do. What they've got to do is extend themselves beyond what they think they can do. And they've got to be quick. A soloist comes in when he feels like it. Anyway that's what he's being paid for. If it's not working out I just shut them up. How? I set up obstacles, barriers like they do in the streets but with my horn. I curve them, change their direction."

Part of the Miles Davis legend is his temperament. He's a jungle of contradictions, cantankerous and belligerent one minute, smiling and generous the next. He hates questions. "If I analyze myself, I won't be able to do anything," he says. "Why am I this or that? I might as well go to an analyst." The answers he vouchsafes are often obscure. "Hell," he says, "if you understood everything I said, you'd be me."

His life offstage is as improvised as it is on. "Just let it happen," he says. If anything is constant in his life apart from music it's his devotion to keeping himself in shape. Every day he's in New York he drives up to Bobby Gleason's gym in the Bronx where his own trainer, Robert Allah, puts him through a rigorous workout. Allah, whose name was McQuillar before he became a Muslim, is a rapier-thin, gentle man, who fought 78 fights and lost only six. He fought Sandy Saddler, Jimmy Carter and Joe Brown as a lightweight and quit the ring after he accidentally killed a man in it. "I'd like to have had Miles as a fighter when he was 20," Allah says. "Even at 43 he acts like 25. He's quick, he's got the reflexes—and the imagination, like a chess player seeing the moves ahead. People come in here who don't recognize him and ask me who my new fighter is."

Wind: For Miles, keeping in shape and expert with his fists is both a practical and symbolic measure. "It gets me away from musicians and helps me think," he says. "It cleans my chest up, builds up my wind and my concentration. And we play real quick so it's good for my coordination."

But beyond that, being able to handle his dukes suits Miles's image of himself as independent and tough and black. He's deeply involved in and often belligerent about racial problems. "It's a white man's world," he says. "The record companies make idols out of white artists. They don't sell black artists like that. Why do movies always show only white sex? Man, you know whites are going to hold onto the power and the money. The white man leaning back smoking his cigar, he's not going to move. He wants everything just the same. He won't do anything he isn't forced to. That's what makes our music different. It comes from a people who have had to learn how to make the white man move."

Davis is by no means indiscriminate in his hostility to whites. In particular, he hates cops. And with some reason. In 1959, he was standing in front of New York's Birdland taking a break during intermission when a policeman told him to move along. In the ensuing argument, a detective slugged him over the head with a blackjack. Ten days ago he was arrested in his red Ferrari for carrying brass knuckles, improper registration, not having a license plate up front and missing an inspection sticker. It cost him a night in jail and $300—$100 fine and $200 for his lawyer. "It wouldn't have happened," says Miles, "if I hadn't been a black man driving a red car. On the way to the station the cop keeps saying 'I've got Miles Davis' like I was Jesse James.

"Cops ought to help people," adds Miles. "The police have got to learn to respect a black artist and a man for what he does. If I could say on my record jackets that these albums can't be sold to the police or their relatives or friends, I would."

Different: Miles is a complex, stubborn, proud man, but curiously without an excessively inflated ego for one who has achieved so much. "I've learned too much from other people," he says. "People who are hung up on themselves usually do the same thing over and over. Because that's the way they feel most comfortable."

If the music he played at the Fillmore East was different from the music on his most recent record, "In a Silent Way," the tapes he played in the sound studio in his Moorish-style living room were different still. One of them, taken from a future record which is tentatively to be called "Zonked," was for his group and electronic tape. "Hear that sound?" he exulted. "Isn't that a helluva sound?" It was. And different. "Sure it's different," he says. "I'm different and that's my music. I was different in 1946, '47 and even '45. You've got to go with life. Put that down. Put it all down. And listen, don't you try to make me into a nice guy."

A NATIONAL TREASURE

by Al Aronowitz

TheBlacklistedJournalist.com, May 26, 1970

Al Aronowitz, often hailed as "The Godfather of Rock Journalism," was one of the most influential rock critics in the music's heyday. His "Pop Scene" column in the *New York Post* heralded such future stars as Elton John, Kris Kristofferson, The Band, Billy Joel, Jerry Garcia, James Taylor, and Janis Joplin. He was also a pioneering journalist who almost single-handedly created what has become known as "participatory journalism," or the "New Journalism," with which writers like Hunter S. Thompson, George Plimpton, and Tom Wolfe would later find immense success.

Aronowitz enjoyed close friendships with scores of musicians, singers, and writers, such as Bob Dylan, The Beatles, Mick Jagger, Janis Joplin, Jimi Hendrix, Jim Morrison, Lenny Bruce, Allen Ginsberg, Jack Kerouac, Neal Cassady—and, of course, the inimitable Miles. Better yet, he *wrote* about those friendships and experiences, capturing some of the most seminal moments in rock history. This piece—in which Aronowitz recalls orchestrating a meeting between the "Prince of Darkness," a jazz revolutionary, and "Pops," a jazz legend, on the latter's seventieth birthday (or so people thought at the time)—was a column Aronowitz wrote for his Web site, www.theblacklistedjournalist.com; it later became part of his memoir of his friendships with Miles and Mick Jagger—the last book he completed before dying from cancer in 2005—aptly titled *Mick and Miles*.

I had to talk Miles into going to the party just the same as I had to talk him into going to Jimi's funeral and just the same as I had to talk him into letting me bring Mick Jagger over to meet him. In Mick's case, Miles ended up not even letting us in the front door, but that's a whole other story which I'll have to tell you some other time. This birthday party I'm talking about was for Louis Armstrong. Probably, it was going to be his last.

So, finally Miles said OK and, as we were on our way, Miles told me a story which he said came from Tommy Flanagan, the keyboard player in Satchmo's band when Satchmo and his troupe were waiting in the VIP Lounge at Orly Airport in Paris for a flight to Moscow. Satchmo and his band were on a State Department "good will" tour when, all of a sudden, Richard M. Nixon, then America's vice president, walked into the lounge with his Secret Service guards. When Nixon saw Satchmo, the vice president immediately rushed up to him, and, almost getting down on his knees, grabbed for Satchmo's hand as if to kiss it. Slobbering all over Satchmo, Nixon began telling Satchmo what a national monument Satchmo was.

"You're like the Statue of Liberty!" Nixon said. "You're a national treasure! I'm your biggest fan, Mr. Armstrong."

It turned out that Nixon was going to Moscow, too. When the flight was announced and everybody started getting up to board the plane, Nixon kept asking: "Are you sure there's nothing I can do for you, Mr. Armstrong?"

The band had a lot of luggage. Louis picked up a couple of pieces and handed them to Nixon, saying: "Yeah! Would you mind carrying these, Mr. President?"

And that, according to Flanagan, was how Louis's band got its stash past Russian customs on that particular trip.

"Pops used to smoke a joint before dinner every night," Miles told me.

To me, Miles, like Satchmo, was also a national monument, another Statue of Liberty and a national treasure, too. Like Satchmo, he was a trumpet player, one of the best who ever lived. I was proud to be going to the party with Miles. I was proud any time I went anywhere with Miles.

At the party, Miles called Satchmo "Pops." So did most of the other older musicians. They were all there when Miles and I arrived at the celebration, held in RCA's brand new Studio A. They were all there, the assembled giants of jazz. They had come to pay homage to the ailing Louis Armstrong in honor of what he thought was his 70th birthday. Like George M. Cohan, Louis always claimed to be a Yankee Doodle Dandy, born on the Fourth of July, but then you'll have to forgive an illegitimate black kid from New Orleans for not remembering his exact date of birth. Satchmo couldn't even remember the exact year. He spent his whole life thinking he was older than he really was. Satchmo always said he was born in 1900. But biographer Gary Giddins eventually unearthed a baptismal certificate proving that Satchmo had been born on August 8, 1901. Still, when you start hitting seventy, what's another year more or less?

The party caught Satchmo by surprise. Why a party now? This was May 26, 1970, and there was still enough time to refloat Noah's ark before the Fourth of July would come around with what Satchmo thought would be his 70th year. The only appointment Satchmo had on his calendar on this particular date was to go to the first recording session he'd scheduled since he'd been stricken by a kidney failure almost two years before. What's another year more or less and what's another recording session more or less? Satchmo couldn't even begin to count the number of sessions at which he'd already played or sung during his forty-seven-year career. But when he walked into RCA's brand new Studio A for his first recording session since September of 1968, he found some 250 of the greatest surviving giants of jazz waiting for him. Also waiting for him was an immense chocolate layer cake.

I remember thinking at first that there was something sad about this party, thrown by old men for another older man who obviously wasn't going to be around much longer. But these old men were all heroes to me. They had created a new and beautiful music, America's very own, which to me equaled the world's greatest classics by the world's greatest masters. These men, too, had achieved artistic immortality. Against crushing hardships, they had persevered. Somehow, they made me think of courageous sea captains ready to go down with their ships but their ships had stayed afloat. Their ships were their music. Here they were, as if with hats in hand, come to pay homage to Louis. Satchmo. Pops. Still, I wondered how many among them had at one time or another looked for a reason to condemn Satchmo. Why? For being too old fashioned? For being too corny? For being too successful?

"God bless Louis!" Billie Holiday once said. "He 'Toms' from the heart."

No, Satchmo had never been a fiery black activist, but he was one of the first of the jazz innovators, taking that genre into the era of the featured soloist and perfecting the blues-influenced brass style of ensuing decades. As Amiri Baraka wrote in *Blues People* when Amiri was still LeRoi Jones, Satchmo's music "moved toward the considerations and responsibilities of high art."

It was Baraka who first really educated me about Louis Armstrong. As for me, I had never been a big fan of Dixieland. But, at a cookout at my house in

Berkeley Heights, New Jersey, many years ago, Satch kept blowing from the outdoor speakers in a twenty-four-hour marathon that a certain radio station was broadcasting as a tribute and I said I wished we could hear something else. Pointing out what a jerk I was and explaining why he could listen to Satchmo's music for a week straight and never once get bored, Amiri enlightened me about Louis Armstrong's contribution to the world. All these jazz heroes at the RCA studio party were there because they knew Satchmo had paved a road for them and they owed him a debt.

"The whole industry is here!" crowed Ornette Coleman, one of the most radical of the jazz avant-gardists. What Ornette's music owes to Satchmo isn't easy for me to discern, but still he radiated reverence for Louis.

"The whole industry" wasn't exactly there, either, but the stars who showed up represented a variety of jazz extremities. This was a tribute Jazz with a capital J was paying to one of its most accomplished elders. With his success, Satchmo had opened doors for so many others. He also had succeeded in living long while making few enemies. He always bubbled with joy and his jolliness was contagious.

Jazz's young radicals might have disagreed with Satchmo's slick show bizzy style and thought he was too jolly "Tommin'," as Billie called it. But it was Louis who broke the show business color barrier, opening a door into which a black couldn't even stick a toe without maybe losing his foot. This was way back in the '20s, when Satchmo became America's first black musician to achieve white mainstream acceptance and acclaim, headlining in venues where no black musician had ever headlined before. Satchmo was the first black musician to star in his own sponsored, weekly radio show, *The Fleischmann's Yeast Program*. Did that make Louis Armstrong America's first black pop star?

It was with his talent, jolliness and charm that Louis Armstrong succeeded. Not only did he have the chops to turn Dixieland into big box office but he had a smile that could melt an ice cap and de-venomize a rattlesnake. Satchmo's philosophy was that he got better results with honey than with vinegar, with courtesy than with confrontation and with cuteness than with controversy. The only time Satchmo ever found it necessary to get vocal about being black was when Arkansas Governor Orval Faubus barred the door of a white school in Little Rock, Arkansas, preventing black kids from entering. Eisenhower was president at the time, and Satchmo, protesting that Ike should've gone down to

Little Rock to handle the situation himself, registered his outrage by saying he would cancel an overseas good-will tour that the State Department had planned for him.

Such an angry public outburst wasn't typical of Satchmo, and his highly appalled business guru, jazz entrepreneur Joe Glaser, expressed disagreement. Glaser thought that this might be bad for Satchmo's image and hurt his business and Glaser tried to get Satch to claim he had been misquoted. Singer Eartha Kitt got into the act by booing Glaser and rooting for Satchmo to stick to his guns. Those were the most controversial headlines Satchmo ever made. That was the extent of Satchmo's black militancy.

Studio A had a Forty-Fourth Street entrance and when Miles and I walked in, Satchmo was sitting atop a stool with a padded back and armrests, looking a little like an egg in an egg cup that's waiting to be broken. A chocolate egg. He was singing into a microphone:

"Here is my heart for Christmasssssss. . . ."

After his kidney failure, Satchmo had been in Beth Israel Hospital for five months and he had spent the next year at his home in Queens recuperating. As I said, this was his first recording session in nineteen months. Another reason all these giants had come to pay homage to Satchmo was that they knew they might not get another chance.

"What are all these people doing here?" Miles asked Louis' wife, Lucille.

"They've come to see him fall on his face," Lucille joked.

"Well, if he does, it's about time," Miles said.

Satchmo himself was buoyant. When I asked him how he felt, he said: "Satchmo never felt better and had less. . . ."

His words danced out like happy bubbles in a toothpaste commercial.

"I'm back on the mound again," Satchmo said. "I'm waitin' for some word from the doctor about when I can play my horn again. But I play it anyway. Every night before supper."

The party lasted only about an hour and then Satchmo had to go to work. Oliver Nelson was conducting and the orchestra was a full one, with more pieces than I was willing to bother counting. Bob Thiele was in the control room, producing. Bob was determined to put out the album on what was supposed to be Satchmo's 70th birthday, the Fourth of July. The album, on Thiele's Flying Dutchman label, was to be called *Louis Armstrong & His Friends* and

Satchmo eventually would receive a telegram from still another "friend," President Nixon. Didn't Nixon say Satchmo was a national treasure, a monument, the equivalent of the Statue of Liberty? The album would end up with Satchmo singing tunes like "Give Peace a Chance," "We Shall Overcome," "The Boy from New Orleans," and "My One and Only Love."

RCA's brand new Studio A was immense, big enough to hold a couple of basketball courts. It had a stage, too. As the party dwindled, many remained as an audience for the session, and there were rows of folding chairs. Tony Bennett was sitting in one. Leon Thomas and Bobby Hackett and Eddie Condon also stayed. Ornette Coleman sat dangling his feet over the edge of the stage, sucking up a whistle every time he thought sick, old Pops hit a home run or made a shoestring catch. Miles told me that it was as if the songs, the arrangements, and the register of the orchestra had been designed to make it easy for Satchmo. So easy that there was practically nothing left for him to do. He didn't have to expend any effort. He just had to crawl around the bases. He could sleepwalk his way across the finish line. But Satchmo fooled everybody by doing some unexpected fancy footwork.

"He don' sound like a dyin' man," Miles said.

To me, Satchmo's performance was the equivalent of George Burns doing cartwheels at the age of 100 while smoking a cigar, but then, what does a jerk like me know? Only a pro knows how to make hard things look easy and easy things look hard. Who else but Pops could have turned "Hello, Dolly" into another American anthem?

The first time I ever went to see Satchmo, I was only seventeen. It was hard for me to get a ticket. He was playing a dance on an amusement pier in Asbury Park and the place was packed. I still didn't know how to dance and I wasn't really one of his fans, but I had to get in to see Satchmo because my best friend was going. My remembrance of Satchmo on the pier is as clear as the sky on a lovesick night in Asbury Park, with a full moon hovering over the ocean. The dance was smoky and mobbed. I remember crowding up to the bandstand along with everybody else just to get a closer look at him. I remember catching glimpses of his head weaving and bobbing with his happy eyes bulging and his cheeks ballooning as he blew his trumpet. I can't remember the tunes he played but Satchmo always played the hits of the day. Still, he never played a song the way it was written and he never sang one as if it didn't belong to him. On the

pier at Asbury Park, Satchmo sparkled. He was ebullient. His smile was contagious. The sound of joy came out of his trumpet. What I remember most about
the dance that night was the happiness.

At the party in Studio A, somebody was telling how Satchmo had started out
singing for pennies on the streets of New Orleans's Storyville section. The other
kids called him Satchel Mouth because his jaw reminded them of the little valise
doctors used to carry in the days when doctors made house calls. They also
called him Gatemouth and Dippermouth. Although he could be heard calling
his trumpet "Satchmo" on a 1930s record entitled "You're Driving Me Crazy,"
Percy Mathison Brooks, editor of *Melody Maker*, England's leading music trade
publication, is credited with giving him that name. Brooks was part of the wel-
coming committee when Satchel Mouth arrived with his band for appearances
in London in 1932. Apparently trying to pronounce "Satchel Mouth" in Brooks'
uptight English accent, Brooks came out with something that sounded more
like "Satchmo," or so the story goes. Laughing, Satchmo's band started calling
Louis "Satchmo," too. Soon, everybody was calling Louis "Satchmo," including
Satchmo himself.

He'd been eleven when a musician named Bunk Jones first taught him to
play the cornet in the back room of the Dago Tony Tonk, a New Orleans night
spot. He hadn't been much older than that when King Oliver had sent for him to
come join the King's band in Chicago. Soon, people started listening to King Oliver records mainly to catch Satchmo's solos. Before long, Satchmo was recording his own records on the Okeh label.

"*DownBeat* called me up to say something about Louis," Ornette said. "I said
I think Louis is the most loved black man in a white man's society, and I think
that's true."

There was a break between takes and Miles walked up to Satchmo, tickled him
on the back and whispered into his ear: "Isn't the orchestra too low for you?"

"You know I don't care about nothing. . . ." Satchmo's voice trailed off and I
couldn't hear the rest of what he said. Both Satchmo and Miles talked in rasps,
gargles and hisses. Miles kept claiming that he and Satchmo both blew out their
vocal chords the same way.

"We blew out our voices playin' for the people," Miles used to tell me.

I guess the kind of voice that both Louis and Miles had is an occupational
hazard for trumpet players. I couldn't hear what they were saying and I don't

know if they could hear what they were saying, either. When Miles headed back into the control booth, Satchmo turned on his stool and said: "Always glad to see you, Miles!"

Back in the control booth, I overheard Newport Jazz Festival promoter George Wein boasting that Miles' presence added significance to the party. After all, Miles represented the jazz revolutionaries. He had been a radical innovator since the Bebop era. Miles was a giant of jazz styles that had long ago left Satchmo outdated. Still, Miles had never had a hit single. Louis had had so many.

"They called Louis an Uncle Tom," Wein said. "Now, it's a different era. That man there," and Wein pointed toward Satchmo, "is true culture. Everything in music is traceable to him."

In a corner, I started talking to Lucille, who told me that her husband had never known how it felt to rest. Suddenly, the orchestra began to play "Mood Indigo" and you could hear Satchmo's voice rasping over the loudspeakers: "Sure is a lot of gumbo in that one!"

Soon, Miles said he was ready to leave. As I followed Miles to the door, he told me: "They take advantage of his age. When you're that old, they really drain you to make you sound as if you're in heaven. It don't matter. He's got so much soul, he makes it sound good anyway."

In the months after the party, Satchmo made a few TV appearances. He played at only one more recording session, held in Nashville in August 1970, a session for a gimmick album of Satchmo singing country and western songs. He died on July 6, 1971, after suffering another heart attack. He died two days after celebrating what he thought was his seventy-first birthday.

FADED BLUE FLOWERS

by Al Aronowitz
TheBlacklistedJournalist.com, September 1970

Billie Holiday first introduced Al Aronowitz to Miles in 1958. During his long friendship with the trumpeter, during which Davis often played his dubs to Al over the phone, Aronowitz succeeded in convincing him to play the Fillmore West, to help celebrate Louis Armstrong's birthday, and to accompany him to Hendrix's funeral. Jimi and Miles hadn't known each other for long, but they'd become close. It was Jimi who had inspired Miles to renounce his past and pursue his musical exploits across fresher terrain. Still, it took some Herculean effort on Al's part to encourage Miles to join him, especially since Davis detested sending off the deceased.

I had to talk Miles into going to Jimi's funeral with me. What the hell, I told him, it was only a few days before he had to be out on the Coast anyway and besides, there'd be a lot of press there and the exposure would be good for him.

"I don't like funerals," he rasped. "*Sheet!* I didn't even go to my mother's funeral."

In the end, he made the plane, Miles, with his hairdresser, Finney, and Jacki, a beautiful fox he had picked up out of the crowd at LaGuardia Airport one day.

They buried Jimi Hendrix in the bright afternoon in a hilltop cemetery amid the sobs of people who hadn't really known him for years or who had never known him. It was a cloudless day. Several hundred kids watched from behind the ropes. Seattle had never understood Jimi, and now it had to open its earth for him. . . .

Miles and Jimi hadn't known each other too long, but in the short time they did they had gotten pretty tight. Jimi was one of those kids who had grown up worshipping Miles as Miles kept getting younger. Which black kid who loved music had never heard of Miles Davis? For as long as Jimi could remember, Miles had been a legend to him, and it was only when he felt secure enough as a legend himself that he came to sit at Miles's feet and ask Miles to record an album with him. Miles said shit, he'd be happy to do the album but he wanted $50,000 for it. For that much of his soul, he wanted that much money. Like when Sidney Poitier tried to hype Miles into doing the sound track for some movie because the movie would make Miles famous.

"Man," Miles answered, "I'm already famous!"

Miles was a big influence on Jimi. Miles was a teacher, but he learned something from Jimi, too. Miles learned something about rhythms and something about phrasing and something about the rock and roll lifestyle. It was Jimi who became the final inspiration to move Miles to renounce the classical forms of jazz, many of them created by Miles himself, and to start playing the rock halls. Miles knew how to stay as young as any kid. What Miles wanted to find out was how come a kid like Jimi could make fifty thousand dollars in one night when Miles still couldn't make ten thousand.

———

> It had been nine years since Jimi left the vast green valleys that
> had sent him off in search of a home he could not find and now
> his remains were back amid the airplane factories, the strip
> mine quarries, the salmon canneries, the steel mills and the
> breweries that had tried to trap him and keep him. . . .

———

Steve Paul was on the plane, Steve, the underground entrepreneur who had once run the Scene at 46th Street and Eighth Avenue, New York's most outrageous cellar rock club. Steve, host to the stars, had become a friend and confidant of Jimi's through the long, hangout nights at the club, where Jimi used to get so drunk and drugged, he couldn't stand up anymore. And still he'd get onstage and jam till dawn. Steve was on the plane with guitar star Johnny Winter, the Albino Whisper, a tender, quiet, bashful sweetheart until he starts picking those

Texas roadhouse blues. Steve and Johnny were married in the music business sense. Steve was Johnny's manager, guiding him to the big time, Mr. Yokel and Mr. Brash.

And then there was John Hammond Jr., who had hired Jimi to play in his band in the Village way back when. It was while Jimi was playing with Johnny Hammond in the Cafe Au Go Go, that Chas Chandler and Michael Jeffrey first laid eyes on the spectacle of Jimi wasting a guitar. Chas was a big star then, one of the Animals. Mike was the Animals' manager. It was from Johnny Hammond's band that they lured Jimi away to England to become the World's Next Super Act.

———

Jimi had become one of the greatest stars ever to make music, a guitar magician never to be equaled, one of the sweetest poets ever to make the language dance. But back in Seattle all they could bury was the memory of a little black kid who used to play on his father's two-stringed ukulele. . . .

———

On the plane it was like a party. It *was* a party. We were all Jimi's invited guests, flying First Class according to his wishes as expressed by Mike Jeffrey, Jimi's manager, in collaboration with Mike Goldstein, Jimi's press agent. We seat-hopped all the way to Seattle, with the two Johnnies getting off on getting to know about each other and me tap-dancing between Steve and Miles, the Black Prince, who was holding court at the table past the airliner's galley. I guess the real reason I talked Miles into coming was because I loved him, too. I wanted his companionship. I was proud to be seen with him just as I had been proud to be seen with Jimi.

When we got to Seattle, Steve, the two Johnnies and I went to the Hilton Inn at the airport, a motel, where Jimi was paying for our rooms. Miles grabbed a limo to the Washington Plaza, the brand new glass, steel and granite showpiece in the center of town, where he checked Finney, Jacki, and himself into a luxury suite. He said he'd pay for his own rooms.

———

At the Dunlap Baptist Church on broad Rainier Avenue in south Seattle, Mrs. Freddie Mae Gautier, a woman Jimi knew well enough to call Mom, presided at the services. She read from Jimi's liner notes on the Buddy Miles album, Expressway to Your Skull:

"*The express had made the bend, he is coming on down the tracks, shaking steady, shaking funk, shaking feelings, shaking life . . . the conductor says as they climb aboard, small we are going to the electric church, the express took them away and they lived and heard happily and funkily ever after and—uh— excuse me but I think I hear my train coming.*"

———

At the motel, our party from the New York plane was amalgamated into a bigger party. There had been other planes—from L.A. and London and even Barry Fay, Jimi's promoter in Denver, had jetted in for the mourning. All of Jimi's sidemen were there, all the roadies and managers who had ridden his express, all the little people along the way, like myself, who had given Jimi whatever breaks they could, the flagmen of his career. Even Nancy, Mike Jeffrey's ex old lady, who loved to draw. Jimi hadn't passed her by either. In the end, he wrote her letters. His first album after he died had her drawing of him on the cover.

———

In the pews were rock stars Johnny Winter, John Hammond Jr. There were also Mitch Mitchell and Noel Redding, both of whom had played with Jimi in the Jimi Hendrix Experience. Drummer Buddy Miles, who also had played with Jimi, collapsed at the coffin when it was opened for the invited guests to pay their last respects. Inside the coffin, Jimi looked waxen and unreal. . . .

———

Jimi wouldn't have loved the party so much as the idea of it, hosting a bacchanal on his own grave. I mean there was plenty of feasting, drinking, smoking, rapping, snorting and picking, with most of the musicians sitting in with the local rock group in the nightclub downstairs. But none of the girls took off any clothes in public and even the craziest of the English contingent kept their manners zipped up. Steve Paul and I had a good time daydreaming about Miles and Johnny Winter touring together. Otherwise, we were less than the pirates we would have been if Jimi had been there, Jimi, the eternal swashbuckling buccaneer, with his plumed hats and ferocious presence, and I sometimes could even imagine a sword hanging from his wide leather belt. Not that the party was lame; but what was missing was Jimi. The biggest excitement came out of a rumor spread by Press Agent Goldstein to the effect that Paul McCartney was going to show up, due any second. The rumor turned out to be so effectively planted that the next day one of the wire service reporters sent a story out to the world saying that Beatle Paul did indeed attend the funeral.

Outside the church there was a crowd of 200, including report-ers, photographers, and TV crews. A half-dozen police cars were parked across the street. A dozen police motorcycles were waiting around the corner. Twenty-four limousines lined the curb. . . .

In Jimi's absence, Mike Jeffrey played host. For Mike, this consisted mainly of sitting in a booth in the coffee shop so people who recognized his power could come over and pay their respects. Of course, aside from his power there was very little to recognize in Mike. I mean he certainly didn't stand out in a crowd, and, unless he was trying to hustle you, you'd have trouble detecting any personal dynamism from his direction. People who talk about him say geniality did not come easily to Mike except for profit. Me, I found Mike easy enough. His problem was that he suffered from an occupational hazard among music business managers known as eclipse. When you're managing a star, the bigger your star grows, the bigger the shadow he casts over you.

The Mike I knew constantly seemed surprised by his success, except when he was safely within his own small circle of hand-picked friends. Mike learned early that when you're a star, nothing you say is wrong. Mike, on the other hand, would rather say nothing than say something wrong. If this made him a cold fish, it also made him a better shark. Being invisible helped Mike become a hit manager. But what he wanted most was to be recognized.

At the Hilton coffee shop, everybody took a turn coming over to his booth. The party was for Jimi but it was Mike's party. Still suffering from eclipse, he presided over the festivities without ever getting in the way of them. Even beaming, he dimmed his light with the cloak in which he was most comfortable: anonymity. To turn Jimi's funeral into a circus was to Mike's advantage because he had a legend to maintain for profit. Jimi still had an album or two in the can and maybe a movie. Jimi was dead but he was still product. I never doubted Mike knew what he was doing. For him the party at the Hilton may have been his finest moment. A year or so later he went down in an airliner that fell into the sea off the coast of Spain.

———

Alongside the coffin were a dozen floral sprays, including one six-foot white and lavender guitar made up with velvet strings. The family had chosen Dunlap Baptist Church because Jimi's nine-year-old stepsister, Janie, was a parishioner there. Janie, in fact, was the only member of Jimi's family who went to church. . . .

———

In the morning I took a cab into the center of the city to meet Miles in his suite at the Washington Plaza. Miles always travels First Class. He had sent Finney on ahead to the Hendrix house in south Seattle to fix up the family's hair-dos for the funeral. Miles will give you his last buck, too, if he cares for you. We sat and had breakfast and then Miles dawdled as he dressed. He was almost ready by the time the chauffeur got back from taking Finney to the Hendrix house. On the ride there, we talked about how Seattle runs at a pace twenty years behind New York; it felt as if we were back in the '50s, maybe even the '40s. It was a comfortable town, but you could see where it could get boring.

At Jimi's father's house, a small, gray, one-family home in a mixed residential district, I couldn't keep track of all the members of the family I was introduced to. Jimi's father looked just like Jimi. And Devon was there. She was one of the most gorgeous women I had ever seen. Devon, dressed in black with a black veil over her face, was one of Jimi's girlfriends.

"Are you playing the merry widow already?" Miles asked her. He, too, would later hit on Devon.

———

"James Marshall Hendrix was born in Seattle on November 27, 1942, to James Allen and Lucille Jetter Hendrix," Mrs. Gautier read from the church podium. "His mother preceded him in death. . . . Jimi, as he later became known to all his fans, felt that his hometown did not afford him the outlet to express himself with his musical ability. . . .

———

Devon was the closest thing Jimi had to an old lady. He left her a widow's pension in his will. She was one of the most beautiful and sensuous of the groupies and one of the most successful, too. I first met her in the '60s when she was hanging out with I forget which superstar, but whenever a rock hero came to New York, the chances were you'd find Devon in his hotel room. They used to recommend her to one another. Her sex was overwhelming. Somebody once told me she was a teacher and I used to wonder of what. In all the times Devon and I talked to each other, we never really got to know what either one of us was all about. We would just gossip.

It got to be amazing how her relationship with Jimi survived. She could never totally belong to anybody, just as Jimi couldn't, but somehow they came to depend on each other. I saw her a few times after Jimi died. She had so spectacular a face and body that she could have charged money just for people to look at her. She was hard not to notice and not to love. I was writing my *Pop Scene* column for the *New York Post* in those days and she kept asking me, "When are you going to write a column about me?"

And I kept saying to her, "When are you going to do something?" I think it was in March 1972 that she fatally overdosed.

———

On the podium Mrs. Gautier read from a poem sent anonymously by a student at Garfield High School, where Jimi had been kicked out for sassing a teacher who had become annoyed because he was holding hands with a white girl. "So long, our Jimi," Mrs. Gautier recited. "You answered the questions we never dared to ask, painted them in colorful circles and threw them at the world. . . . They never touched the ground but soared up to the clouds."

———

After Jimi's funeral, I went to Monterey for the pop festival and then spent some time with Miles in San Francisco, where he was working in a club. I was backstage at Winterland with the Grateful Dead and the Jefferson Airplane when word came that Janis had been discovered dead in her motel room in L.A. I didn't know what it all meant then and I still don't know, but even as I write this there's a moth beating itself to death on the electric bulb of my lamp. And in a little plastic cup on my desk near my typewriter there are two dried out flowers, faded blue, from Jimi Hendrix's graveside.

THE UNMASKING OF MILES DAVIS

Interviewer: Chris Albertson
Saturday Review, November 27, 1971

Former disc jockey, jazz journalist, record producer, and host of the PBS weekly television series *The Jazz Set,* Chris Albertson is the acknowledged authority on Bessie Smith and author of the definitive biography, *Bessie* (revised and expanded edition, 2003). A longtime contributor to *Stereo Review*, *DownBeat*, *Saturday Review*, and other publications, he has written extensive liner notes for jazz and blues albums (for which he won two Grammy Awards) and has produced a wide array of recordings and radio and television programs. He is currently working on his autobiography.

When Miles Davis returns from a six-week tour of Europe and takes his quintet into Philharmonic Hall this week, chances are that a good percentage of his audience will consist of young black people. This is not a writer's prediction based on a typical Miles Davis following—no one has determined just what that might be—but a request Miles made in a phone call from Paris four weeks ago: Jack Whittemore, his agent, was to take half of Miles' fee, purchase tickets for the concert, and hand them out to young black people who otherwise could not afford to attend. "Miles has never done anything like this before, but nothing he does surprises me," says Whittemore, admitting that he doesn't quite know how to go about distributing over $2,000 worth of free tickets to the right people.

Such unusual gestures are as typical of Miles as they are atypical of most performing artists; they come as a surprise only to those who know the enigmatic trumpet player from a distance. Since his first appearance on the music scene some twenty-six years ago, Miles Davis has been the subject of controversy; endearing with his music, offending with his personality. That is to say, his personality as it is most commonly interpreted, for the forbidding mask of hostility that in many minds characterizes Miles is just that: an image fostered by his own, deliberate lack of showmanship, and sculptured by reporters who have failed to recognize a serious artist at work. We don't, after all, expect Rostropovich or Casadesus to warm up their audiences with small talk, and Miles Davis is as serious about his music as were Brahms and Schubert.

The music performed by Miles Davis today has undeniably evolved from that labeled "jazz," which New Orleans pioneers played sixty years ago, but there are other elements contained in it, too, and if Miles' music is jazz, then so is Stravinsky's *Ragtime for Twelve Instruments*. He himself feels that jazz is "a white man's word" whose application to his music is tantamount to calling a black person "nigger." Accordingly, though he still must give performances in noisy, smoke-filled night clubs, Miles approaches his work with the dignity it deserves.

During club or concert appearances he never addresses his audience nor announces his selections, generally wears clothing that reflect future fashion trends—*Gentleman's Quarterly* named him "Best Dressed Man" ten years ago—saunters off the band stand or to the rear of the stage when not playing, and occasionally turns his back to the audience while focusing attention on his fellow musicians. "I have been with him on several occasions when he left the stage during a performance," says Robert Altshuler, Columbia Records' publicity director. "He either crouches or ambles to the side of the audience and you realize that he is deeply concentrating on everything that his musicians are playing—he is digging his own band, digging it in the way a Miles Davis fan would. He simply becomes a part of his own audience."

Club owners and concert promoters have been known to go into a rage over Miles' seeming detachment, but conformity is not in his vocabulary and, despite the constant criticism, he has for twenty years remained the dark, brooding, wandering loner who doesn't care whether he is regarded as an eccentric genius or a bellicose bastard, as long as people listen to what he says through his music.

The son of a well-to-do dental surgeon, Miles Davis has never been poor, but money cannot cure the inherent stigma that society has attached to people of dark skin and, faced with prejudices that sometimes are so subtle that only their victims can detect them, he has always sought to fight back on his own. "I am not a Black Panther or nothing like that," he explains. "I don't need to be, but I was raised to think like they do and people sometimes think I'm difficult, because I always say what's on my mind, and they can't always see what I see."

One thing Miles never fails to see is someone taking advantage of him. "Back in the days when he was only getting a thousand dollars for a concert, Miles was booked into Town Hall," recalls Jack Whittemore. "The tickets were selling very well, so the promoter suggested doing two shows instead of one. As was customary in such cases, Miles was to get half fee, five hundred dollars, for the second concert, but when I approached him with this he looked puzzled. 'You mean I go on stage,' he said, 'pick up my horn, play a concert, and get a thousand dollars. Then they empty the hall, fill it again, I pick up my horn again, play the same thing, and get only five hundred?—I don't understand it.' I told him that this was how it was normally done, but he was not satisfied. Finally, he turned to me and said he'd do it for five hundred dollars if they would rope off half the hall and only sell half the tickets. When the promoters heard this, they decided to give him another thousand for the second concert."

If Miles is "difficult," it is because his honesty and candor are such rare traits in the show business world that few people know how to deal with him. His monumental disdain for the complimentary small talk and instant familiarity that entertainers are exposed to, and his absolute refusal to indulge in such trivia, has earned him the reputation of being unapproachable. "I have found," observes Altshuler, "that when Miles meets someone new—people from the press I've introduced him to—he will check them out first. They don't always know this, but Miles is actually laying down the ground rules for a totally honest exchange of questions and answers, and he will accept his interviewer only if he can be sure that his time is not going to be wasted with inane questions." As one might expect, Miles is reluctant to appear on TV talk shows.

"Dick Cavett and Johnny Carson don't know what to say to anybody black, unless there's some black bitch on the show and she's all over them," he told me while conducting a guided tour of his unconventional but comfortable Upper West Side residence. "It's so awkward for them, because they know all the white facial expressions, but they're not hip to black expressions, and God knows they're not hip to Chinese expressions. You see, they've seen all the white expressions, like fear, sex, revenge. White actors imitate other white actors when they express emotions, but they don't know how black people react. Dick Cavett is quiet now when a black cat is talking to him, because he doesn't know if the expression on his face means 'I'm going to kick your ass,' or if 'right on' means he's going to throw a right hand punch. So," he continued, pointing out the oddly shaped, multi-level blue-tile bathtub, "rather than embarrass them and myself, I just play on those shows and tell them not to say anything to me—I have nothing to say to them anyway."

Miles makes a good point. Intelligent, relevant questions are rarely directed at black guests on TV's talk shows, and the media's handful of established hosts relate to his music about as well as Nixon's "silent majority" relates to the problems of Bedford-Stuyvesant residents. We stepped down into the circular bedroom where a television set, dwarfed by a gigantic bed, silently radiated an afternoon ballgame. "I just put it on because I have nothing to do," volunteered Miles as he waved his hand towards a long row of flamboyant clothes and boots in dazzling colors. "I have these made for me." When CBS flashed the image of its night host on the little screen, it served as a cue for Miles. "Merv Griffin is embarrassing to me," he said. "I felt like yanking his arm off last year." He was referring to the 1970 Grammy Awards ceremony at Alice Tully Hall, during which, after a superb performance by Miles' group, Griffin—the evening's master of ceremonies—brushed him off with a remark that was disrespectful of his music. "The trouble with those cats," said Miles, "is that they all try to come off to those middle-aged white bitches."

Such remarks don't exactly produce invitations to guest on late-night TV shows, but Miles aims his fire without such considerations. Even Columbia Records—with whom he has enjoyed a good and fruitful relationship since the mid-Fifties—has been victimized by his public candor. In a recent statement, published by a black weekly, Miles—who refers to himself as the "company nigger"—suggested that his label was not affording black artists equal opportunities in terms of exposure. As we seated ourselves comfortably in the round sunken living room, I asked if there had been any repercussions from Columbia. "No," he replied, "Clive [Davis, Columbia's president] asked me why I had said that, and I said 'Was I telling a lie, Clive? If you can say I'm a liar, I'll retract that statement.' You see, all those records I have made with them have been a bitch, and they come out being rich behind all this token shit."

"You would think that he's not grateful," says Clive Davis, "but I just know he is. I'm not sure that it's his mind that he speaks; I'm not sure that he just doesn't tell people what they want to hear, because it takes a certain amount of research before you go off making such statements. I'm prepared for all of Miles' statements, none surprise me. I do mentally treat him differently, not because he's black—because we have such a tremendous number of black artists—but because he's unique among people, and you expect the unexpected from Miles Davis."

Clive Davis admits that he is not totally unaffected by Miles' criticism. "It bothers me because I think we have really done a tremendous amount to be creative along with him, and we work very closely with him so that we make sure that he sells not only to jazz audiences and to contemporary rock audiences, but to R&B audiences as well."

Despite his complaints Miles readily admits to having an unusually close relationship with Columbia, which is borne out by his long tenure with the label, and the fact that the forty-five-year-old superstar of black music could easily find another home for his recording activities. "The Internal Revenue Service is always after me," he says, "but I just send their bills on to Clive. I got one for $39,000, but he took care of it." When asked to verify this, Davis gave a diplomatic reply: "Miles is treated very well by Columbia Records," he says. "I think he's really appreciative of it, too—we don't get Internal Revenue bills from Chicago or Blood, Sweat & Tears."

The recent upsurge in Miles Davis' popularity is mainly due to an album entitled *Bitches Brew*. Released in the spring of 1970, it was the subject of a well-coordinated national promotion campaign aimed more at the young rock fan than at the established Miles Davis follower. Of the close to thirty Miles Davis albums that have accumulated in Columbia's catalogue over the past fifteen years, *Porgy and Bess*—with sales figures approaching 100,000—had been the most successful; other albums have averaged around 50,000 and recent releases have barely crawled to the 25,000 mark, but *Bitches Brew*—a two-record set—has sold over 400,000 copies in this country alone.

The wide stylistic gap that separates *Porgy and Bess* and *Bitches Brew* is reflected in the sales figures, but it is not just the sound of his music that Miles has changed, for he has also updated the group's appearance. Surrounded by a young interracial group of musicians sporting afros, long hair, headbands, dungarees and dashikis, Miles has transformed himself into a trendy, youthful figure. With his flared pants, leather boots, tasseled Western vest, and love beads, he points his shiny horn downward and roams slowly amid the complex-looking electronic equipment. It is no coincidence that the current Miles Davis band has the look of a modern-day rock group—he is determined to win over a new generation of fans, and judging by album sales, the plan is working. Miles' new music is an abstraction of everything he has played before; it is as if he were summing it all up for us, but we know that he won't let it end here—this is merely the latest plateau. At the same time, it is a testimony to Miles' artistry and forward thinking that none of his past recordings—going back to his revolutionary 1949 Capitol sessions—sound outdated in 1971.

If rock groups are not envious of Miles' musical accomplishments, they perhaps should be, for many of them have yet to approach the stage of development reached by Miles and collaborator Gil Evans in the Fifties. One can't help but wonder if, ten or twelve years from now, anyone will have more than a nostalgic nod for the current efforts of today's musical pop heroes. There is bitter irony in the fact that Miles has to take second billing—as he did last year—to a group like Blood, Sweat & Tears, which sells records in the millions and turns youthful audiences into a frenzy of excitement with musical ideas borrowed from Miles' past. "I can't be bothered with these groups," says Miles, recalling with some amusement how he turned down promoter Bill Graham's request that he retract a negative statement about Blood, Sweat & Tears. "If they can't stand constructive criticism, to hell with them. I'm honest in what I say, I don't lie, so I don't have to watch my words or take them back."

There are those who feel that Miles' attacks on rock groups are unfair and that he, in an odd sense, owes these performers a debt of gratitude. They see his appearances last year at the Fillmores East and West—Meccas for the rock cult—as a turning point in his career, but they seem to lose sight of the fact that these concerts, along with Columbia's promotional efforts, would not have sold the public on Miles Davis if he had not had something substantial to offer. For over twenty years, Miles has pointed music in new directions, reaching unexplored plateaus, then forging ahead before others could catch up with him. "He has never been bound by convention," says Teo Macero, who has produced virtually all of Miles' recordings since 1958. "You wouldn't expect Miles to go back and do something the way he did it years ago anymore than you would expect Picasso to go back to what he was doing in his 'blue' or 'rose' periods."

One tangible result of Miles' recent commercial success has been the signing up by Columbia of several black musicians who last year would hardly have been able to get as far as Clive Davis' eleventh floor office. Explaining this change in policy, Clive Davis makes one momentarily forget that he is running a highly competitive commercial business: "I am very eager to allow Columbia to be used by the most forward looking American jazz artists, to explore what kind of synergy can come out of jazz and rock. What do the jazz giants, the leading jazz figures of today, have to say? What is their reaction to the fact that, in attempting to fuse jazz and rock, Chicago and Blood, Sweat & Tears have reached millions of people all over the world while they, without such an attempt, only reach a few thousand with their music?" He mentioned that the label has signed Ornette Coleman, Jack De Johnette, and Weather Report—an offshoot of Miles' group—and that it was recording Charles Mingus. "Just as Columbia sponsored a Modern American Composer series in classical music—not having any less reverence for Stravinsky, Mahler, or classical music performed by the New York Philharmonic or the Philadelphia Orchestra—so we are here exploring a very exciting new development in music, to see where it will go. I don't know where it will go, but I think that by opening up the company to this kind of exploration of music by brilliant talent, we are providing a tremendous service."

Columbia's aims are obvious and Miles is not fooled for a minute: "It's smart to be with the niggers sometimes. I know what made *Bitches Brew*, but they need guidance: Mingus needs guidance; Ornette needs guidance; nobody's going to tell them what to do because then they might call them white bastards. They have to tell Mingus what to do, otherwise he'll do the same shit all over again, and they have to tell Ornette that he cannot play the trumpet and violin. Motown shows you where it's at, man."

It is difficult to imagine anyone telling Miles Davis what to do with his music, but he is just as receptive to constructive criticism as he is ready to give it. "Miles lets you be as creative as you want to be," says producer Teo Macero, "as long as it doesn't screw up his music. A lot of artists say, 'Man, don't touch my music, don't do this, I don't want any electronic sound, don't use a Fender bass, and so forth,' but Miles is so far ahead that he's on the same wavelength as you are, which makes for a great deal of excitement. When he plays, he does it with such intensity that every note is a gem. He doesn't make any mistakes; if he doesn't like something he did, it is usually because it didn't capture the right feeling. We never discuss the music or how things went in front of anybody else; he either calls me out into the hall or we sort of talk in the corner, and I try to refrain from talking about the piece over the studio talk-back system. That's something I've learned by working with him over the years. Like his private life, he keeps it to himself; I never ask, because if he wants to tell me something, he'll do it."

The physical aspects of producing a Miles Davis album are as unconventional as his music. As Macero explains, there are no takes one, two, or three, "because there's something new that pops into the music every time, whether it's deliberate or just by accident—no one seems to know quite for sure. The group is constantly building toward a final goal and we don't stop the tape machines like we used to do in the old days—they run until the group stops playing. Then we go back, listen, and decide between us what should be tacked to what—it becomes a search and find routine, and finally it's all there, it's just a matter of putting it all together. There are a lot of tapes for each album, but we may use only the material from two or three sessions."

Two albums, *Miles Davis at Fillmore* and the sound track for the documentary film *Jack Johnson*, have been released since *Bitches Brew*, but neither shows signs of doing as well commercially. This, of course, provides an incentive to make the next release particularly interesting, and it looks as if *Live and Evil* (one word is the reverse spelling of the other) will be just that. Scheduled for a December release, it is the distillation of ten to fifteen reels of tape, selected from an original working pile of thirty reels. "The album is partly live, and it has an ethereal evil, where the mind is clouded and all these things are happening," says Macero. "It's like a wild dream." Artist Mati Klarwein, who was responsible for the unusual *Bitches Brew* cover, has been commissioned to give the new album a similar look.

If *Live and Evil* becomes another *Bitches Brew*, there will undoubtedly be more demands on Miles Davis' time, a commodity he values and likes to spend as a part-time pugilist working out in a midtown gym, swimming in some appropriate waters, sleeping in his oversized bed, or simply relaxing with friends amid the international decor of what has been termed "an architect's nightmare"—his house on West 77th Street.

Unimpressed by critics ("I don't know any, because I never read what they say") and disc jockeys ("If we didn't make any records, they wouldn't have anything to do"), Miles periodically threatens to quit the music business to avoid the exploitation which he admits is "the name of the game." Some day, he will undoubtedly do just that, and then a smile the public never knew may emerge from behind the mask.

MILES

Interviewer: Leonard Feather, 1972
From *From Satchmo to Miles* (Da Capo Press, 1984)

Over the course of his prestigious career, British journalist Leonard Feather authored eleven books on jazz, including the renowned reference *The Encyclopedia of Jazz*. The jazz community, including Miles, respected and liked Feather, who contributed scores of liner notes for jazz LPs. He was also a composer and lyricist whose compositions were sung and performed by a range of prestigious luminaries including B. B. King and Mel Tormé. Davis often sat down with Feather and revealed to him his candid thoughts on racism, the evolution of jazz, and his musical contemporaries. Most notably, Feather was famous for his Blindfold Tests in *DownBeat* magazine, in which Miles participated several times.

Miles Dewey Davis III has learned as well as any musician alive how to make music, women, money, and headlines, not necessarily in that order of importance but probably in that chronological sequence.

The various sobriquets he has acquired along the way—Prince of Darkness, Public Enigma No. 1—attest to his ability to build around himself an aura of cultism and mysticism.

He inspires young musicians who are awed by his presence, instills fear in the hearts of young secretaries at Columbia Records whom he has called white bitches, leaves reporters ignored or confused, talks in absolutes and with seemingly total conviction. His words are at variance with his actions, particularly in the area of race, and some of his statements are total contradictions of others.

He has been called bitter, hostile, bigoted, capricious, undependable, often by some of the same observers who at other times have found him shy, warm, generous, sensitive, and witty. After denouncing white American society, he has emulated its most materialistic values by acquiring all the appurtenances and luxuries his millions could bring him over the years: the $15,000 Ferrari; the $100,000 town house on West Seventy-Seventh Street; the vast Italian-style wardrobe, including compensatory high-heeled shoes.

Much has been made of his background: unlike most black and many white musicians, he was born into a middle-class family with bourgeois values, and was urged by his mother to take up some genteel instrument such as the violin. That these advantages have not protected him from racism or other forms of dehumanization Davis considers irrelevant. "You don't know how to play better just because you've suffered," he says. "The blues don't come from picking cotton."

He is a maverick in much more than his social origins. It has been axiomatic through the history of jazz that once established, the great individual styles, whether conceived by Armstrong, Eldridge, Hawkins, Hodges, Young, Gillespie, or Peterson, have remained basically unchanged through the years, evolving only within the original framework. Gillespie solos recorded in 1945 and 1971 are clearly recognizable as the work of the same artist. Davis, on the other hand, has changed so radically that most listeners not familiar with all his work would refuse to believe that a recent solo, on one of his rock-dominated records, was played by the same trumpeter heard on, say, "Out of the Blue" in 1951.

Davis, for all his changes of direction, is today more than ever a player of unquestionable originality and has an almost hypnotic influence on his contemporaries, as Gillespie had in the 1940s. Miles was the first to make a definitive switch from trumpet to flugelhorn, an instrument that has since become a double for hundreds of trumpeters. He was the first to make use of modal themes, a development later associated more closely with John Coltrane, but actually dating back to the late 1950s when Coltrane was a sideman in Davis' group. Davis' early career found him a bebopper who had listened closely to Clark Terry and Gillespie; in a second phase, as a central figure in the breakaway from bop to cooler and more orchestrated conceptions through his collaborations with Gil Evans, John Lewis, Gerry Mulligan, and others on the *Birth of the Cool* recordings (1949–50); in a third stage, as leader of various small bands, quintets and sextets, and overlapping the latter, as partner with Evans in a series of large-scale orchestral albums that are assured a permanent place in musical history. Still later came the first intimations of "space music," and not long afterward the flirtation with rock.

With each of these directional shifts in the group style came substantial changes in Davis' entire approach to the horn. According to him each new move has represented a step ahead, a development evolving directly out of the previous period. Other musicians are sharply divided concerning the accuracy of this self-analysis.

Davis revels in the present and eagerly courts the future; in effect, although at times he may deny it, he rejects his past.

LF: When you hear the old records you made with Gil Evans, or the combo albums when Herbie Hancock and Wayne Shorter were with you, how do they sound to you today?

MD: I don't listen to them.

LF: Is that because you no longer find anything interesting in them?

MD: The records sound funny to me.

LF: Wouldn't you advise young musicians to go through those stages first before getting to what you're into now? These guys that you have now, didn't they at one time play songs with definite beginnings and endings?

MD: Yeah, you have to come up through those ranks. They can always do that; but you don't hear anybody doing that old shit with me. You know, some guys are still playing all that shit we did years ago, things I did with Bird and stuff; they're still using those clichés and calling it jazz. Black guys as well as white guys. I hear it over and over again—shit that I've even forgotten.

LF: Well, that's natural, Miles, as long as they get into something eventually.

MD: No, it's not natural.

LF: You could just as well say that Dizzy is still playing the blues and "Night in Tunisia" and all those things. Does that make him inferior?

MD: How is he going to be inferior? How is he *ever* going to be inferior?

LF: That's what I mean. So why shouldn't he continue to go on like that as long as it's valid?

MD: He can do anything he wants to.

LF: Do you believe the era of the 12-bar blues and the 32-bar song is dead?

MD: No, you can add something to it. But when I write something, I don't think of anything I've ever heard. I don't try to be different; it's just that I figure, when whatever I wanted to write is finished, I stop. I don't count the bars. What's complete to me might not be complete to your ear; 'cause I never resolve anything that way. I hate to. But I'm not rejecting anything. You're not losing anything with what we're doing now; you're gaining everything you lost, because you heard all that other shit over and over again.

LF: A lot of young people haven't heard it. The kids that heard you at the Fillmore or Shelly's Manne Hole may not even know about the Gil Evans albums, let alone the Capitol albums. I think it's wrong that they should be unfamiliar with the important innovations of the past.

MD: There's so much more to music than just that. Like what I'm doing now, you know?

LF: I'm saying that they should also recognize what you did then, because you accomplished something that was important to you and to jazz at that time.

MD: I don't know whether they recognize it or not. Anyway everything that I do is recognized until somebody else does it.

This last observation is irrefutable. Whether or not today's rock fans are conscious of it, some part of each Davis contribution has eventually filtered through into the mainstream of jazz. This means that he has manifestly changed the entire course of an art form three or four times in twenty-five years—an accomplishment than no other jazz musician can claim.

The Davis family has to its credit at least three generations of impressive achievements. Miles Dewey Davis the First was a well-to-do black man who at one time owned 1,000 acres of land in Arkansas. Miles II became a substantial landowner himself in addition to pursuing a lucrative career as a dentist and dental surgeon. Miles Dewey Davis III was born May 26, 1926, in Alton, Illinois. Soon afterward the family moved to East St. Louis, where Miles II increased his wealth still further by breeding hogs.

Pride of family was a conspicuous trait in the Davis household. Doc Davis once said: "The Davises historically have always been musicians. I would have been one myself, but my father forbade me to play, because Negroes at that time could only play in barrelhouses. By genetics and breeding, Miles III is always going to be ahead of his time."

LF: How many were there in the family?

MD: I have an older sister, Dorothy; she's married. My brother, Vernon, was born in 1929.

LF: How old are your own children now?

MD: Cheryl is the oldest, then there's Gregory, and Miles. They're all in their twenties. I was married when I was sixteen. I have a grandson—he's five; he and Cheryl live in St. Louis.

LF: You were pretty close to your mother, weren't you?

MD: No, I've never been close to none of my family. Me and my mother fell out when I was thirteen. We were close at one time; we could talk to each other, but you know, I wasn't going to take none of that shit from her just because she was my mother.

LF: What kind of shit?

MD: Just real bullshit. It was a matter of either talk straight to me or not at all. When she did, we became real tight.

LF: How was your relationship with your father?

MD: Not bad. He just told my mother to leave me alone. He bought me a trumpet for my thirteenth birthday, and I'd only been playing two or three years when I had a chance to leave school and go on the road with Tiny Bradshaw's band. I went home and asked my mother . . . she said no, I had to finish my last year of high school. I didn't talk to her for two weeks.

LF: What advantages did growing up black and middle class give you over growing up black and poor?

MD: You're gonna run into that Jim Crow thing regardless of how wealthy you are. I can't buy no freedom. Having money has helped me once in a while, but I'm not looking for help. I'm even the one that's the helper, helping people by playing my music. There's no excuse for being poor anyway. You see, you're not supposed to wait on anybody to give you nothing. My father taught me that.

LF: How old were you when your parents separated?

MD: I don't remember, but I remember I sent my sister to school, to Fisk, when I was about sixteen—I was making $85 a week with Eddie Randall's band. That was just before I went to New York.

LF: How did you get along that far musically in just a couple of years?

MD: I just got onto the trumpet and studied and played. It would have been that or something else; a lot of black people think that to keep from being Jim Crowed and shit like that you have to be a professional man and know a little bit of something. But then if you want an engineer or an architect or something, who do you get? You don't go to a black man.

LF: Were there a lot of kids in school with you who became professionals?

MD: Yeah. One of them is going to run for Mayor of Compton, Cal. East St. Louis was so bad that it just made you get out and do something. . . . See, I believe if you don't go to school you can still educate yourself. I don't think you need formal schooling to get an education. There's always a library. You know, I can't *believe* the library they got in New York.

LF: Were you a good student?

MD: Well, I taught my sister mathematics. See, if I had a book, I could look at it and remember the whole page. It came to me like that. I can remember anything—telephone numbers, addresses. Even today I can just glance at them and remember. That's the reason I used to take care of band payrolls; I could remember all the tabs and shit.

Music was easy. When I was a kid, I was fascinated by the musicians, particularly guys who used to come up from New Orleans and jam all night. I'd sit there and look at them, watch the way they walked and talked, how they fixed their hair, how they'd drink, and of course how they played.

Then of course I played in the school band. Around that time I met Clark Terry. He was playing like Buck Clayton in those days, only faster. I started to play like him. I idolized him.

Clark Terry, five years Miles's senior, grew up across the river in St. Louis. "The first time I ever set eyes on Miles," says Terry, "was in Carbondale, Illinois. His music teacher, who was a drinking buddy of mine, had told me about him. 'I've got a little cat over there in East St. Louis who's a bitch,' he said. 'You really got to hear him' I said OK, OK, I'd hear him sometime.

"Not long afterward I was working in a May Day affair when all the schools would compete against one another in athletics. He was in this school band, and he came up to me and very meekly said, 'Pardon me, Mr. Terry, but would you tell me something about the horn? I'd like to know how you do certain things.' And I was so preoccupied with all the beautiful schoolgirls around that I said, 'Why don't you get lost—stop bugging me,' which is something I never normally do. Miles was maybe fifteen then.

"A few months later, in St. Louis, I was on my way to an after-hours jam session at the Elks, a place with a long staircase. On the way up this long flight of stairs I heard this new sound, new trumpet. I thought I could recognize everybody's style, but this stumped me. So I walked up to the bandstand and there was this little fellow. I said, 'Hey, aren't you the cat I ran into at Carbondale?' And he said, 'Yeah, man, I'm the cat you fluffed off that night!' I was in the profession a long time before he was, and I guess he used to come across the bridge many times to listen to bands I was in. I know he credits me as his first influence and I'm flattered, because he's not a cat that passes out compliments too easily.

"He was a nice, quiet little kid then, and I think the changes in him are a cover-up. Deep down, basically, he's a beautiful cat. Many people have misunderstood him and don't know the true Miles.

"If he seems to go to great lengths to conceal it, he's probably been given a bad time by people who've mistreated him and he feels he doesn't have to accept these things anymore. I can understand this, because there were times in my own childhood when I was abused by Caucasians, so I could have all the reason in the world to be anti-Caucasian and make a career out of paying people back for things they've done to me. I've been attempted-to-be-lynched twice, and spat on, and had my clothes ripped off and been beaten, but I just refuse to lower myself to that level. Maybe many more things happened to Miles than to me, and some of them he just can't forget."

If Miles does not talk about childhood traumas, it is certainly not because they never existed. "One of the first things I can remember," he says, "was when I was a little boy and a white man was running down the street after me hollering, 'Nigger, nigger!'"

He is said to have been deeply hurt again when, living in a white neighborhood with his black middle-class parents, he was stopped by a white bigot who told him, "What you doin' here? This ain't no nigger street." Miles's father once told friends that his son would have won the first prize in the high school music competition, but traditionally whites had a hold on that honor.

Before leaving high school Miles had one brief fling in the big time, playing for three weeks as substitute for one of the regular trumpeters in the Billy Eckstine orchestra. This placed him in the exalted company of Dizzy Gillespie and Charlie Parker. (Eckstine recalls it differently: "When I first heard Miles, I let him sit in so as not to hurt his feelings, but he sounded terrible; he couldn't play at all.")

Mrs. Davis wanted her son to go to Fisk University, a predominantly black institution in Nashville, well known for its music department and renowned for having produced the Fisk Jubilee Singers. But Miles knew that this would be pointing him in the wrong direction for jazz. He opted for Juilliard and, with his father's blessing, headed for New York.

"I spent my first two weeks looking for Charlie Parker," he recalls. "That's who I wanted to learn from. I knew all that Juilliard shit already—I'd studied it all myself.

"Originally I went there to see what was happening but when I found out nothing was happening, I told my father to save his money. I stayed about a semester and a half. Shit, I did all the homework for summer school in one day."

"Isn't that," I suggested, "because you just naturally had a bright mind and a good feeling for it?"

"I had nothing on my mind *but* study. I wasn't even fuckin', man, you know?"

"I thought you said you were married when you came to New York?"

"Yeah, but at that time she was pregnant."

Whatever the state of his education Davis soon drifted into the bustling Fifty-second Street scene of the mid-1940s and found a friend and sponsor in Charlie Parker. For a while they roomed together and Miles followed Bird around on gigs. "I'd make notes of the chords and stuff I was hearing, write 'em down on matchbooks, then next day at Juilliard, instead of going to class, I'd spend all my time trying out those chords."

Before long Davis was out of Juilliard for good and a regular member of Parker's quintet. As the early recordings show, his technique still had a long way to go; he had little control in the upper register and often fluffed in the middle. Over the years an elliptical sense of self-editing developed that enabled him to play less yet say more.

As a close associate of Parker he was inevitably brought into contact with the drug scene, yet to most observers around Fifty-second Street he was the abstemious, mild-mannered youth who neither smoked nor drank. A year or two elapsed before he became a part of the narcotics world. Heroin was then rampant among the young beboppers, but Miles, to all outward appearances, remained cool, taking care of business on the Bird job and subsequently with Coleman Hawkins' small band, on the road with Benny Carter's orchestra and with Billy Eckstine. By this time he was so improved, Eckstine says, that he was able to take over the parts previously played by Gillespie. He stayed with

Eckstine until the band broke up in 1947, later working in the singer's small combo. It was during this period that he made headlines with his first arrest for possession.

"As strong as that man may seem to be outwardly," says Harry "Sweets" Edison, "his inward character may be a little weak just one time, and that's all it takes."

Although his private life was to remain chaotic for several years, Miles continued to progress as he became part of a workshop band, one that involved the use of two instruments never before heard in the new jazz, French horn and tuba.

"Gil Evans and I spent the better part of one winter hashing out the instrumentation for that nine-piece band," Gerry Mulligan once recalled. "But Miles dominated the band completely; the whole nature of the interpretation was his."

Miles's version of the band's evolution was predicated on his desire to play with "a light sound . . . because I could think better when I played that way. Gerry said to get Lee Konitz on alto because he had that light sound too. That whole thing started out as just an experiment; then Monte Kay booked us into the Royal Roost on Broadway for two weeks.

"As for that *Birth of the Cool* shit, I don't understand how they came to call it that. Someone just dropped that label on me. I think what they really mean is a soft sound—not penetrating too much. To play soft you have to relax . . . you don't delay the beat, but you might play a quarter triplet against four beats, and that *sounds* delayed. If you do it right, it won't bother the rhythm section."

The nine-piece band was short-lived, lasting for two public appearances and three recording dates, but it marked the beginning of the close, enduring friendship and association between Miles and Gil Evans. It was to bring out in Davis a lyricism, a soaring and ecstatic sound for which Evans provided the perfect setting.

"Gil has a way of voicing chords and using notes like nobody else," said Miles. "We work together great because he writes the way I'd like to write. In fact, years ago I used to do arrangements and give them to him to look over. He'd tell me my charts were too cluttered up, that I could get the same effect using fewer notes.

"Finally I decided the best thing to do was let Gil do the writing. I'd just get together with him—sometimes not even in person, just on the phone—and outline what I wanted. And he always has such a complete feeling for what I mean that it comes out sounding exactly like what I had in mind."

For younger jazz fans who know Davis only from his recent work, an entire new-old horizon may be opened up by the endless mixture of orchestral sounds, and the stark, mournful spareness of Davis' horn, in such masterpieces as *Miles Ahead, Porgy and Bess*, and *Sketches of Spain*. Davis and Evans were reunited in parts of the *Miles at Carnegie Hall* album and on a later LP called *Quiet Nights*, but the first three are the definitive works. (All five are still available on Columbia.)

Miles's career might have gained immediate momentum after the *succès d'estime* of the first (Capitol) collaboration with Evans, but the narcotics habit proved a formidable roadblock, wrecking his home life, limiting his musical development, and reducing him at times to a near-derelict.

"I remember one day on Broadway," says Clark Terry, "I found him sitting in front of one of those ham-and-eggs places. He was just wasted, actually sitting by the gutter. I asked him what was wrong and he said, 'I don't feel well.' After buying him some ham and eggs I took him around to my hotel, the America on West Forty-seventh Street. I was getting ready to leave on the bus with Basie's band, and I told him, 'You just stay here, get some rest, and when you leave just close the door.'

"The bus waited longer than I'd expected, so I went back to the room. Miles had disappeared, the door was open, and all my things were missing.

"I called home, St. Louis, and told my wife to call Doc Davis to see if he could get Miles, because he was obviously in bad shape and had become the victim of those cats who were twisting him the wrong way. And you know what? Doc Davis was very indignant. He told her, 'The only thing that's wrong with Miles now is because of those damn musicians like your husband that he's hanging around with.' He was the type of guy who believed his son could do no wrong. So he didn't come to get him."

As Miles found himself facing a bleak future, it became a case of physician's son, heal thyself. "It took me four years to break the habit," he told an *Ebony* reporter. "I just made up my mind I was getting off dope. I was sick and tired of it. You can even get tired of being scared. I laid down and stared at the ceiling for twelve days and cursed everybody I didn't like . . . I lay in a cold sweat . . . I threw up everything I tried to eat . . . then it was over." He had kicked the hard way—cold turkey.

Nonetheless illness continued to plague him. He had an operation for nodes on the throat. Warned by a doctor not to use his voice for a while, he began speaking too soon; as a result he was reduced to the famous whisper that has become chronic, a source of psychological and physical discomfort, and a subject he prefers to avoid.

The post-heroin years marked the start of an invigorated, productive phase. In addition to the large orchestral ventures with Evans, he headed a series of combos, each of which had its own catalytic effect on jazz.

In 1955, at the Newport Jazz Festival, he earned a rousing reception, scoring most strongly with a down-home swinging blues called "Walkin'." The recorded version of this number, on Prestige, became a classic. In the view of many critics it set the pace for a trend away from the cool phase, which Davis himself had done so much to initiate, into a period of funkier and more aggressive music. Even more influential was his *Kind of Blue* album, recorded after his switch to Columbia Records. Three members of the sextet heard on that LP were to develop as individual forces on disparate levels of jazz creativity: John Coltrane, who took Miles's modal pioneering many steps further and blended it with other idioms; Cannonball Adderly, and Bill Evans. (The other definitive unit flourished in the mid-1960s with Wayne Shorter, Herbie Hancock, and Tony Williams, all of whom also subsequently became leaders.)

"While I was in the band," Coltrane said, "I found Miles in the midst of a new stage of musical development. It seemed that he was moving to the use of fewer and fewer chord changes in songs. He used tunes with free-flowing lines and chordal direction. I found it easy to apply my own harmonic ideas . . . I could play three chords at once; but if I wanted to, I could play melodically. Miles's music gave me plenty of freedom."

Davis' method of assembling cohesive groups of major artists, usually finding them at the most crucial points in their evolution, is deceptively casual. Herbie Hancock, whose case is typical, recalls their first meeting, when Donald Byrd took him to the Davis house.

"I was introduced to Miles as Donald's new piano player. Donald said, 'Herbie, why don't you play something?' So I sat down and played a ballad. Miles said, 'He's got a nice touch.' And that was that until the following year, when he called me up and asked me to come over to his house.

"Tony Williams was there, and Ron Carter and George Coleman. I knew he was looking for a new group, so I figured this was an audition. We concentrated on one tune, 'Seven Steps to Heaven.' The next day we rehearsed some of Miles's older things but concentrated on a second tune. Miles didn't even play. He just came downstairs with me, said something to George, and then went back upstairs. I guess maybe he turned on the intercom and was listening to us.

"The next day, as I heard later, Miles called up Gil Evans and Philly Joe Jones and said, 'Hey, come over and listen to my new band.' On the third day Miles came downstairs and played a couple of notes, but he soon went back up. After we finished running things down, I'm still thinking that I'm auditioning, so Miles comes downstairs and says, 'You have to be at Columbia studios tomorrow afternoon at two.'

"It took me completely by surprise. I said 'Wait a minute—what? I thought you were auditioning. Are we recording tomorrow?' He said, 'Yeah.' I said, 'Does that mean that I'm in the group, or what? He said, 'You're making the record, ain't you?'

"I left his house floating on a cloud. Just through that offhand conversation, I had a job that turned out to last five years and then enabled me to go out on my own."

During the incumbency of Hancock, Wayne Shorter (who replaced George Coleman), Williams, and Carter, Miles veered further and further away from his 1950s concept of playing structured popular songs and jazz standards. Although he continued for some time to hold on to "'Round Midnight" and a couple of others, most of the themes now were freer and more adventurous works written by members of the group. They became points of departure for displays of intracommunication that were tantamount to ESP—which logically became the title number of a 1965 album. Performances became longer as Davis pioneered in the concept of segueing from one theme and mood to another, so that an entire set at a club or concert would be a continuum.

Working at an ever-higher level of abstraction the quintet became more completely an expression of the leader's dominant personality as key sidemen left. The use of electric keyboards and bass, and of two or three percussion instruments, expanded the compass of the music still further. The switch from a floating, free rhythm to the incorporation of rock became a controversial element but one Davis sincerely believed in.

Herbie Hancock points out: "Miles has been going in his present direction ever since the time when I jumped on the electric piano. Back in 1968 the album *Miles in the Sky* had a hint of rock. The next year *In a Silent Way* showed the shape of things to come with its two or three electric keyboards. The essential difference was in the rhythmic complexity. *Bitches Brew*, which shook everyone up in 1970, was totally different from *In a Silent Way*, yet you can hear the parallel; it blended all the complexities of the new modern jazz with an underlying rock beat.

"The next album, *Miles at the Fillmore*, showed how much he can be fed musically not only by his musicians but by the whole environment, the vibes of the people. This is something I totally respect. . . . But of course it didn't sound like John Mayall at the Fillmore or anyone else at the Fillmore. Miles was still playing Miles.

"The value of what Miles is doing now is that he is, in effect, setting up a criterion of excellence in the direction of rock that nobody else has achieved, in terms of instrumental efficiency, interaction, and all of those things that just hadn't happened too much in rock before.

"I realize that a lot of people were turned off by the strong rock element, especially in the soundtrack of the film he did, *Jack Johnson*, which was pretty much straight rock with Miles thrown on top. Obviously this had to be controversial to many of the people that were into his music during his traditional jazz days, but then periods shouldn't be compared. I don't think people should expect him to go back and play 'Stella by Starlight' again because it would only inhibit the direction he's going in.

"Sure, the best of music is timeless. But to the artist who is performing it the music has to be a reflection of where he is at any given moment, and where he is depends on the individual. Say, in the case of Oscar Peterson, there is a certain predictability about his playing, but his growth seems to be internal, whereas Miles's is external. There's room for both attitudes."

Hancock's view of Davis is of course an inside glimpse, offered by a musician who for years was an integral part of his music. Those on the outside have mixed reactions, especially musicians who were once regarded as Miles's main influences.

"I have listened to those recent albums time after time," says Dizzy Gillespie, "until I started getting cohesions. The guy is such a fantastic musician that I know he has something in mind, whatever it is. I know he knows what he's doing, so he must be doing something that I can't get to yet.

"He played some of it for me, and he said, 'How do you like that shit?' I said, 'What is it?' and he said, 'You know what it is; same shit you've been playing all the time,' and I said, 'Have I?' I said, 'Look, I'm going to come by your house and spend several hours and you're going to explain to me what that is.' But we never did get together. I'm sure he could explain it to me musically, though of course you can't explain anything emotionally.

"Miles should be commended for going off in a completely new direction, he's just as brave as shit. That's what it is, stark stone bravery, to have something that his fans all over the world liked so much, and then turn around and go on an altogether different course. Shit, I don't think I got that much guts. Sometimes I find myself playing those same old licks I used to play, till I get stale as a motherfuck. When I play something exactly the same way I did it some other time, I figure, 'Oh shit, you're getting lazy.' But I can no more change my spots. . . . Miles can, though.

"He has a knack of grabbing one of those notes in the chord, like, suppose you have a B flat minor sixth chord with a C in the bass, Miles would stop on an A flat or something like that—and hold it! He picks the dynamic notes to lay back on. He had the same thing going on in *Bitches Brew*; he had a blues thing going, and he grabbed one of those notes, and when the chord changed he grabbed one of those other strange ones and held it.

"Whether it'll last, what he's doing now, that's not up to me to judge. You can't judge your contemporaries; you can only say what strikes you at the moment, but you can't assess the validity of the message. Time alone judges that, so I just sit here and wait until . . . well, if he's hooked that far in front, wait for time to catch up with it. Because I had the same experience with Ornette Coleman until somebody gave me an album one day and I sat down and really listened. I used to make jokes, like I'd say, 'Ladies and gentlemen, we're going to play "Hot House" and Ornette is going to play "Night in Tunisia" at the same time.' But now I realize he had something to build on.

"Miles has even more to build on. Not only has he got me and Yardbird and Freddie Webster and whoever else inspired him, he's also got himself, to reach back and get different things. The guy's a master, so I wouldn't come out and say that I don't like what he's doing now.

"Besides, it would be out of line. Could the King of England criticize the King of France?"

Gillespie's comments may subconsciously reflect an attitude that has been lucidly explained by Herbie Hancock.

"People become accustomed to a style that's been associated with a certain individual," he says, "so when they want to hear his music, they listen with these preconceptions. This is the wrong way to go about getting involved with anything. You're better off, listening to any music, not expecting anything, because the artist you listen to may be a completely different person when you confront him at a different time. Miles is a perfect case in point. There might be a particular area of his development that you prefer, but if you walk in looking for it, you'll be disappointed. If you just go in saying, 'Let me near what's going to happen,' then you can be objective and dig what the man's output is for its own self."

Other Davis-watchers take the position that his change in direction has been at least partially pragmatic.

"I can understand exactly why he's doing these things," says Clark Terry. "Miles is the kind of man who has always wanted to stay abreast of the times. He's smart enough to realize that this is what people are buying, and if this is what they're buying, why shouldn't he sell some of it?

"Maybe he's doing it sincerely, but I do know that it's a much more lucrative direction for him. I happen to know that there was a period when in spite of all his many possessions—investments, home, car—there was a period when he needed to bolster these; he really needed to get into a higher financial bracket. And there was an opportunity for him to get into this kind of thing, so he took the opportunity to jump out and do it.

"I don't know whether or not I'm musically mature enough to understand it. I do know that there are people in that area who are incompetent, and it's an avenue where they can parallel people like Miles who have studied and worked hard. Others can reach this point through a short-cut method. Nobody could do that when Miles was playing more lyrically. I loved him much more at that time, when he was more in depth as far as chord structures and progressions. Ain't nobody around can play more melodically than Miles when he wants to. In a sense it's a waste to see him not using all his knowledge."

I asked Terry, "What do you think people hear in it that is making him so successful in widening his audience?"

"What they hear in it is less significant than what they don't hear. What they don't hear, because it's not there, is the real balls of jazz, the chord progressions, the structures, and so forth. They are not musically mature enough to cope with this and Miles is smart enough to put something where they can reach it on their own level. If they're not hip enough to know what's happening—say, the way Miles was playing with Bird years ago, with swinging groups—if they're not hip enough to grasp that type of thing, they're going to grasp whatever is simple enough for them to cop. And the simple thing for them to cop happens to be that one-chord modal bag that is so fashionable."

Other trumpeters of Terry's generation share his viewpoint. "I guess he's trying to change with the times," says Harry "Sweets" Edison, "but personally I liked the way he sounded when he had Philly Joe Jones, Cannonball, Wynton Kelly, and Paul Chambers, around 1956—that was a magnificent bunch of musicians.

"I listened to him on *Bitches Brew* and there was just too much going on for me to really enjoy his playing. I don't think a man of his distinctive ability needs to do that kind of thing. Also, Miles is such a good writer, but what he's doing now doesn't sound like he's putting into it all that he's capable of.

"I'm not going to underestimate him; I'm sure he's true to his own convictions, but I feel he could still play the way he played years ago, with the same feeling, and people would appreciate it."

Quincy Jones, the composer and former trumpeter, who has known Davis for twenty years, has made a close analytical study of Miles's progress. "When we were kids," he says, "we ran around with a notebook copying off all the Miles and Bird solos. Most of us didn't jump on Dizzy, though, because he was just too much to try to emulate, so we'd try to grab hold of Miles.

"Miles has always been concerned with growth, with perfecting one thing and then taking on a new challenge. That's what keeps you feeling young, man. Nobody wants to stay the same."

Asked whether he felt that to retain one's basic image was less important for an artist than the continual development of new identities as in Davis' case, Jones replied: "I think you have to trust that same mojo that led you into the first style, and go from there. It's fortunate that Miles is flexible enough to have given us the kind of contrast that separates *Miles Ahead* from *Jack Johnson*. I think he's blessed, to have that scope, that range."

Recently, as Jones points out, there has been a curious shift of focal points in the thrust of the new jazz. "A decade or two back, the velocity and animation were usually carried by the melodic instruments on top, while the rhythm section laid down the bass like a canvas, remaining essentially a time-keeping device. But in the last few years that has been reversed. Any record you hear now, the horns almost have to play time, because the complexity has moved to the basement now, and you can't take that kind of complexity on top with what the fender bass players are doing nowadays. Too many passing notes. If you play too many alterations in the top, it cancels out the freedom in the bottom.

"With this change of roles, I think Miles is trying to see what his same lyrical and innovative mind can do. We know it's the same guy, so we have to trust our group leader. He's putting himself on a different menu, and I dig it. Every step he has made, he's always been right, and always ahead of his time, so I think we'll end up in good shape.

"I think we can expect further changes. At some point he may decide, 'Hey, the rhythm section I used on *Bitches Brew* and *Jack Johnson* was too loud,' and he'll use his wah-wah pedal and amplifier on the trumpet to match it; or he might say, 'What if we dropped the volume of everything down,' and he might bring more lyricism in. Anything can happen."

Herbie Hancock concurs. "The music of the past is not necessarily old hat, but I can understand how Miles feels, because people come up to me and ask me to play 'Watermelon Man' and that's not where I'm at now, I don't want to play it. Miles isn't up there to please everybody, or anybody. He's there to be honest, that's all; and he has to be taken for what he is."

Miles Davis remains seemingly impervious to the controversy that surrounds him. He has often been quoted as indifferent to criticism and has claimed he never reads anything that is written about him, yet there have been many cracks in the wall he has built around himself. One review (of a record made during his appearance at a rock festival on the Isle of Wight) clearly got through to him. From Milan he called the *Melody Maker* in London: "What kind of man can call me arrogant? I know where you're at. You shouldn't be a critic. You are a white man looking for white excitement, but there are more subtle forms of excitement." He went on to express contempt for the entire rock scene.

Obsessed with what seems to him to be a necessity to analyze everything in racial terms, he once told Don DeMichael, in a *Rolling Stone* interview: "Rock is social music. There's two kinds—white and black—and those bourgeois spades are trying to sing white and the whites are trying to sound colored. It's embarrassing. It's like me wearing a dress." One wonders to what extent his rebellion against the "bourgeois spade" background (that is, his own parentage) is conscious. One wonders too how he explains the fact that many of the early rock groups to which he gave serious attention (Jimi Hendrix, Sly & The Family Stone) were racially integrated.

Whatever his true feelings about the rock of whites and bourgeois blacks, he has made a palpable and self-admitted attempt to compete with the rock musicians on their own level. On listening to a record by Cream, he said: "They sure play loud. If they're gonna play loud, I'm gonna plug into an amplifier too." It was one more psychological step toward the Fillmore and the Isle of Wight.

The reception of Davis by rock fans has varied quite conspicuously from job to job. At the Hollywood Bowl in 1970 his group was the supporting attraction in a program starring The Band. The latter was wildly received; Miles, opening the show, played continuously for forty-five minutes and walked off to tepid applause.

His own analysis of the stage at which his music had arrived around the turn of the decade is essentially that it does not call for analysis.

"See, Leonard, what you're missing, I'm not doing anything, it doesn't need an explanation. I'm reacting to what's been done and what's supposed to be happening today. Everything you've ever heard, all that shit is condensed, you know? All the clichés are so condensed that you can play "Body and Soul" in two bars.

"If some musicians don't understand it, they just don't have that kind of an ear. Everybody I get is special. If I wanted to play songs that have a definite beginning and an ending, all that calls for is an ordinary working musician. Keith Jarrett, Jack DeJohnette, all the guys I've used have changed the whole style of music today. You should know that.

"You ought to try playing some of the things we do. I could show you how. The other day I wrote down some chords and stuff for George Wein to play, and I had him playing like Keith!

"You know what I don't like? It's the playing between solos. They don't blend or nothing. . . . In my group we play a lot of polyrhythms and everything, you know, a lot of different keys off of keys and scales off of scales. You ought to study it.

"I know you wrote that my group is loud. Well, that's just the times we live in. Everything is loud; everything gets higher. You take a symphony orchestra. You cannot write for two violins. You can't hear that shit. How many do they use? Dozens. They don't use one bass fiddle—they use twelve. It's the same thing. Anyhow, I still play way down sometimes, but you can hear it—every note.

"One of the things you learn in my group is, you leave drummers alone, 'cause drummers have their own inside thing. And do like I did Herbie Hancock, take out all those fat chords and shit. And Keith—I just put him at the piano and let him go. Keith wasn't playing like that before he joined me.

"A lot of what we have in the group has been developed in clubs. I love the possibility of just freaking off on your horn in a nightclub. In Shelly's I really found out something. Actually it was a learning period in there, when I played everything and made the band play everything they could possibly play.

"That's what's good about working clubs. You play a first set, OK; second set, OK; third set, OK—and they're playing what they know, right? Then the last set they start playing what they *don't* know; which is out of sight! They start thinking, which is worth all the money in the world to me. Thrills me.

"I worked Shelly's just to help keep the place open. I lost about ten pounds in that motherfucker. I made $4,000 a week there, but I went in weighing 139 and came out weighing 129. Then I was asked to play Boston and I said to myself, if I go to Boston I'll weigh 121. I haven't worked since. That was three, four months ago."

LF: What was all the talk in the press about your retiring?

MD: What I meant was, I got a tour in Europe. I'll make about $300,000 on it. Then I won't work again until the spring and I'll make a spring tour. No more week here and three weeks off and a week there. I'm through with that shit.

LF: How about festivals?

MD: I don't care. They're all such bullshit. Just one-job things.

LF: How are you going to keep your men together?

MD: I can always get a group. The men I need, I can keep on salary while I'm laying off.

LF: Will you ever again do anything like you did with Gil Evans? Or have you put all that behind you?

MD: I can't get with that. But we have a new instrumentation for a big band that's outa sight.

LF: What does it consist of?

MD: If I tell you that, every motherfucker will be copying it. Quincy would be the first one. Quincy's always trying to pick my mind.

The slighting reference to Jones is indicative of Davis' attitude toward an overwhelming majority of musicians in every field. In judging others he cannot overcome the temptation to expect them to measure up to his own levels of originality, proficiency, and sophistication. This leaves him with very little outside the purlieus of his own music that he can enjoy and respect without reservation.

His assessment of pop and rock stars vacillates according to his moods. He has often pointed out that rock musicians are limited by their lack of harmonic knowledge and generally poor technical musicianship. He has made mildly complimentary remarks about Crosby, Stills, Nash & Young, and The Who. Concerning Blood, Sweat & Tears he has blown hot and cold. On one occasion he called the group "a pretentious imitation of me and Gil Evans," but at another point he declared that B S & T was "the only group I know that really gives people [at the Fillmore] something musically." Asked to name his preferences in the field of pop composing, he said: "Elton John and James Taylor write good songs. Valerie Simpson writes good songs."

In the fall of 1971 Miles was in Los Angeles for several weeks. As he does wherever he goes, he spent much of his time in a local gym. He has been on a serious health kick for several years, has his own personal trainer, and a white terry cloth robe with his name emblazoned on the back. Proud of his physique, he thinks nothing of working out with a heavy speed bag, sparring for several rounds, skipping rope, then doing as many as a hundred or more pushups and situps.

In his spare time he might be found watching ball games on a small black-and-white television set in his room at the Chateau Marmont, overlooking Sunset Boulevard. This fading relic of the old Hollywood is his home whenever he visits the West Coast. One afternoon, after dispatching his lissome girl friend on a shopping tour, he was in the mood to talk about his contemporaries, his social attitudes, and his plans, such as they were, for the future.

LF: What live music have you heard lately that impressed you?

MD: I never go out to nightclubs any more. When I go, I know what to expect. It's what I can hear in my head without going.

LF: Are you going to hear Herbie Hancock's group at Donte's?

MD: I don't want to hear it. I can't even listen to that, as much as I love to hear Herbie play. I can't stand the trombone . . . and Eddie Henderson—I just don't like to hear trumpet players that keep playing like Freddie Hubbard. You know, it's the way you look at something happen that enables you to be your own self, if you're not lazy. It's easy to play a cliché. A cliché should be your musical foundation, but it shouldn't be what you do.

LF: What do you think of Tony Williams' group?

MD: Tony needs somebody to solo, other than himself. Larry, the organist, he's all right, but you know, you shouldn't bother a soloist. Like, I never bother Keith. Sooner or later Tony will get tired of not hearing what he wants to hear.

LF: What does the music of Pharoah Sanders say to you?

MD: It doesn't say anything to me, because Pharoah's not doing anything.

LF: How about Ornette Coleman?

MD: If you hear a guy, he has to be with someone that's right for him. Like, I heard a white guy with Buddy Miles, and the way Buddy plays, the white boy was playing out of sight. Now if he was playing with another white boy playing drums, he wouldn't sound like that. When Ornette was playing with Leroy Vinnegar and Billy Higgins everybody was together. But I don't know *what* he's doing now.

You know, the horn doesn't sound like it's supposed to sound. To me it's not the right background. So I check him out, and if he doesn't have the right background he's a sad motherfucker. And he's not a trumpet player. That's something that takes years to develop. As for his violin playing, he's not going to scare Ray Nance.

LF: Have you listened to the Joe Henderson combo?

MD: Joe Henderson can play his ass off. He used to play with me. But in general there ain't much happening that I want to hear. All the groups are trying to play like somebody I know. I don't want to hear clichés: I don't want to get back into the past. What's important is what's happening now, the new music and the music of the future. I don't even want to think about what I was doing myself last year.

LF: Haven't you heard any rock groups that interest you?

MD: I haven't heard anything coming from the white kids with the long hair and shit. I like to hear the Motown sound and James Brown, them funky singers.

LF: You put it on a racial basis, yet some of your most rewarding associations have been interracial.

MD: You don't understand. What I want to hear doesn't come from a white musician.

LF: Including Gil Evans, Bill Evans, Dave Holland?

MD: No, I don't mean like that. What I want to hear, like rhythm and blues, it comes from black musicians all the time.

When you get guys that aren't prejudiced, like Joe Zawinul and John McLaughlin, I hardly ever look at their skin; they don't make me look at their skin. But when I hear a rhythm section with Tony or Jack on drums, or Buddy Miles, they do some shit that you just don't find in a white drummer.

A choreographer I know went to Africa with Harry Belafonte; he tried to copy some of the dances to bring them back to teach, and he said he just couldn't break it down. And he's a hell of a choreographer. It's something they have that you just can't figure out, it's a natural thing.

LF: Do you think you can tell from listening to a record whether a musician is black or white?

MD: I think you could. I still can.

LF: Would you like to do a blindfold test to prove it?

MD: If I happen to be driving along some place and I hear something—not something that you put on—if I hear something, if I say he's white, he's white; you can bet your money on it.

LF: Suppose it's a mixed group?

MD: What difference does it make anyway?

LF: You said you could tell the difference.

MD: It's because I'm black, Leonard. I'm not white. I wouldn't turn on Al Hirt, but a white guy would.

LF: I wouldn't turn on Al Hirt's show, and it's not because I'm white or black. On the other hand, if it were the Bobby Hackett show you'd turn it on.

MD: Not necessarily. . . . If Herbie Hancock was on television at the same time as Al Hirt, who do you think I'd turn on?

LF: Who do you think *I'd* turn on?

MD: You'd turn on Herbie.

LF: Damn right I would, and not because of black or white, because he's a better musician.

MD: Why do you say Herbie's a better musician than Al Hirt?

LF: A musician who appeals to me more. Beg your pardon. (It had slipped my mind that a few years ago, Miles had told me: "Al Hirt is a very good trumpet player; and he's a nice guy. It's a shame they made him into a television personality—fat and jolly and bearded and funny. I guess if he was thin he wouldn't have to do it. Harry James is a good trumpet player, and he never did no shit like that." Still respectful of Hirt's musicianship, Miles was taking exception to my simplistic "better musician" explanation.)

MD: Herbie Hancock would be good for a TV program. He's the most patient guy I've ever seen. He plays all kinds of styles; and he's a nice-looking guy too, you know? Why shouldn't he have his own show?

What I'm saying is, it's not just Al Hirt, I mean because a guy is white, white people will follow him. You understand?

LF: Some white people follow him.

MD: I'm not saying all this to be the great black father. I'm just saying that our roots are black and that's where they'll remain, and I can't help it.

When I hear a white guy, or when I look at a white girl that's supposed to be attractive, I don't feel the same thing that a white person would feel. I can understand a white girl seeing a white guy, and her screaming because she's white. But if I see a black girl screaming over a white guy . . . I'm just saying their roots won't let 'em do certain things.

There are mixed marriages that work. I'm not talking about that shit. I'm just saying that white people cater to white people and black people cater to black people. It's just a normal thing. One dog will fuck another dog.

LF: Don't you nevertheless believe that integration is the ultimate solution?

MD: I don't know whether it is or not. I think things will just come. If they work, fine. If they don't work, we just gotta accept it. You see black kids and white kids playing together, and they don't get fucked up until older people come in. Interracial couples, when they dig each other, they dig each other; it's just that outside pressure.

LF: Your ideal world basically is still an integrated world, isn't it?

MD: Right. But I think it won't work . . . Most black people would like to see everybody integrated, you know? A lot of black people want to be like white people; they think there's a level that they should be on, that white people have a level that they want to try to reach. That's sad, you know?

People can live together, but all that old shit hasn't stopped. As long as they keep on showing Army films with an all-white Army, it's not going to stop. That's a joke.

They fucked my son Gregory around, man; he went into the Army. He had to knock out a couple of white guys in St. Louis. He said, "Father, I'm going into the Army, and when I come back, if they start any shit, I'm not responsible."

LF: The Army gave him a very bad time?

MD: Shit yes, they Jim Crowed him in Germany. He's a fighter, you know, he won four titles. He brought back all those trophies. He can break your fucking neck and not even think nothing of it. He's not afraid of nothing. He would say it was supposed to be broken. He's a Muslim. He just wants to learn black things.

I can understand how he feels. If a white man bothers me, man, I don't want to touch him because I don't know what I might do. I might kill him.

Davis' need to keep his cool was never more frighteningly illustrated than in an incident that took place on a hot summer night in 1959, when his group was playing Birdland. After escorting a young white girl out of the club to a taxi, he was standing on the sidewalk when a patrolman came by and asked him to move on. When Miles said, "I'm not going nowhere—I'm just getting a breath of fresh air," the patrolman threatened to arrest him. Miles said, "Go ahead, lock me up." When the patrolman seized his arm, a scuffle ensued during which a plainclothes detective passing by began hitting Miles with a black-jack. With blood dripping all over his clothes, he was taken to the police station where, with his distraught wife, Frances, at his side, he was booked on charges of disorderly conduct and assault. At a hospital, ten stitches were taken in his scalp. After a lengthy series of legal maneuvers, a three-judge panel ruled that the Davis arrest had been illegal and the charge against him was erased. Miles decided to sue the city, but eventually dropped the whole matter in disgust. At the time of the incident he commented that it might never have happened if the girl he was escorting to the cab had been black.

LF: Have you been practicing while you've been out here?

MD: Uh-uh.

LF: Aren't you afraid your chops won't be up when you start again?

MD: Hell, I've been playing since I was thirteen. The older I get, the stronger I get. I still have the same mouthpiece I had when I was thirteen.

LF: Do you still have the urge to play, to be creating right now?

MD: I *never* have the urge to play; just sometimes when I hear something, I want to play with it.

LF: That's liable to continue as long as you live.

MD: That's what I'm saying.

LF: As long as there's something around that you can hear and want to be part of, then, you're not going to be just doing nothing.

MD: Right.

LF: The big difference between you and someone like Diz is that he will sit in with any kind of band, Dixieland or whatever, but you still have your own thing that you want to play with.

MD: Diz may do that, but he won't stay there a long time.

LF: No, he just likes the change of pace.

MD: Right.

LF: With your children gone and no wife, don't you miss having a family around you?

MD: I don't believe in families. Like, if I die, my money ain't going to go to people just because they're close relatives. The people that are closest to me are the ones that helped me be able to do what I do, not just because somebody's my brother. If I had a lot of money, I wouldn't leave everything to my brother or sister just because they're related to me.

LF: Don't you feel close to your daughter or your grandson?

MD: No, I don't. Do you?

LF: I have no grandson, but I feel close to my daughter. I think most people feel a closeness because of family ties.

MD: Family ties are a lot of bullshit. That's what's fucking up this world. Sitting down at tea and all that shit. It doesn't go that way. In the first place, who wants to eat that much?

LF: That's not your nature, Miles, come on! If your daughter were sick and needed you, you'd go out and help her.

MD: Help her do *what*? No, man, that ain't nothing. If you said, "Miles, I need $500," and I had it, I'd send it to you, because that's the way I am. Money ain't shit, if it helps you and I don't need it for anything else, why shouldn't I send it to you?

LF: I don't see how I would deserve it.

MD: I mean I don't have anything for my family. I don't live for my family, I live for myself.

LF: But logically that should apply to your marriages too. Why did you get married if you don't believe in families?

MD: Because they asked me. Every woman I ever married asked me.

LF: Why didn't you have the strength of will to say no?

MD: Because I figured it'd make them happy.

LF: You just made an admission. You're willing to do something to make somebody happy.

MD: Of course!

LF: That's the same thing I was asking about your daughter.

MD: That's not what I'm saying, Leonard. I didn't say I wouldn't go out there. If she had any trouble I'd go out there to see what was wrong with her. I still don't have any family ties. If one of them would die or anything, I don't know how I would act; you wouldn't see me acting like they do on television. When my mother was sick I went to see her in the hospital; I knew she was dying of cancer. But when she died I didn't go to the funeral.

LF: What do you want to be doing ten years from now?

MD: Nothing. If I don't have a deal that is lined up like I want it, ten years from now, I'd give up.

LF: What does nothing mean to you? Sitting watching television? Going to the gym?

MD: Right now I want to find out where I want to live.

LF: You're thinking of moving out of New York?

MD: I don't know where I want to live. But the best time I ever had in my life, other than playing trumpet, was when I was out in the country riding horses.

LF: Do you still have a feeling for the country?

MD: Yeah, I like space, man.

LF: You should probably buy some more land.

MD: I don't want to have to search. I don't know where to buy.

LF: It sounds to me as though you're not that interested any more, or not deeply concerned, about continuing in music.

MD: I didn't say that.

LF: That's what you said in effect when I asked you what you wanted to be doing ten years from now.

MD: If I started thinking about music—now—then I'll have to play the trumpet. But the minute I don't think about it, I can be contented doing nothing.

Although the possibility seems remote, it is not inconceivable at this stage of his life that Miles Davis may extend his present policy of semi-retirement into almost total inactivity. For a quarter of a century he has to some extent controlled the direction of jazz, expanding the minds of his listeners along with the scope of his music. How long he can continue to grow, and take his audience along with him, is a secret as inscrutable as Miles himself seems to the young music student observing him at a distance.

For the present, though, his music remains as pervasive a force as ever, more challenging than yesterday when it seemed incomparably more complex than the day before. Now, as always, it mirrors the personality of the man, of his words and his actions. Although, as our conversation revealed, he is emotionally vulnerable, he prefers to keep his defenses up and cultivate the image that had led *Jet* to refer to him as "Terrible-tempered Miles." For all his displays of anger, cynicism, arrogance, and heavy sarcasm, he is no less capable of tenderness, generosity, and idealism. The psychological convolutions through which he moves toward these emotions are no easier to figure out than the processes involved in the creation of one of his uncompromisingly innovative solos or compositions.

In the light of Miles's life as an avocational boxer, a comment by Clark Terry seems singularly apposite: "I have a feeling that Miles is rather like Sugar Ray Robinson on the ropes, when he wants to psych out his opponent. Ray had a way of leaning on the ropes and faking, to the point where the opponent would say, 'I've got this cat now,' and then Ray would grab one hand with the rope and whale like hell with the other hand, and in most instances he'd floor the other guy. Miles uses all kinds of psychology in dealing with people, and he has found it to be lucrative."

As Quincy Jones once observed, "Miles is always trying to hide all that warmth, beauty, and romanticism; it's a tough job for him, and it shows through when he plays." And Dizzy affirms: "Basically Miles is very shy; that's the whole thing. You know, I know him probably better than he knows himself. I was talk-ing to his daughter Cheryl in St. Louis, and I said, 'Did you know that your father is really a very bashful man?' and she said, 'Yeah, I've always known that, but nobody else can dig it; he puts up that front to cover up the shyness.'

"But what I really respect about him is he won't be a phony for anyone. He was the first one that came along in our business and figured he didn't have to smile at everyone, didn't have to tell no jokes or make no announcements, didn't have to say thank you or even bow. He figured he could just let the music speak for him, and for itself. He succeeded in doing this, and you can't fight success. I say more power to him."

An ironic aspect of this phenomenon to which Gillespie did not draw atten-tion is the extent to which Miles' personality has built a mystique around him and has contributed to the hold he has on the public. The irony lies in the fact that three or four decades ago Louis Armstrong, whose attitudes were anti-thetical to Davis' in almost every conceivable way, also owed his commercial achievements in large measure to his personality.

Armstrong, accepted first by musicians as the supreme instrumental catalyst of his day, later reached the masses by being, onstage, exactly what they wanted him to be. Davis, after gaining similar in-group acceptance, went on to acquire his material luxuries, and massive income-tax problems, by doing precisely the opposite: defying the public to like him, insisting that he be accepted solely for the intrinsic value of his music.

That he has attained this objective is a measure of the distance traversed by pure jazz in barely half a century, from the level of entertainment and comedy, "happy music" aimed primarily at the lowest common intellectual denomina-tor, to its present eminence as a musical idiom admired and dissected by serious students all over the world. It is an accomplishment never before registered by any of the lively arts. The jazz world may well take pride in the role played by Miles Davis—black, volatile, rebellious, and resilient as jazz itself—in bringing about this phenomenon in the twentieth-century music scene.

—Hollywood, 1972

MY EGO ONLY NEEDS A GOOD RHYTHM SECTION

Interviewer: Stephen Davis
The Real Paper, March 21, 1973

Stephen Davis is the author of *Jim Morrison: Life, Death, Legend; Old Gods Almost Dead: The 40-Year Odyssey of the Rolling Stones;* and the classic *New York Times*–bestselling Led Zeppelin book *Hammer of the Gods.* He is the coauthor of memoirs by Mick Fleetwood of Fleetwood Mac, The Band's Levon Helm, and Aerosmith. His journalism has appeared in *Rolling Stone,* the *New York Times,* and the *Boston Globe,* among others.

Miles Davis, the jazz trumpeter, was fined $1000 in Manhattan Criminal Court yesterday after pleading guilty to a weapons and possession charge. He was arrested Feb. 23 in an apartment house he owns on Manhattan's upper west side.
—*New York Times,* March 2, 1973

"Look," Miles's bearded manager says, "the whole thing is finished and we got him off for only a thousand. I think he'd rather just forget about it. What happened? I'll tell you two stories; here's the one you can't print. Miles and his girlfriend L. get back to his house around one in the morning, both really fucked up, at least Miles is. He can't find his keys, he's pissed off, he starts punching the door to his house. BAM BAM BAM. He empties his pockets looking for the keys and a bag of coke falls out and spills on the floor. Miles owns the building, but one of his upstairs tenants is drunk all the time, and he hears Miles trying to break down this heavy door and figures the place is getting ripped off. The drunk calls the precinct and a couple of cops come over, a sergeant and a patrolman. As soon as she sees the cops L. throws her handbag in a corner. The cops come in. The sergeant knows Miles, knows he owns the house, and at that point the search should have legally stopped. There were no longer any grounds for the cops being in the building.

131

"The cops see L.'s bag laying in the corner and asks who it belongs to. Miles and L. tell the cops they never saw the bag before. Which legally gave the cops the right to pick up the bag and search it as abandoned property. So they open the bag, find some more coke and a loaded .22 automatic, and they immediately bust the two of them.

"So at three in the morning I get a call from some Irish desk sergeant. 'We have Miles Davis down here and he's using you as his one phone call.' Miles gets on the phone and says, 'Neil, get me outta here. They're treating me like a nigger.' The cop grabs the phone away from Miles and tells me he can't allow anyone to talk like that over the phone. I hang up and call the lawyer and everybody else and go back to sleep. And somehow, being Miles, he gets them to let him make a second phone call at five in the morning. 'Neil, get me outta here! Wake up a fuckin' judge or something.'

"That morning I talked to the district attorney about dropping the charges because of the bogus arrest, and he tells me it's impossible to drop the gun charge on a black man in New York City when cops are getting shot on the streets every day. Have you ever heard such bullshit in your life?"

This narrative is related by Neil Reshen, Miles Davis's recently hired manager, in the vestibule of Miles's building on West 77th Street. Neil rang the bell five minutes before but there was no response. Also in attendance is Waylon Jennings, a client of Reshen's who is tagging along in the hopes of meeting the reclusive trumpeter. Reshen rings again. Silence. "Anyway, it's over," he continues patiently. "We got him off. Miles is in a good mood today. Ask him whatever you want. Getting busted doesn't bother him for too long. He's been harassed by these fuckers for so long he probably doesn't think about it anymore."

There's a huge gash in the door where an enraged Miles tried to kick it in the night of his bust. Reshen rings again. A woman's voice over the intercom asks who's there. She lets us in—light complexion, green scarf covering her hair—and shows us into a vestibule without a word and vanishes. The room is a Moroccan grotto, all arches and dark grey dripping plaster. One room is a waterfall. It's so dark we can hardly see the massive gong hanging from the ceiling. On the coffee table are a broken trumpet, a broken wah-wah pedal and a paperback copy of *Jonathan Livingston Seagull*. From the gloomy interior of the house emerges the legendary Finney, Miles's valet and hairdresser, who had seen much action with the late Jimi Hendrix. Finney has large, half-closed eyes and hair wound into tight little pigtails hanging from his head. At two in the afternoon it's evident that the establishment is just waking up. Finney tells Neil Reshen to go upstairs and tells Waylon Jennings and me to wait down here.

What am I doing here? I'm here because Miles Davis is jealous. Miles Dewey Davis, 47 years old, the richest and most successful jazz musician in the world, a musical innovator who has been creating new modes of music approximately every four or five years since his breakthrough cool tonalities in 1949, is envious. Most of the young musicians who have played with him over the past few years have formed successful bands of their own. John McLaughlin's Mahavishnu Orchestra, the Tony Williams Lifetime, Wayne Shorter and Joe Zawinul's Weather Report, Jack DeJohnette's Compost, and Keith Jarrett's many albums as a leader and soloist compete with Miles's recent albums and in many cases outsell them. Miles doesn't like these musicians reaping the rewards and accolades that he feels responsible for. (Miles's two most recent albums, *On the Corner* and *In Concert*, heavy with the dense electro-funk of guitarists Pete Cosey and Reggie Lucas, both got less-than-rave notices from everyone save San Francisco critic Ralph J. Gleason.)

So Miles fired his manager of 17 years and hired Neil Reshen, who specializes in artists deemed "difficult" by their record companies. Miles demanded Reshen hire a press agent. Reshen called Columbia Records and told them that Miles was pissed off. Columbia's publicity office called me and several other writers. I had approached them about interviewing Miles a year earlier, and had been told that Miles wasn't talking to anybody. Now here was another chance and I jumped at it, hopeful that Miles wouldn't go through one of the last-moment changes of temperament for which he was so famous. To say that Miles Davis had the reputation of being sullen was to pay him a compliment. He was said to be a violent and malevolent son of a bitch with a cinder for a heart and a cash register for a mind. All one had to do was listen to him play his horn to know that couldn't be true.

Waylon is talking. He's nervous. He's wearing a black cowboy hat and boots. He's an Outlaw, a big country music hero. He's in awe just to be in Miles Davis's lair. Neil Reshen comes back down, looking relieved. "Miles is gonna talk to you," he whispers. A pair of bright red patent leather Italian loafers begins to descend the staircase, followed by sockless black ankles and legs in tailored dungarees. Miles Davis negotiates the stairs gingerly, taking each step in half time. A few weeks ago he totaled his white Ferrari Dino on the West Side Highway, breaking both legs and landing him in the hospital for ten days. Miles makes it to the bottom landing, looks at the three of us and rasps in his blown-out croak of a voice, "Where's the cat from Nashville?" Waylon strides over and shakes hands. Neil introduces me. Miles looks carefully and pantomimes a fearful mock cringe at what he sees: longhaired rock journalist in denim shirt and uncool sweater. Hiking boots. Tape recorder. He's quaking with bogus trepidation, putting on a show. But wait, he's smiling, and we shake hands, his grip firm and dry. I'm in heaven.

Miles leads us through the ground-floor dining area to a glassed-in conservatory overlooking the enclosed courtyard in the back of the house, with bare ailanthus trees and lawn furniture. Egyptian hieroglyphics and mystical rune frescoes adorn the outside walls. On a sofa surrounded by greenery are the drawings for the cover of the forthcoming *Big Fun* album, drawn by artist Corky McCoy in the streetwise style of *On the Corner*: jivey dudes popping fingers and talking trash, sinuous black goddesses whose buttocks bulge out of tight skirts, whose nipples pop out of giant African tits. One of them avidly fellates a trumpet ten times her size. Miles picks up the rendering and gasps to Neil, "Here, man, sell these motherfuckers to Columbia."

Neil looks surprised. "I thought they already had the artwork for the cover."

"That's right," Miles croaks. "These are the ones we're not gonna use. Sell 'em to Columbia anyway." He snorts a laugh out through his nose. Miles hasn't had a voice in years, I've been told, but he's less reticent about it now than he used to be. Back in the fifties he had an operation to remove polyps on his vocal cords. One story has the surgeon slicing through his vocal cords. Another has Miles screaming at an errant club owner while he was recuperating. He speaks in a hoarse whisper that occasionally breaks into a high-pitched voice when he says yes or no to a question.

Neil and Waylon are ready to split. Miles hands Neil a thick sheaf of his mail to look over. Miles refuses to read his mail. Neil handles everything.

Now we're ready to talk. I've been primed with tapes of new music—a cassette of bluesy, percussive mixes dated 2/14/73 with Miles playing organ.

(These tapes, which have never been on a record, are similar to "Rated X" and "Billy Preston," which appeared on *Get Up With It* in 1974.) We're in this glass-enclosed porch with a hospital bed that Miles bought after the accident, a hospital serving table and a wheelchair. Miles seats me in the wheelchair, propping up the leg supports and lifting my legs into horizontal position. "Now you can see how I've been living for two months." Miles pours himself a Heineken, lights a Marlboro with a silver lighter and settles back into the folds of the hospital bed, smiling, ready.

How are your legs feeling today?
"They're OK. Getting better all the time." Miles sits up, pulls up the legs of his jeans and shows the vivid scars around both ankles. Then he looks up, apprehensive. "Did you listen to my tapes?" His huge eyes bore into mine.

Yes, of course, talk about what you're doing.
Well we got the long blues thing with drums and different times and shit. On that I tried to show my piano player what was happening, and it wound up sounding so good with me playing on it that Teo Macero wanted to keep it that way. I was playing the same way on the organ that I would on the trumpet, playing in the same spaces. So I just told him to lay out. I thought the thing would wake up that way and it did.

Do you structure your sounds to affect your audience a certain way?
I'm not thinking about anybody but myself when we play. [Miles laughs ruefully.] I mean, how is my audience gonna move me? I know that if I don't move myself, then it's no good. I don't ever think about that audience shit. Man, I play with fuckin' *blinders* on. The way that we play now, it's too hard for me to think about stuff like that. In Detroit the other night we played for two hours and fifteen minutes without stopping. I lose about five pounds, six pounds. I'm fuckin' wringin' wet.

I can hear the ghost of Jimi Hendrix in some of this music—
When I say "like" Hendrix or James Brown, I mean that I tell the guitar player that if he likes Hendrix or Sly, and I like Hendrix and Sly, to play something like that, just to open it up. It can't sound exactly like them because it'll have

a little more music and shit in it. What we play on top wouldn't be like what Hendrix'll play on top. What Sly and them need is a good soloist. What Jimi needs—needed—was good rhythm, which he never had until he got Buddy Miles, you know, the Band of Gypsies.

You don't *look* for any kind of particular sound. It's already there. All that shit is out there for you to pick up on.

The critics who don't like your new band say you're trying too hard to appeal to the Rock market.

I ain't thinking like that, man, about no fuckin' market. Shee-it. [Miles scowls, doesn't like the observation.] Listen to what I say. Hendrix had no knowledge of modal music; he was just a natural musician, you know, he wasn't studied, he wasn't into no market, and neither am I. Columbia tries to get me into that shit but I don't let 'em do it. They wanted to put some of my music on some kind of sample record of some of their black music, and I said fuck that shit, man. Leave my music alone.

Aren't you satisfied with Columbia?

Uh uh, man, by no means. I ain't satisfied. They don't do anything for you unless you're white or Jewish. Except maybe when I got out a new album or something. By now I don't even talk to them anymore. For instance: when I showed 'em the new cover by Corky McCoy, they told me it won't help sell any albums. And I *told* 'em how to merchandise nigger music, man. Put Chinese on the covers. Put niggers on the covers, put brothers and sisters on 'em, whatever they're gonna call us next, that's what you put on the covers to sell us.

Corky McCoy's my best friend. I just called him up and told him what to do. In fact, he was afraid to do it, and I . . . you know, look at those covers, man. He just *lives* it. *Black life!* It's different from white life, Chinese life, whatever. My life's *different* from yours.

How come [bassist] Michael Henderson is the only musician from your last band to be in your present lineup?

What about Mtume? He stayed in too. Uh . . . Michael had a funky sound, you know, and I been teaching him for awhile. [Henderson was hired by Miles out of Stevie Wonder's touring band. James Mtume Foreman played percussion.]

Like if he's in E Flat and I play an A chord or maybe a C or a D he doesn't get ruffled anymore, like he used to. He sticks where he is. He's used to all my stuff by now.

But I got to change bands, you know. You're not gonna use guys like Keith [Jarrett] or Jack [DeJohnette] forever. I mean they're all capable, but after awhile, you know, they're gonna lose it. It gets to be all the same. You hear Keith now, man, he lost it.

Do you ever listen to what the musicians who used to work with you—John McLaughlin, Weather Report—are doing now?
Never.

Do you ever feel like you have your own school?
Yeah, all the time. But you know, when they're playing real good, I also feel like I'm *in* a school. It works both ways. You might show a guy something and he takes it and learns. I just don't listen to what the guys are playing now because I already know what they're gonna do. Like John [McLaughlin]: I got him his drummer. I got him his manager. I know what he's gonna do. He's got two sides to him: a lotta sides actually. I know how soft John is, or can be. That's the way he plays when he plays with me. That's what I like about him.

What about the influences your musicians have on you. Joe Zawinul, for instance, is credited with being responsible for some of your recent directions, with In A Silent Way.
Let them [the critics] say it. I don't care what they say. As long as I been playing they never say I done anything. They always say that some white guy did it. I just let 'em say it. Shit, whenever Joe or somebody would bring in something that they wrote, I'd have to cut it all up because these guys get so hung up on what they write. They think it's complete the way they write it. Like the way he wanted that *In A Silent Way* was completely different. I put it in a mode, no chords or anything. I don't know what he was looking for when he wrote that tune, but it wasn't gonna be on my record.

So now they all play the tune the way I had it. Even Joe's own group [Weather Report]. Shit, a little melody like that, why make it so important? It's just a little sound—let it go.

Miles, are you at all religious?
Um um. By no means. You mean *God*, and stuff like that? It's a big joke to me.

What do you think of musicians like Pharoah Sanders and Alice Coltrane, who seem to play their music in a religious context?
I never think of 'em. Religion just don't come into it. You've got to study music. You can't just be religious and the stuff just pops out like that. They're giving people the wrong impression. I mean, there's music that comes out of being in a religious group, like the Staple Singers, or James Cleveland. Billy Preston and stuff like that. That's one way you can learn, in church.

Were you brought up in church?
No. If you ask me, that's just the shit the white man uses to con black folks. All forms of religion are a big con. People are just scared to die, man. Everybody dies.

Are you afraid to die?
No. [Miles laughs out loud.] All these lectures—"Protecting Your Inner Karma," and all that shit. How many people even know they have one? I mean, think of all the guys that go to the [Vietnam] war: they go for no reason and kill somebody that they don't even know, and then you come back and a guy calls you a black motherfucker or something, and you have a reason to smash his head in and you do it and you're a criminal and you have to go to court, but you don't have to go to court for going in the army and killing fifty people that you don't know.

It's easy to do . . . kill somebody. I mean the police do it all the time and nobody says a fuckin' thing. They don't go to church and say, "I'm sorry I killed that guy."

Miles stops talking for awhile and stares at a little group of three trophies that stand next to his bed. Each is an Army boxing trophy, a little gold-plated fighter brazenly leading with his right. Miles resumes:

They're trained like my son was trained—to kill. These trophies . . . my son's. He was a champion boxer in the Army. In Germany. He comes back, a white guy pokes fun at him because of his color, and the first thing my son does *is try to break his neck.* You know? And I *tried* to *tell* him about that shit.

But he's a Black Muslim, and he says, "What do you think I'm supposed to do, father, let that guy stand up and say that to me? They sent me into the Army to kill somebody I don't even know, then they won't give me a job, they make fun of me." I mean, it takes all the spirit out of him.

Miles looks down and closes those huge eyes for a moment, revealing a poignancy I couldn't have envisioned in his features after studying them closely during the dozen of times I've seen him on a bandstand. Then his face quickly resumes its scornful, noncommittal mien.

Once I saw a mark on his arm, and I said, "What you wanna do that shit for?" And he said he just did it once, for his girlfriend.

He's in jail now.

Where?
In St. Louis. I got to get him out, fast. So I never think about that religion shit. And when I do, it makes me mad, you know? People have to respect me. I know they respect *me*, there's no doubt about it, because they can't do it themselves. Otherwise there'd be five *On the Corners* out.

Columbia. Shit. I got guys like Motown offering me five hundred thousand a year and shit like that. Atlantic Records wants me. Columbia don't pay me shit.

Why do you continue to record for them?
Because I can't get out of that contract. I mean, they don't even try to go into the black neighborhoods and sell records. They tell me, "We want to introduce you to a new audience," but that audience is always white! Sheeit! It'd be a sad fuckin' day if there was no Sly Stone, wouldn't it?

You've never had a problem finding your audience, have you?
They find me. It makes me mad when Columbia says, "We want these [new] people to hear you." I don't audition for no white man, and for no black man either for that matter. I don't give a fuck if they like it or not. All I tell 'em to do is

sell the music *black*, not to put no white girls on the cover with no pants on and stuff like that. Sell it black. Like I like Sly, man, James Brown, James Cleveland. I like to look at black people—Jim Brown, Ray Robinson, people you never even heard of. I don't listen to the Rolling Stones and any of that shit. [Miles looks at me reproachfully.]

Well, do you listen to R&B?
I'm from *St. Louis*, man. That's all we played in St. Louis. The only reason my records sound the way they do is because I studied music. It's my background. We always played the *blues* in St. Louis. Bands came up on the boats from New Orleans, guys came from Kansas City and Oklahoma City, all playing the blues. I mean there's some funky shit in St. Louis even today. You can still go to any little town in Kentucky that has a black nightclub and hear a real good band that nobody ever heard of, musicians that can't get out of town and just lay around. They can't all go to New York or San Francisco because there ain't enough there for all of 'em.

Why did you come to New York in 1944?
To go to Juilliard. To get out of St. Louis. To find Charlie Parker. See, we were working in a club in St. Louis and right around the corner was a hospital for the heart and no black people could go in there. One day I finally said I have to get the fuck out of this town.

How long did you stay at Juilliard?
Till I found out that nothin' was happening. All that shit I had already learned in St. Louis. And outside of school I was with Charlie Parker, and I met guys like Gil Evans, and George Russell, John Lewis, Dizzy . . .

How did you meet Charlie Parker?
I sat in with him one night in St. Louis when he came through with Billy Eckstine's band. They had a trumpet player I really liked named Buddy Anderson and he had to stop playing because he started to hemorrhage and they called me to play. [He smiles fondly.] Actually, they didn't have to call me because I was already there. I knew his part and just started to play.

Who was your main teacher?
Buchanan. Elwood Buchanan. Then I had a teacher here in New York, who was
with the Philharmonic, named Vachiano. He always used to tell me to play for
him and I said man, I'm paying you for the lessons, show me something. Then
I had a teacher named Gosta who was really something, man. He could run the
chromatic scale seventeen times in one breath, all the way up the horn and all
the way down.

*You never seem to play with any vibrato. Did that come from one of these
teachers?*
Buchanan. He didn't believe in it. He said that all the white guys used it and the
best guys were the black guys that just played straight sounds.

Who were your other influences when you were coming up?
There're a dozen of 'em. A whole lot. The main one must have been Clark Terry.
My teacher played like him. There was a guy from New Orleans named Cape-
heart. There was another one but I can't remember his name. Ray Nance. Buck
Clayton. You listened to everybody and took the parts you liked. You watch how
they hold the horn, how they walk. I mean, you're 15 and looking at them like
this. [Miles makes his eyes nearly pop out of his head.]

Would you say that Charlie Parker taught you to play a certain way?
He never said nothing. He just told me to play.

I think you made your first record with him in 1945. You were nineteen years old.
Yeah. I felt like this. [Miles quakes with fear.] I was nervous, man. But I had to
get over being nervous fast because he was never there and I had to rehearse the
band. Which I was used to doing in St. Louis. I was the musical director of the
band in St. Louis when I was 15. We played shows and shit. Eddie Randall and
the Blue Devils, we were called.

How did the famous Birth of the Cool *sessions happen?*
I wrote John Lewis a letter, he was in Paris, and I told him that I had an idea and
that he should come back. Everybody just wrote something and we did it.

Did you have a name for that music? People called it cool jazz, or chamber jazz.
No, man, it's the white folks that need those labels. I mean they named Dizzy's music "Bebop." [Miles frowns.] I can't believe this shit sometimes. They always turn it around. They always put some white guy, make him the top, say it was his idea and all that shit. Like you can see what Weather Report is doing even today. I don't see how they can sound bad, you know? But I know they're limited because I know how both Wayne and Joe play.

Here's my secret, man: I don't tell no one my secrets. Nobody knows all the instrumentation I had in *On the Corner*. They're just guessing. I want to make the fuckin' critics *think*. Not even Teo [Macero] knows all the stuff that's on that record.

I'm confused about when you made what you consider the first "Miles Davis" records.
They were on Savoy, around '46. But I made records when you weren't supposed to make them because they had a war on and were trying to save rubber. They're releasing that shit from those days, you know—"Take One! Take Two!" and that shit.

When you look back on those days now . . .
I don't look back on them. Never. I don't have any place in my head for that stuff. I only look ahead.

We talked for about three hours. Invited back the next afternoon, I returned to the house on West 77th Street with photographer David Doubilet to finish the interview and make some photographs for my article. Miles again sat me in his wheelchair and spread himself on a sofa to answer more questions.

You seemed bitter yesterday when you were discussing Weather Report.
I don't mind people imitating me. If they're kind of polite, they say where the shit comes from. You take Weather Report and people say they got a style all their own, and they *don't*. They took the *Silent Way* shit, you know? But I guess they gotta do that on account of their wives get after them. I mean I've let a lotta guys go on account of their wives.

Are you married now?

[His face breaks into a grin.] Who the fuck am I gonna marry? I wouldn't marry somebody if they had a gun at my head and about five million dollars here on the fuckin' table. First place, I'm too difficult to live with and I know it. Second place, women just go off into themselves. . . . Some girls you can get along with, no questions, no headaches, they don't wanna change you.

Like when I was in the hospital for ten days I had a girlfriend call me up, and she said who's with you now and I said a couple of girls and she said I'll be over when you get rid of them. I said you must be jokin', I'm not gonna put any of these people out on account of one bitch. You know what I mean? *It wasn't as if I'm layin' in the bed fuckin' em.* They just come to see me because I'm fucked up. I ran my car into a pole on the highway.

There was talk that someone broke your legs for you . . .

[Miles frowned, looked at me sharply, and laughed, but it was more a derisive snort.] Why should they break my legs? If they wanted to really hurt me, all they'd have to do is hit me on the mouth.

[Miles is silent for a minute. He purses his lips.]

Here, give me your hand. [He took my extended forefinger and placed it on his upper lip, which was pursed tightly as if its owner was spitting into the mouthpiece of an imaginary horn. I felt a large, circular muscle spring up under my fingertip, a huge protuberance. I had to blink with disbelief as I considered the space I was being allowed into. I took my hand away. Miles smiled.] That comes after thirty years of playing the horn.

While Doubilet was getting in close to photograph Miles's lip, I asked him what he thought of the current music scene.

White people have their own white gods who they worship. I don't know who they are because I don't follow the scene that carefully any more. But I seen some of those shows, you know, where the boys look and dress like girls. [This is in reference to David Bowie, the New York Dolls and the then-fashionable Glam or Trash style.] I mean, I can see whites digging Country & Western and that shit, but now it's just like the guy's ass, and see how he moves. It's not music, man, it's entertainment. So they should sell it as that. Burlesque, only with boys. Ha. Which is all right, you know. When I go to Paris I go to all those shows because they really do it right.

Do you ever get tired of playing music?
No man, I don't. Music is like a curse for me, and I feel like I have to go through with it. What I don't like is being hustled. I mean, I put out good music: why should I be hustled? Like the other day—I'm supposed to do an encore and I don't want to do it and my road manager says, "Get back on the stage, motherfucker." But this wasn't like any "motherfucker" I'd ever heard before. It was a white "motherfucker" with too many Rs in it

I said to him, Man what the fuck are you talkin' about? But I had to cool it because I knew I might break his jaw and I'd be right back in court. Right? I had to tell Neil [Reshen] about it. I said, You talk to him because I'd break his neck or something. I'd just take his head and smash it against the wall. Shit. I just wanted to play the job, make everybody satisfied, and *leave.* Which I did.

I know. Everybody says I'm a violent guy, but nobody talks to me like that, not even my mother, man. Now *she* understood me, and we got to be the best of friends. I mean, me studying music at the age of 14 meant to her that I wasn't no idiot. She knew she couldn't just say anything to me and expect me to believe it because she was older than me.

Did she give you a bad time when you left home and went to New York?
No. What could she say? My father—he was a dentist, an oral surgeon—said to her, "Leave him alone." When I left he told me, "You need anything, let me know. I'll send you $50 a week allowance." But I was already making $85 a week when I was 15. My parents got a divorce when I was young and I helped send my sister through school. My parents . . . [He smiles again.] Mothers and fathers are something else, man.

We took a break and Miles told us to follow him up to his bedroom, where Finney was busily steam-curling the hair of an extremely attractive young woman. Miles turned on two large color TVs to two different newscasts and told us to look around. "You should have a fuckin' notebook," he cackled. He lay back on the large circular bed in what looked like Miles Davis's bedroom as conceived by the Playboy *Advisor. Miles switched to an old movie and became absorbed. I walked into the big closet. The massive wardrobe spilled off racks and shelves onto the floor in a phantasmagoria of cloth and color—cool Italian silk suits from the Blackhawk days, beautiful tweeds, luxurious gray and charcoal gray flannel suits, more recent denim ensembles, chamois shirts, buckskin pants, an array of high heeled silver boots.*

Miles motioned for the photographer to check out his bathroom. I asked what for and Miles crossly replied, "I don't know. Tell him he can jerk off if he wants." We walked into the bathroom to find Miles's immense ten-foot bathtub, big enough for three, all blue-tiled and surrounded by mirrors. I asked if we could photograph him and his friends in the tub and he looked at me like I was stupid. "Sheeiitttt," he said.

He asks to see the camera, and starts to talk photography. "I got lots of pictures of naked bitches I took in here, man. They all dug it, you know? I got pictures of them doing funky things to each other and everything.

"I mean, I ain't no collector. *I don't look at 'em or anything. I just* got *'em." Miles muses on women. "There's a lot of women comin' around here lookin' to give away their pussy and sex but I don't fuck 'em, at least not all of 'em. I don't fuck bitches that want to fuck me. It doesn't appeal to me. I have to fight off that shit all the time."*

So now that this police business is settled, are you going back to work?
Shit. There's always too much policin' going on, 'specially policin' of kids. If I were a judge and they busted Sly, I'd say to the police that brought him in, "What the fuck are you doin'? Let that motherfucker out so he can make some more music to keep those black folks happy so they won't *really* start a fuckin' riot." I mean they're so stupid. Why should they bust Sly. He ain't sellin' no dope. He ain't sellin' shit. All he has to do is write two notes and that'd be enough.

Do you think drugs can help you at all? Or is it poison?
Certain drugs might help you make up your mind, you know? They don't help you to play, because you've got to study to do that. But if you're hesitating about playin' something, sometimes it can help you to go ahead and do it without any hesitation, 'cause you'll be concentrating on the music.

I like your attitude.

Well, I can see where, say, a writer like you might take a drug and it might help you make up your mind if you had five or six choices and it could help you settle for one. But there's no telling what happens with drugs. When you take drugs and you got nothin' to do, that's when you get into trouble. If you don't put all your energy in something, you get paralyzed. Like this. [Miles freezes, seizure-like.] Who wants to be like that?

Do you listen to records?

No man, they're all in here. [Miles taps his head.] Everything. I got a place for Lightnin' Hopkins. I got a place for Stravinsky. And right here [Miles taps his frontal lobe in the middle of his forehead] I got a place for SSSIllyyyyy.

How come you're not stuck in 20 years ago like most of your generation of jazz musicians?

I figure it like this. I never look down or talk down to any musician because he's 19 or something. I don't sell anybody short. I'm always listening. Yesterday's dead, man.

What do you see in the future?

Tomorrow.

Why wouldn't you appear at the Newport Jazz Festival last summer?

Well, I didn't wanna be no Newport Nigger. I mean that shit is just a big party, like a reunion. They don't do anything or try to play anything new. I'm not like that. I want the new stuff all the time. I'm not into myself that way. I don't listen to my old records. I'm not into gold records and trophies and awards and being on covers of no magazines. My ego doesn't run like that.

What does your ego run on?

My ego only needs a good rhythm section. I mean, my band now, man, they have so much fuckin energy, and I got to bring it out of them, or it doesn't work.

Time to go. I shut off the recorder and David Doubilet packed up his cameras. I asked Miles if he ever read anything about him that he liked. "Ralph Gleason," he rasped. "He understands me." I asked him if he read a recent article in The Saturday Review *titled "Miles Davis—The Man Behind the Mask." Miles smiled and began pulling at his handsome face, stretching the skin, tugging at the combed-back hair, pulling his new moustache. "This ain't no mask," he said.*

INTERVIEW AT NORTHERN ILLINOIS UNIVERSITY

Interviewer: Jimmy Saunders, 1975

Geniuses are generally difficult to approach for interviews, and Davis was no exception. Jimmy Saunders, a writer/musician who first met Miles back in 1964, thought he had a pretty good chance of getting him to talk when the Davis group played a concert at Northern Illinois University in DeKalb. So when the Godfather of Jazz Rock arrived, in full-length fur coat and three-piece satin suit, Saunders asked for a short interview. Miles agreed. Right after the concert they got to talking about colleagues in the jazz field, white folks vs. black folks, and religion.

SAUNDERS: How do you get up for this kind of thing—for gigs, interviews, and so on?

DAVIS: I don't make interviews.

SAUNDERS: Well, the gigs, then.

DAVIS: Black folks.

SAUNDERS: That's what gets you up?

DAVIS: Drummers. My musicians. What they might play, and what they might play after that. (*Laughs.*)

SAUNDERS: Well, you've always surrounded yourself with great musicians, like 'Trane.

DAVIS: When I first went into the studio with Coltrane, they asked me, "What are you doing with a sad-ass saxophone player like him?" So I said, "Just shut up and get behind the controls—before we leave." (*Laughs.*) When I first got Sonny Rollins, they said the same thing. Fuck them folks. They don't know shit. You know them blankets they used to put in front of the drums in recording studios? I made them take that shit from in front of Art Blakey's drums, man. They don't use that shit no more. Drums are supposed to be heard—everywhere!

SAUNDERS: Speaking of drums, what do you think of the music Billy Cobham is playing now?

DAVIS: Aw, man, I don't want to get into talking about other people's music and shit. That's what them goddamn critics do.

SAUNDERS: He and McLaughlin were both with you—

DAVIS: Well, John played different when he was with me.

SAUNDERS: He seemed to lay back more.

DAVIS: Naw, naw. He didn't lay back with me. See, you can't lay back when you play, because you don't help the rhythm section. You got to keep goosing them. I don't worry about playing the trumpet, man, because I *know* how to play the trumpet. But a horn ain't shit without the rhythm section.

SAUNDERS: Having to lead such gifted musicians must put you through a lot of changes. Like Herbie Hancock—

DAVIS: Herbie wanted to quit, man.

SAUNDERS: Why?

DAVIS: Because once in Chicago he said, "Miles, sometimes I feel like it just ain't nothing to play." And I said, "Then just don't play nothing." He's a great musician, man, and he knows what's happening. But you can't be a nice guy. He's a nice guy. But me, I ain't nice. I don't care if you don't like me—as long as you can play.

SAUNDERS: What about Wayne Shorter?

DAVIS: He fell in love, man. He started playing pretty, syrupy music. Ain't no fire there no more.

SAUNDERS: Weather Report doesn't move you, then?

DAVIS: Foggy. It's foggy.

SAUNDERS: The things that Weather Report has done are more structured than what you're doing now. Your band is a really free, extended-improvisation group.

DAVIS: But there's control. We might write a melody around the drums. We might write a melody around one chord. Whatever we do, it's controlled.

SAUNDERS: But you're constantly creating—

DAVIS: That's the name of the game. I'm forty-eight, but so what? Am I supposed to stop growing? If I live to be seventy years old—

SAUNDERS: You still going to be playing?

DAVIS: I don't know. We might get up there and just hold hands. We have rehearsals like a five-hour rehearsal of non-reaction. . . . Like, if I say, "Ba-bop-ba-ba-ba," you don't say, "Bop." You don't do that. You don't say nothing.

SAUNDERS: You wrote on Joe Zawinul's first solo album that he was extending thoughts you'd both had for years—

DAVIS: Listen. Zawinul is like Sly and Mingus. They write things and they fall in love with them. You know what I mean? I don't write things for myself. I write for my band. When you write things for yourself, your ego takes over. I ain't never going to ever damn-fool myself into believing that everything, or any one piece I write, is that good—and I ain't going to let my musicians tell me that shit, either. I don't have no yes men around me.

SAUNDERS: Do you ever read reviews of your music or concerts?

DAVIS: Never.

SAUNDERS: Why?

DAVIS: Because white folks can't review black music. I don't review their music. Could I review *Fiddler on the Roof*? Or would I?

SAUNDERS: I'd like to go back to your comments about Shorter. Do you really think the fire has gone out of his playing?

DAVIS: You can't come, then fight or play. You can't do it. I don't. When I get ready to come, I come. (*Laughs.*) But I do not come and play.

SAUNDERS: Explain that in layman's terms.

DAVIS: Ask Muhammad Ali. If he comes, he can't fight two minutes. Shit, he couldn't even whup me.

SAUNDERS: Would you fight Muhammad Ali, under those conditions, to prove your point?

DAVIS: You goddamn right I'd fight him. But he's got to promise to fuck first. If he ain't going to fuck, I ain't going to fight. (*Laughs.*) You give up all your energy when you come. I mean, you give up *all* of it. So if you're going to fuck before a gig, how are you going to give something when it's time to hit?

SAUNDERS: This might be somewhat far-fetched, but are you a religious cat, Miles? Are you into God and Jesus?

DAVIS: Ain't no fucking Jesus, man. Get out of here. Shit. Do you believe in God and Jesus? I believe in myself. I believe every man is Jesus and God. If there was a Jesus, and he came down here, he'd get put in jail—drinking wine, beer, smoking shit. White folks fill you up with all that shit about Jesus, and then you get out there believing that holding hands we shall overcome. If there was a God, he would be in the cancer wards, in the hospitals—or over in Korea and Vietnam.

SAUNDERS: One more question. You've got a concert tomorrow night in Boston; are you going to make it?

DAVIS: Man, shit. I'll be up all night thinking about what we did tonight and trying to think of something else for the band to do.

AT THE MOVIES WITH MILES

Late 1976 / Early 1977
by Mary Bringle (April 2007)

After feverish years of constant touring and recording stretching from 1968 until 1975, Davis's health began to suffer, and he'd developed a fierce addiction to cocaine. For the next five years Davis had, by and large, put down his trumpet and maintained an air of seclusion in his Manhattan brownstone apartment. Gil Evans, who had attempted to coerce Davis into recording some music with him, remarked, "His organism is tired. And after all the music he's contributed for thirty-five years, he needs a rest."

Novelist, mystery writer, and short-story author Mary Bringle has written more than a dozen books, including her most recent novel, *Carmen*, and the classic *Hacks at Lunch*, selected for inclusion in *100 One-Night Reads: A Book Lover's Guide*. In the latter half of the 1970s Bringle was a guest at just another mundane Upper West Side party—that is, until Miles, who'd also been invited, rang the bell. This piece was written especially for this book.

Sometime around 1976/1977, my husband and I visited our friend Carole, who lived on West 77th Street off Riverside Drive. Carole was having a few friends over, and since we had no babysitter that night we brought our six-year-old son with us and put him to sleep for the night in the bedroom of Carole's daughter.

When the doorbell rang, Carole was busy in the kitchen and asked me to answer. A shadowy figure, mumbling something in a gruff voice, stood at the door. I recognized Miles Davis, Carole's neighbor on the block, a musical genius I much admired but had never yet met.

Carole's former husband, an interior designer, had apparently helped to personalize Miles's apartment on 77th Street. (According to Carole, Miles had wanted a bathtub contoured to his buttocks, so he could sit in the perfect mold of his body and enjoy his bath. The logistics of this plan bewildered me—did Miles have to sit in plaster of Paris, which was later magically converted to a porcelain imprint? However it was done, I thought it was a wonderfully narcissistic and sybaritic idea. It must've been uncomfortable for the next owner of the apartment, though, so I imagine the Miles Davis bathtub was ripped out and consigned to the junk heap of history when it should've been preserved in some Museum of Decadence, like the wine glasses shaped to Marie Antoinette's breasts.)

His guttural voice growled again.

As I stood aside to let him in, I heard what he'd been saying, which was: "You want some cocaine?"

At the same time he was holding up a needle and seemed to be volunteering to inject me in the windpipe, an experience which was very low on my wish list of pleasurable activities. I said, "No thanks," probably seeming like the squarest female he'd ever met, and led him down the long hall to the apartment.

A quiet but unmistakable presence, he sat in the room.

Soon, he was asking, in the same cracked ruined voice, if any of us wanted to see some movies. Carole, aware of what kind of movies he had in mind, declined cheerfully, but Miles got up and went to the door, only to reappear with some earlier incarnation of a video machine and the promised movies, which he began to show. He seemed as uninterested in his cinematic antics as the guests, who politely turned away at the sight of grainy, homemade porn tapes. We all seemed to realize that Miles was simply trying to entertain us, if not with injected coke than at least with his amateur porn. But it was early in the evening and we hadn't even had dinner yet.

His timing was all wrong.

At some point I became aware that my son had stumbled out of the bedroom and was glued to the flickering images on the small screen. I led him quickly to the bathroom and, afterwards, settled him back to sleep in the bedroom.

I thought that was the end of it, but never underestimate the memory of an intelligent six year old. Several months later, we were in London and found ourselves at a large record store on Oxford Street. Our son zeroed in on a particular record jacket and shouted for all to hear: "That's Miles! He brings *movies!*"

He seemed to like Miles when we played his tapes in our car on a long drive to California, but never understood it was the same benevolent chap who had smiled at him across a room when he stumbled up from sleep, as if they were just guys together enjoying a wholesome evening at a friend's place.

HANGIN' OUT WITH DAFFY DAVIS

Late 1970s
by Eric Nisenson, preface from *'Round About Midnight: A Portrait of Miles Davis* (Updated Edition, 1996)

In addition to *Ascension: John Coltrane and His Quest, Open Sky: Sonny Rollins and His World of Improvisation,* and *Blues: The Murder of Jazz,* the gifted jazz writer Eric Nisenson published two books on Miles, *The Making of* Kind of Blue*: Miles Davis and His Masterpiece* and *'Round About Midnight: A Portrait of Miles Davis,* from which the following, originally the preface to the updated edition, is taken. From 1975 to 1981 Davis temporarily retired from music and became almost completely reclusive. Nisenson was the only jazz writer able to get close to him during this time. A recipient of a Guggenheim, Eric Nisenson died in August 2003.

I have idolized Miles Davis since I was about fifteen years old. I idolized him in the same way other kids worshipped Mickey Mantle or Elvis, or the Beatles a little later. I tried to get as many of his albums as I could afford back then, read everything I could get my hands on, and continually told Miles stories to my friends, most of whom couldn't have cared less. I do not think that even my imagination at its most febrile could then have conjured what would come years later: that when my phone rang, especially late at night, I would groan, "Oh no, it's that damned Miles again. Why can't he leave me alone?" And I would pick up my phone to hear that famous whispered growl demand, "Bring your white ass down here, Eric. Now."

Back when I was a teenager, even the idea of meeting Miles Davis seemed preposterous. His reclusiveness was part of his legend, as was his supposed hostility to white people. Yet I always had the weird feeling that if we met we could be friends. Maybe it was because I felt as alienated as he did. And I understood why he did the things he was always being criticized for—not announcing tunes or introducing the members of his band, turning his back to the audience when he played, refusing to compromise no matter what. I found it wonderful that Miles refused to cooperate with *Time* magazine when they were planning to do a cover story on him. Who else would have the guts to turn his back (excuse the pun) to a cover on *Time*? Only Miles, who kicked their photographers out of the Village Vanguard when he was performing there (instead *Time* put Thelonious Monk on its cover). This was my kind of guy.

In the late seventies I moved into an apartment on New York's Upper West Side after having lived in San Francisco for several years. Although I had a day job working as a college textbook editor, I spent a lot of my time at the nearby home of my friend the great bassist Walter Booker. Bookie had converted part of his huge apartment into a recording studio, and when he wasn't touring with Sarah Vaughan or Nat Adderley, he recorded sessions with some of the finest musicians in jazz. Bookie looked at me as a kind of "historian" for his studio, someone who would record the unique musical events and the interplay of the musicians, many of them jazz legends, who constantly passed through. Needless to say, I was often enthralled and amazed by the music and musicians who went in and out of Bookie's home and studio. His place had become kind of a jazz salon where virtually every great jazz musician came by at one time or another. And one night Miles Davis dropped by.

I was actually scared of meeting him—afraid that he would make a nasty insult or simply be rude to me. But he was wonderful—talkative, funny, warm, and friendly. He walked up to me to shake my hand and acted as if he knew me. I had this strange sense—as if we had known each other in some previous life. He was much shorter here than he had seemed when I had seen him perform, and his intensely intelligent, probing, wary eyes pulled you in as if they were bright embers at the center of his pitch black face. The controlled muscularity of his movements were like those of the large wild cats, cheetahs and tigers, that he enjoyed watching fight on film. But there was no doubt—none—that he attracted attention whether or not you knew who he was: he was a walking definition of "charisma."

I knew enough not to say something like, "Gee, Miles, I really like that *Sketches of Spain* album." I knew Miles hated that sort of crap. I just shook his hand and said I was glad to meet him, wondering if he could tell how awed I was just to be in his presence.

But Miles and I hit it off immediately, which in some ways astonished me but in other ways seemed obvious and natural. We were both sly, basically loners. (Miles immediately picked this up—he had developed the perception of a fighter in that he was able to suss out somebody's character very quickly. Once I introduced him to a guy who wanted to be my agent. Miles shook his hand, the guy said a few words, and Miles turned to me and said, "He's a liar." He turned out to be—unfortunately—quite right.)

Miles knew how to use his voice—that famous whispered growl—to his advantage, as a way of pulling in those around him. He obviously knew that he was hard to understand unless one listened carefully, so he made everyone focus on what he was saying.

Miles invited me to see his home and a couple of days later I took him up on his offer. I called before I left and Miles repeated his invitation and asked if I could pick up a six-pack of Heineken when I came over. That seemed innocent enough, but I didn't know at the time that this was the beginning of a kind of indentured servitude. When I came to Miles's 77th Street house (it had been converted from a church) he was in the outer entranceway, a disgusted look on his face. "The Con Edison guy came here and asked me if he could talk to the owner of the house. He thought I was the janitor! I told him, 'You're looking at the owner, you white motherfucker.'" It was obvious that Miles had never become inured to such casual racism, that running into it was still shocking and profoundly upsetting. Later on, whenever Miles came to visit me, I had to go back to the street with him in order to hail a cab. Even Miles Davis could not get a New York City cabdriver to stop and pick up a black man, especially at night. I, of course, had no problem.

This took place during the late seventies, the period of Miles's so-called "retirement." In the early seventies Miles had been at a creative peak, breaking away from the post-bop which he had played for most of his career and creating perhaps his most revolutionary music. He valiantly toured and recorded, despite several overlapping physical ailments, often performing on crutches. But in 1975, Miles gave in to the toll on his body and entered into a period of supposed retirement. He was ostensibly healing mind and body, but he was really on a self-destructive roller coaster, staying up for days at a time on cocaine and then crashing with barbiturates. "If I can't stay up for three days at a time, hell, I might as well forget about it," he used to say.

Miles's 77th Street house was a five-story building; Miles lived in the first three stories, and the top story was rented to a homosexual couple. The floor right above Miles's top floor was empty mainly because Miles was so sensitive to sound that just hearing footsteps or loud conversation bothered him. Later on in our friendship Miles offered me the apartment at a reasonable rate, but I was warned by someone who knew a previous tenant that living right above Miles was a very bad idea; I would have had to make all my guests take off their shoes before they entered, and if I watched TV or listened to my stereo I would have *had* to listen through earphones. Otherwise Miles would raise hell about the "disturbance."

The interior of the house itself seemed to be a reflection of Miles's state at that time. It was like a *Playboy* pad gone to seed. For instance, there was a large projection television—but a couple of bulbs were burnt out and so it was like watching a 3-D movie without the glasses (interestingly, Miles usually had the channel set on a particular listings station that used jazz as background music; so jazz, not pop, was the music most constantly heard there). And in the bathroom was a tub big enough for two, but with a huge crack. There were boxes all around the house, almost as if Miles had just moved in (although he had been living there since the sixties). Even Miles's piano, on which he worked out ideas and composed new pieces, was in sorry shape—terribly out of tune with a few keys totally unplayable.

Of course, the house did not look so bad inside because Miles kept it dark all day long. He was a dyed-in-the-wool "night person." This too was a reflection of his mood in the late seventies. He had stopped playing because of a series of overlapping health problems, which he had fought against valiantly in the early seventies, regularly touring and recording, but which simply became too overwhelming in 1975.

Miles and I hit it off right away, perhaps because I immediately caught on to the fact that what some called "rude" or "insulting" was really his way of testing people, playing with them to see if they were hip enough to be trusted. With me that meant a continual series of mock anti-Semitic jibes. It was obvious to me that Miles was actually completely unprejudiced, and he looked on racism, of any kind, as inherently ridiculous. His nickname for me was "Jewish bastard," and he used to say things like "I'm having a party this weekend and you're invited, Eric. Yassir Arafat is the guest of honor." Of course, the funniest part of that crack was the idea of Miles putting on any sort of party during this reclusive period. Once Miles said to me, "Okay you Jewish bastard, call me nigger, go ahead. I've been called that a million times."

I replied, "Well, Miles, if you've been called that a million times, I better call you 'wop.' That's it, you little wop." Miles was stymied at his own game. This kind of playful jousting was one of his favorite activities, and I was able to hold my own most of the time. However, Miles often tried to get me to box with him, throwing light punches which I refused to return (Miles was, of course, a trained amateur boxer). I was at least a foot taller than him and he continually wanted to show how somebody his size could physically deal with someone like me. I conceded to him that he undoubtedly could, but he kept on trying to get me into a little back-and-forth anyway.

Almost from the beginning Miles confided things to me that few knew, particularly the extent of his physical problems. He was in intense pain frequently and was often emotionally discouraged. Our jousts seemed to cheer him up, and I felt glad to be of aid. Once we became friends it became hard for me to think of him as I once had, as a musical legend. He was my friend Miles now, amazingly enough.

I soon found myself in the position of being his errand boy. He would call me up (he seemed to know the moment I got home from work) and invite me— actually, command me—to come over and bring groceries or pick up a package at the pharmacy or cash a check, or any other errand that needed doing. And a few times he had me pick up little packages from one of his coke dealers who lived a block away from me.

I hated doing that, for a number of reasons. I had little interest in coke myself—it made me nervous and uncomfortable. I seem to be allergic to most intoxicants; I don't even drink coffee or alcohol in any form. I always turned Miles down when he offered me some coke (he made it a practice of insisting that if someone did some of his cocaine, that they do the same huge amount at one time as he did—I shuddered at the thought). My main concern was for Miles's health, not my own safety. But he would explain to me in great, and quite poignant, detail the reason for his use of coke. It distracted him from the pain better than anything else, he told me, and it elevated his spirit. Without it he sank deeply into depression over his physical state; without it, he told me quite earnestly, he had no reason to continue living. "I've done everything, been everywhere, done so much shit, there's nothing to look forward to." Except, he made clear, the coke. I tried to get him to see psychiatrists, get some treatment for his depression. But he would hear nothing of it. He knew exactly what he wanted out of life. Yes, I should have been stronger, but I suppose I still looked at Miles, even in this state, as an idol, a god. And I did what this god wanted me to do. What can I say?—he got to me. I never made a nickel from delivering anything to him (if anything, I lost money for bus and late-night cab rides), including the coke, which I only had to deal with when he couldn't get his dealers to deliver.

Much of the time, however, Miles just wanted company—desperately. Although a lovely young girl was living with him at the time—whom I will call "Daisy"—she did not provide much intellectual fodder for a mind as brilliant as Miles's. He had also discovered that I was virtually a walking and breathing encyclopedia of his life and career. He was proud of the fact that he had forgotten so much—to him, that was the mark of a true artist and innovator, for if you cannot remember the past you are forced to continually create something new. But he did need to retrieve information from time to time that he had forgotten.

Soon, visiting Miles often became deeply depressing. He was so jaded, so world-weary and cynical, he almost seemed to be living at the heart of the void. A friend of mine begged me to bring him to meet Miles. But after we left Miles's home, my friend said, "I don't ever want to see him again. I'll just stick to listening to his music." I understood how he felt, but I also had deep compassion for Miles.

I don't remember how we first started talking about collaborating on Miles's autobiography. It seemed as much his idea as mine, although such a project had been a fantasy of mine long before I met him. At first Miles was not too sure. "If we do this book," he told me, "I'll have to say in it that — — (a famous black entertainer) is a flaming faggot." (Incidentally, Miles was not at all homophobic—he was friendly with several homosexuals, including those who rented the top apartment in his building—and of course there have long been rumors that he was bisexual, although I never saw anything to bear them out.)

"No, Miles, you don't have to talk about him. Talk about those you respected like Charlie Parker."

"Charlie Parker," Miles declared, "was a hog." He then told me the story about the cornbread that is in this book.

"Well, okay, what about Coltrane?"

"Coltrane," Miles declared, "was a hog. You see, a genius like that, he has to be selfish. That's just the way geniuses are." As Miles said this, he was putting about half a gram of cocaine up his left nostril, deftly illustrating his point.

Finally, Miles agreed to do it, if the advance was sufficient. Thus began our "interviews," which were more like discussions, and, for me, like pulling teeth. Miles would start talking about Bird on the 52nd Street scene of the "Birth of the Cool" band ("Why," Miles asked rhetorically "am I called anti-white when my first band was almost all white?"), but then he would say, "That was so long ago, who cares what happened that long ago?" I tried to convince him as well as I could, telling him that lots of people did. He would not let me use a tape recorder for some reason. When someone asked him how I was supposed to remember all that he had said, Miles replied, "Eric will remember it. He doesn't need a tape recorder"—which was partially true. However, it certainly would have been easier with one. If I hid one in my briefcase or put a small one in my pocket, Miles was always able to ferret the damn thing out.

Miles had a very ambivalent attitude toward his past. At times, he was proud of his accomplishments; at other times his illustrious past almost seemed like a weight around his neck. For example, I knew Jimmy Cobb, Miles's former drummer (and, incidentally, a greatly underrated player) pretty well. Jimmy had found a tape of Miles's group with Coltrane from its 1960 world tour, the group's last. But when he tried to give it to his old boss, whom he had not seen for a while, Miles wouldn't even open his door, telling Jimmy through the intercom just to slide it under. Jimmy, who used to be close to Miles and is a very sensitive person, simply left. He did give it to me, however. The music, particularly Coltrane's, was really extraordinary, so I invited Miles over, telling him I had something I had wanted him to listen to. Several days later, returning from a trip to Connecticut, Miles dropped over. I asked him if he wanted to hear the tape; at first he said no. I told him who it was and he said he still did not want to hear it. Then a little later, in the middle of a conversation that had nothing to do with music, Miles said, "Put it on, Eric."

The first tune was "So What." Miles groaned. At the beginning of the trumpet solo, Miles acted as if he were on the bandstand, grumbling to the bassist Paul Chambers, "Play the right fucking notes, Paul." He turned to Daisy and said, "Hey, that's some pretty good trumpet playing, don't you think, Daisy? I wonder who that is." I doubt if even Daisy was unaware who was playing the trumpet.

But when Coltrane came on, Miles really got sucked into the music, exclaiming when Trane played a brilliant series of ideas or a particularly roiling arpeggio. Miles moved his body to Coltrane's solo, more caught up in this music than I had ever seen him. When it was over, Miles stood up to go, indicating to Daisy that it was time to leave. I said, "Wait, Miles, there's a lot more on the tape."

Miles looked at me with more sadness in his eyes than I had ever seen and said, "How could you do that to me, Eric? I thought we were friends." Needless to say, I was devastated.

From experiences such as his ability always to know when and where I had secreted a tape recorder, I often wondered just how powerful Miles's mental powers were. Believe this or not, but on more than one occasion when I called him on the phone he answered by saying, "Hey, Eric, what's up?" And on more than one occasion he heard, or sensed, Daisy a block away walking toward the house (the drapes were drawn and he had been talking to me, sitting on his huge curved couch, his back to the window, so there was no way he could have seen her). "Go downstairs and open the door. By the time you get down there and undo the lock, she will be at the doorway." Needless to say, he was correct. Real *Twilight Zone* stuff.

Miles now had great leverage with me. If he wanted me to do something, and I was hesitant, all he had to do was threaten to pull out of the book. Eventually I began to ease the amount of control he had over me. If he said, "I want you to pick up a six-pack of Heineken and get over here now," and I told him "absolutely not," he would usually reply, "Well, that's it Eric. Just forget about the book. It's all over." But I knew that he would call back an hour later, a day later, or sometimes two days later, and once more make a demand, as if nothing had happened.

Sometimes Miles's imagination worked overtime in figuring out a ploy to get me to run him an errand or just come over and keep him company. Here is a particularly bizarre example. It was late—after one in the morning—and I was at my girlfriend's place. We were just going to bed when the phone rang—somehow, Miles had obtained my girlfriend's phone number—and he wanted me to pick up some coke for him, because none of his dealers would deliver. I hated that particular errand, especially late at night. I was dog tired to boot and had the beginnings of a flu. Miles went through his usual threats, but I would not budge. "All right," he muttered, "this is the end, Eric," and hung up.

A few minutes later the phone rang. It was Daisy this time wanting to talk to me. "Eric," she said in a virtual monotone, "Miles says that unless you get over here now he's going to kick your white Jewish ass." I could clearly hear Miles's whisper in the background telling Daisy exactly what to say. "Well, Daisy," I replied, "you tell Miles that I'll see him tomorrow so he can kick my white ass then. It's cold outside and there is no way I'm going to run around, especially for Miles's poison. And tell him that I'm coming down with the flu, Daisy." I got the feeling that, as was often the case, Miles did not need coke as much as company. How deeply saddening—one of the great geniuses of this century truly desperate just for a little company at one-thirty in the morning. "Okay," said Daisy, obviously embarrassed.

A few minutes later Miles called again. This time he talked to my girlfriend. He told her he knew exactly how to give me a treatment for my flu that would get me well in a matter of hours. But of course I had to come down there for the treatment (which had something to do with soaking in a bathtub with some special salts). I told my girlfriend to tell Miles, "No dice."

Finally I crawled into bed, thinking—foolishly—that Miles had certainly given up for the night. But a few minutes later the phone rang yet again. I told my girlfriend not to bother answering it, but she did anyway. What a surprise—it was Daisy with a terrible emergency—Miles had fallen down his stairway! I have to come over right away!

"Oh my God, Daisy, that's terrible. Listen, call 911 immediately. Do you want me to? I'll call them for you." I heard that whisper in the background. "No, uh, Miles wants you to pick up something for him and to come right away." Another whisper. "This is an emergency."

"Sounds pretty bad, Daisy. But you have to call 911 right now, I can't help him. Understand? Miles has to get treated as soon as possible."

Hesitation. "Uh, okay." And she hung up.

And yes, a few minutes later the phone rang yet again. I answered it this time. "Eric," said Daisy—I could hear Miles's whisper in the background—"Miles wants you to know that he did not really fall down his stairway."

"Oh, really?"

"No, Miles says that he just doesn't like bullshit."

"Tell him, neither do I, Daisy, neither do I."

If all this seems like a game, of course it was, at least to a degree. On a number of occasions Miles would have me come over, supposedly just to discuss the book, and then after five minutes or so say, "Okay, Eric, I want to be alone. Get the fuck out of here." His house was about ten blocks from mine, not just around the corner, so I did not find this particular ploy very amusing.

I cannot say that Miles did not return my favors. One time I went to his house right after a horrific haircut. Miles insisted on recutting my hair, telling me that I was the first white guy whose hair he had cut. And when he had the straight razor against my neck, he cracked, "Now I've got you where I want you, white boy." Real funny stuff, Miles.

Another night Miles and I had a lengthy argument about the book. I wanted his old friend Bobby, his long-time boxing trainer, to help with the book, since he had known Miles for so long. But Miles was adamant, furious that I would even broach the idea. "He's just a boxing trainer. He doesn't know about any other shit." I thought that was very unfair to Bobby, who was not only highly intelligent but who had been close to Miles over a period of many years. He had even toured with him on several occasions, so I thought he would be helpful in jarring Miles's stubborn memory. But Miles insisted that if Bobby was part of the project, he would pull out.

As I was leaving that night, Miles told me to wait for a minute. He went into his bedroom and came back with a pair of his boxing gloves and an old jockstrap. I knew it was his way of saying, "Okay, I'll allow you in the same ring with me." I was being accepted on existential terms by Miles.

Miles constantly surprised me. For instance, he was a superb chef. One night he invited me over for what he claimed was "the best fried chicken you will ever eat." He was right. And he was knowledgeable on a wealth of subjects. He discussed literature with me, comparing the great writers to the great jazz masters. Although I had never seen Miles read, he knew who the important American writers were—he mentioned as "the masters" Hemingway, Steinbeck, Fitzgerald, and Faulkner. He told me that there was one writer he simply could not stand—Herman Hesse. He once had a girl living with him who loved Hesse and had all his books. Miles gave her an ultimatum—get rid of the Hesse books or leave. I was not sure whether Miles hated Hesse because of his pretentious style or just because he was German (although he never mentioned Thomas Mann or any other German writer). But he had the same low regard for Hesse as a writer that he did for such musicians as Stanley Turrentine and Oscar Peterson ("Oscar had to be taught how to play the blues" was his dead-on comment).

Sometimes Miles's generosity took strange twists. Somehow he heard that I had had a big fight with my girlfriend and he invited me over to talk about it. As soon as I walked in he told poor Daisy to give me a blow job "to cheer Eric up." Daisy—who until recently had been living a relatively sheltered life in the Midwest—was horribly embarrassed by this sort of thing. "Not tonight," I told Miles, "we've got a headache." I was pretty sure that if I had been unhinged enough to take Miles up on his offer, he would have caused me great bodily harm.

By the way, I have heard many rumors about Miles's supposed bisexuality. I never witnessed anything that made me think he was anything other than heterosexual—he certainly never hit on me—but he thought of himself as being beyond sex. He told me a story about a brief affair that he had with a woman in Chicago. According to Miles, right in the middle of lovemaking, he realized that sex completely bored him—so, as Miles told me, he withdrew from the situation, explaining to this poor woman that he simply had no more interest in this sort of thing. I wonder if she ever recovered.

I am not so humble that I am not able to repeat what Miles said about me to my girlfriend. Early one afternoon he came over to visit, which he rarely did. He was having problems with Daisy, he told me, and he wanted my advice. While I was out of the room he said to my girlfriend, "I love your old man. He reminds me of Gil Evans, a white guy with no prejudice." Being compared to Gil Evans by Miles Davis—I could have died with a smile on my face when my girlfriend reported it. (He would never, of course, say something like that directly to my face.)

Miles seemed facetious about most matters, and he could be very funny. His sense of humor could be downright silly. One time I started a sentence, "Miles, I . . ." and he interrupted me, saying, "Eric, I'm really sick of being called Miles. Call me Daffy from now on. Daffy Davis."

But there were dark moments too. His jaded outlook on life often made me depressed, and many times he sank into deep blue funks. And the darkest moments concerned his treatment of Daisy. One night he called me up and asked me to come over. I had not heard from him in a few days and I could tell from Miles's voice that there was a problem. When I got there, he was by himself. He had broken Daisy's jaw, he explained, and she was hospitalized. "So, what do you think, Eric. Am I an asshole?"

I was furious; Daisy was one of the sweetest, most innocent creatures on earth; she cared deeply about Miles although she was about thirty years his junior and did not really know who he was. "Yes," I said, "you're a damned asshole, Miles. How could you do such a thing?"

"I meant to pull my punch. I know how to pull my punch."

This was Daisy's crime: a few nights previously, one of Miles's dope dealers came to the house with his girlfriend. Miles gave the girlfriend a red hat of his. After they left, Daisy said to Miles that he had never given *her* a red hat. And that's what did it.

Miles had a private telephone line put in her hospital room. Although it was after midnight, he decided to call her, despite my protest. When she answered, Miles asked what she was doing. Well, she was trying to sleep, of course, despite the pain in her jaw.

It was obvious that Miles felt bad about this incident, just as he probably felt bad all the times he had beaten and abused women throughout his life. Miles is, of course, one of the great jazz heroes, but few jazz writers have mentioned this aspect of his personality. The jazz world is notoriously male-dominated, a place where few women are truly respected. And most jazz writers are male, too. So the fact that this musical genius has brutally abused women—and this was very well known throughout the jazz community—has apparently not been thought worthy of mention.

Can you imagine if, say, Stan Getz had routinely brutalized blacks, how he would have been portrayed by the jazz press? I doubt if such a "little idiosyncrasy" would have been avoided. And yes, I am as guilty as anybody else. There is little in the original edition of 'Round About Midnight about this aspect of Miles's life. But now, after the O. J. Simpson affair, I really think it is time to view such activity for what it is—sick and evil. I guess when I wrote this book I still thought of Miles as a friend, but there is really no excuse. It amazes me how people like Miles can scream about the evils of racism—rightly so—and then continually abuse women. What utter hypocrisy.

This incident deeply troubled me, and in many ways our relationship was never the same. Daisy moved right back in with Miles when she was released, which I could not understand. One day I said to Daisy that she seemed a bit depressed. "What's she got to be depressed about?" growled Miles. "She's in her early twenties and I'm fifty-two." I thought, she's got plenty to be depressed about, Miles.

Eventually I put together enough materials from our "interviews" to create a proposal. I talked with several publishers, but they all wanted to know the same thing—would Miles participate in publicizing the book? Miles had been very explicit about this, so I had to tell the truth: he was so reclusive during this point of his life that he could not even come to the publisher's office to sign a contract. Most publishers had no interest without Miles's participation in the publicity. I was offered a relatively small advance, but Miles refused—he knew that he deserved at least six figures since, in his words, "I've got a million dollars worth of information." So the publisher offered me a deal to write an unauthorized biography. I told Miles about this and he expressed no problem with my doing such a book. He even let me continue, from time to time, to ask him questions about his career.

My editor for the original edition of *'Round About Midnight* was Joyce Johnson who, besides being a superb editor, was also a fine writer herself (some of her most fascinating work concerned her long relationship with Jack Kerouac). Joyce despised Miles simply from what I told her, and pretty soon it became obvious that she did not like me much either. From my current perspective, I think I know why: I obviously greatly admired Miles despite his despicable treatment of women. It is a great human dilemma—can we love parts of a person and simply ignore that which is repugnant? Now I believe Miles's brutality toward women simply cannot be denied or avoided. (By the way, it was Joyce's idea to call the book *'Round About Midnight*. I was not crazy about the idea since it is the name of a well-known composition by Thelonious Monk. I wanted to just call it *Miles*— which was, of course, the eventual name of Miles's autobiography.)

Several years later when Miles did get a large advance to do his autobiography, he was well out of the reclusive mode of his supposed "retirement" and he agreed to publicize the book; he even did that incredible *60 Minutes* interview with Harry Reasoner, something I cannot imagine him even considering during his "retirement."

I stopped seeing Miles, for the most part, when Cicely Tyson came back into his life. I was a little surprised about that—Miles used to do nothing but complain about her. I was equally surprised to see him hanging out with Bill Cosby when I had seen him get livid at Cicely for giving Cosby his phone number. But I believe that the part of Miles that still wanted to survive saw in Cicely a strong woman who could push him to actively turn things around in his life—which is exactly what she did. However, she insisted that Miles drop his old friends, completely change his environment. Naturally, there were those such as myself who felt that we had been good friends, that we had tried to discourage Miles's self-destructiveness. But maybe she was right, as painful as it is to admit it. Maybe Miles had to be cut off from everyone who "enabled" him to get high, no matter how unwillingly. And she did save his life, inarguably. Later, Miles would explain that she wanted complete control over him and did not want him to have his own friends. I do not know whether or not that was true. But even if it was, Miles owed her a tremendous debt.

Miles cut me off very sharply and I, like a number of other friends, was hurt. I had been very careful when I wrote *'Round About Midnight*—really, far too careful—about intruding on his privacy. So there was virtually nothing about his treatment of women or his voluminous drug use (although he had few compunctions about describing these things to interviewers and in his autobiography). However, I was told by many who had long been on the jazz scene that Miles did this all the time, often for not much reason at all—Jimmy Cobb is an excellent example. One person told me that sooner or later Miles did this to almost everybody close to him; for some reason I thought that I was an exception.

But the bottom line is that I owe Miles an enormous debt. He went out of his way to try to teach me how to think at the highest level of creativity. Miles was trying to show me the *way* of the artist—his attitude was definitely that of master and student. He was not teaching me any specific technical points about the work of an artist, but rather the existential terms—the stance and consciousness of the artist (although many of his lessons I had to suss out for myself—such as the gift of the boxing gloves and jock strap).

Despite his inexcusable treatment of women, despite the way he treated me at the end, despite even those final years of his life when he seemed to turn his back on most of the things he had once believed in, Miles changed my life for the better, and changed the lives of all who were moved by his music. A number of musicians told me that it was listening to Miles that made them dedicate their lives to music.

In the following book, you will read his story as close as I could get it to the way he told it to me. It was my first book, and therefore a great learning experience. Some sections I had to get completely through secondary sources, but I tried to bring in Miles's own point of view, at least as it was filtered through my own, as much as possible—except when my own voice can be clearly heard, mainly in the discussion of the music itself, which is fairly perfunctory anyway.

Knowing Miles Davis was without doubt one of the highlights of my life and I have no doubt it will remain so until my dying day. I hope that the reader of this book will glean at least some of the profound lessons I learned from him and his wonderful music.

MILES DAVIS'S HOUSE—
TELEPHONE INTERVIEW, N.Y.C.

Interviewer: Kishur Manwar
Originally broadcast on "Miles Beyond" for KWMU-FM,
Washington University, August 3, 1980

Toward the end of Miles Davis's self-imposed retirement he began opening up a little. This phone call made to Miles's home is a humorous look at how he treated some interviewers, like a cat toying with a mouse before abandoning it altogether.

Phone rings and Miles answers.

MD: What do you want?

KM: Well, we tried to get in touch with you and we couldn't. . . .

MD: My brother lives right there, and my daughter's there [in the St. Louis area].

KM: Well, we weren't able to get in touch with you and I, myself—

MD: My ex-wife lives down there.

KM: Yeah, I talked to her when she was here in March.

MD: Who?

KM: I talked to your ex-wife.

MD: Which one?

KM: I talked to her when she was at the S. I. U. Jazz Festival that they had out here.

MD: Who? Betty?

KM: Right, Betty, that's her name, yes, and she was out here and I tried then to set up an interview with you, and she didn't think that you would talk to us then. So, like I said, I'm really appreciative that you are talking to us.

MD: My daughter hasn't told me about it, my aunt, and my brother, they all live right there in St. Louis, and my ex-wife.

KM: Well, we're not that well known. We are a public radio station and we *are* college students that *do* play jazz.

MD: How come no one in my family knows about it?

KM: That I can't answer. I don't understand why nobody really knows about it. Can I start by asking you some questions?

MD: Yeah, go ahead.

KM: OK, first of all I'd like to know how would you contrast your direction of music when you started out playing to the way it is now?

MD: [sighing] Oh boyyy . . . well, can't you tell the difference, man?

KM: Yes, I can tell the difference, but—

MD: Answer it yourself.

KM: Well, I would like for you to say—

MD: I'm not like that, man. I don't want to talk about it.

KM: OK, I can understand that. If there are some things that you would like to talk about, feel free to do so. Whatever you want to talk about, or whatever message that you feel people should know about you.

MD: Then my [unintelligible]. . . .

KM: Pardon me?

MD: Don't give me that much free range of things to talk about or else I'll wanna talk about V.D. [venereal disease]

KM: [nervously laughs] Well, whatever it is that you want to talk about, I'm leaving it strictly up to you.

MD: [balking at the opportunity] I don't need that.

KM: I know you don't do this kind of thing a lot, so—

MD: I hate it.

KM: Well . . .

MD: I just wanna know what is "Miles Beyond." What kind of station it is.

KM: OK, well . . . "Miles Beyond," as I said, we cover mainstream and contemp—

MD: I don't know what "mainstream" means.

KM: Mainstream jazz, my definition would be *that* jazz that has—

MD: Firstly, jazz is a nigger word, right?

KM: Right.

MD: It means "nigger."

KM: OK, well let's—

MD: You say "jazz" you automatically are thinking "nigger."

KM: Well, not necessarily, Miles. I mean I think jazz is music myself, I don't think that there should be a label.

MD: Of course not.

KM: OK, can I ask you what do you think jazz is?

MD: I don't think it's nothing, man. I never thought it was while I was playing it, as playing jazz.

KM: So in other words you just thought of it as playing music, right?

MD: If you're gonna shut up man, I'll tell you.

KM: OK.

MD: First off, while playing in St. Louis, the white folks wouldn't even listen to so-called jazz, because they thought of it as niggers fuckin' and all that shit. So since then, that's a nigger word, it's a nigger thing. So I just wanted to divorce myself from the white . . . from the honkies in St. Louis. That's about it.

KM: OK. Is there anything else that you want to say about your music style? Or, the way you play, or what message you try to get across.

MD: Not music, man. I want to talk about them white honky motherfuckers in St. Louis right around the corner from the Heart Foundation and invite people there. I felt very bad about that and I got out of St. Louis. Or sometimes it was at the Rhumboogie [a club in downtown St. Louis frequented by the black community]. St. Louis is a *lousy* town.

KM: How has your music been accepted in other towns besides St. Louis?

MD: They accept it in St. Louis! They love it in St. Louis!

KM: Yeah, they love it *now* in St. Louis, as I love it now in St. Louis, but I mean when you felt St. Louis was closing the door on you.

MD: I didn't say that.

KM: OK, it's just, just—

MD: People love the music. It's just the white folks, they Jim Crowin' us. That's an old-assed phrase.

KM: I'd like to ask you something about Charlie Parker and John Coltrane.

MD: What?

KM: How did they both influence your playing, if indeed they did.

MD: What do you mean they influenced my playing?

KM: I mean—

MD: I taught Coltrane and Bird and shit to get high and go to sleep.

KM: What artists do you think have picked up on your ideas of how music should be?

MD: You through yet?

KM: Yes.

MD: What you mean?

KM: You know, you had a message in your music—

MD: Nah.

KM: . . . or direction in your music.

MD: Come on, man. That there's no good musicians out there is a shame.

KM: OK, I'm not a musician myself so I can't comment on—

MD: The only good musician I know that is out there that can write is Stockhausen. He's in Germany.

KM: Have you played with him before?

MD: No and until you listen to the music, you shouldn't discuss it.

KM: OK, all righty.

MD: See? Then why bother calling me up?

KM: But see, I focus more of my attention on the music that you did—

MD: You focus more of your attention on the music that I made when? When I was twelve?

KM: No, the music that you did with Philly Joe Jones, Paul Chambers—

MD: Oh shit.

KM: . . . uhmm before that, Charlie Parker—

MD: [undecipherable]

KM: Pardon me?

MD: Anything I did now?

KM: Well, the *Circle in the Round* album with Chick Corea and Herbie Hancock. I mean—

MD: I wrote on it, motherfucker!

KM: I know you did, I know you did. You've—

MD: Chick didn't play on that, Herbie did. You don't know who's on the album, huh?

KM: Yes, I know who's on the album, Herbie Han . . .

MD: Chick Corea.

KM: Tony Williams, Ron Carter, John McLaughlin you played with—

MD: Find *Circle in the Round.*

KM: Pardon me?

MD: The *Circle in the Round.* Wrong. You must be thinking about country songs. The *Circle in the Round* I like, there's a whole bunch of good songs.

KM: Could I ask you about uh . . . I know that you wanted Jimi Hendrix to play with you because you liked—

MD: *They* wanted *me* to get him a new band. That's where that went. And they were paying me to find him a new band.

KM: Did you like his style of music or his style of playing?

MD: Of course.

KM: Did you at one point and time want to play with him? Or—

MD: No. I didn't want to get in the way.

KM: OK. Miles, from talking to you this might be a hard question for me and for you as well, but, if you could give me some insight on—

MD: Is it "Am I a freak?" Yes.

KM: OK. What direction do you think jazz is headed in? Or music itself? I mean is it headed in the type of, or the style of music that you would have wanted it to be in?

MD: People I know, that I like, that play like Herbie, Corea, Wayne Shorter, Tony Williams, that's about all the people I know that have advanced musically.

KM: Do you feel as though they've advanced because of your influence?

MD: Of course.

KM: OK. Do you think—

MD: I talk to Chick every night.

KM: Are there any other musicians that you think will follow, say, in your direction or in the direction of Chick and Herbie and Tony and Wayne Shorter?

MD: Nobody has that much knowledge, ya know? Gil Evans probably, and Dylan is on the way down. But the rest of 'em don't have that much knowledge. They have no knowledge and skill, different things in musical terms.

KM: Like, I'm gonna say it again, is there anything that you want to mention as far as your background or what you're doing now? Anything like that?

MD: Yeah. Why don't you learn something about me before you call me?

KM: What do you want me to know about you?

MD: When you tell me something about some music you know, you should do some research or something, you know. I mean when I want to know every album by someone, I would do my research. I would do like four months of research.

KM: I respect that. I've listened to your music like I said . . .

MD: I mean if I called you, I'd do some research on you so I knew what I was talking about.

KM: OK, I'm gonna be honest with you, this, as a whole, was—

MD: St. Louis was pretty good, you know.

KM: Right. I did an interview with Lester and he talked about you two weeks ago. He was just here with the Art Ensemble [of Chicago].

MD: Yeah, they play pretty good.

KM: Yes. Well, I wanted to get across again that I am more interested in what you say and what you say about music more than anything else because I feel that I, myself, personally feel that you were an innovator in music. I hope you take that as a compliment because I am deeply grateful to you for having the chance to talk to you and get some insight.

MD: There's a lot of you guys playing out there tonight, today. Who was that guy that wrote that Diana Ross song?

KM: Chic? What's the name of the Diana Ross song?

MD: I don't know. I know the words.

KM: Well, are you talking about the latest Diana Ross album?

MD: Yeah.

KM: OK. I know that Chic produced the album, but I don't know the—

MD: And Michael Jackson's latest album [*Off the Wall* from 1979 and produced by Quincy Jones] which I think is a motherfucker.

KM: Yes it is. It *is* a very good album.

MD: You have to listen across the thing, because those jazz musicians aren't doing shit other than just playing what they're hearing. They play the same fucking thing over and over again. The same clichés.

KM: And you're getting sick of hearing it?

MD: I don't listen to it.

KM: You don't listen to it. What mainly do you focus your listening to?

MD: Everything but that.

KM: Everything but that. Classical? Is that included with that?

MD: Yup.

KM: OK.

MD: Rachmaninoff, Stockhausen. Everything.

KM: Has any type of classical music that you've picked up on, has that influenced your style of writing or—

MD: All of it! Chopin, all that stuff.

KM: More so than the jazz?

MD: I just told you.

KM: OK. Do you think that at any time in your career that you have left, that you will perform again?

MD: Maybe. They offer me so much money now I can't refuse it.

I JUST PICK UP MY HORN
AND PLAY

Interviewer: George Goodman Jr.
New York Times, June 28, 1981

When *New York Times* contributing editor George Goodman Jr.
interviewed Miles Davis, it was a fortuitous moment for both interviewer
and interviewee. For Goodman it was a coup of sorts.

Since his last album, *Get Up with It*, in 1974, Miles had retreated into his
"retirement," which lasted nearly seven years. During that period he wrote
no music nor recorded any tracks. Instead, he struggled to recover from
several serious illnesses: polyps in his throat, hip surgery, a stomach ulcer,
gallstones, and a leg infection that came close to requiring an amputation.
In the words of producer and pianist George Wein, who visited Miles during
one of the latter's hospitalizations, "Miles is not one to detail his suffering,
but you could see the agony on his face." Perhaps to deaden the pain or to
blunt his frustration and rage or to combat the pervasive boredom and the
sharp eruptions of near panic, Davis returned to using drugs of a wide
variety. Despite their initial palliative effect, the large quantities and long-
term use only complicated an already complex web of physical dissolution
and psychic debility. His recovery was especially demanding, and a lesser
man might have succumbed or resigned himself, but Davis had never been
such a man.

During that period Miles had shunned reporters and refused requests for
interviews, so Goodman could be proud of netting so notoriously difficult a
fish. This was also a coup of sorts for the trumpeter, who was just
re-emerging after a long absence, about to perform live again with a small
electric group, and releasing his first album in seven years, *The Man with
the Horn*. With so much riding on this return (besides Judy Garland, how
many comebacks can one artist manage?), Miles looked to large, powerful
venues to service his needs for publicity, and as he had in the past (*Playboy,
Newsweek*) and would later (*60 Minutes*), he chose shrewdly a venerable

publication with a wide mainstream readership, the *New York Times*. And although he showed his usual irreverence and irritability toward the representative of that institutional dinosaur, Davis and Goodman walked away after enacting a fair exchange for both parties.

And the reader benefits for it.

(This piece, with slight changes, was reprinted in *Ebony*'s October 1981 issue.)

The way Miles Davis tells it, whether dealing with his music or his women, all he needs to do is put aside the past. Sitting in the darkened living room of his West Side brownstone, just after the recent announcement that he will resume his performing career with two appearances next Sunday at the Kool Jazz Festival at Avery Fisher Hall, the acclaimed 55-year-old trumpeter is explaining his philosophy of art as well as life. The two performances will mark his first public appearances in five years.

"The way to stay young is to forget, to have a bad memory," says Mr. Davis. "You know, when a woman says to me: 'Do you remember when we were lovers, five years ago?' I say, 'No.' Guys come up to me with their arms outstretched, I say: 'What's that for?' And they say, '1947, Chicago, remember? We got high together.' I say: 'No. Get out of my face.'"

This is one of his rare interviews. Mr. Davis—acknowledged in the jazz world as one of the all-time greats—seems wary. "Everything you do, you want to do, but then you don't want to be reminded of it," he says. "Childhood? Who wants to remember that? I was born like this."

Mr. Davis is looking fit and speaking with mischievous humor in the rasping whisper of a voice that is a Miles Davis trademark. He is wearing a red jump suit, tan Western boots and a white cap; and a small tape recorder is playing excerpts of a freshly made Columbia Records release, his latest work with a group of young sidemen he plans to take on a concert tour after the performance at Lincoln Center.

"To me, it's old. I can't stand it," Mr. Davis says of the music on the recording. His visitors include two women friends and Teo Macero, his record producer at Columbia Records. A Juilliard-trained composer and saxophonist, Mr. Macero has worked closely with Mr. Davis on nearly 30 different recordings since the artist first signed with the company in the 1950's for a reported annual fee of $300,000.

Mr. Davis explains that a variety of debilitating physical ailments, including a throat condition which necessitated several operations, and trouble with a hip which called for additional surgery, had caused him to stop performing five years ago.

"When I laid off, I wasn't thinking about music at all," the trumpeter says with his characteristic disdain for the past. "I gave music a break because I didn't feel like it." Though Mr. Davis does not dwell on his ailments, family members say he underwent surgery for removal of gallstones, for the treatment of a stomach ulcer and for a leg infection.

"Miles is not one to detail his suffering," says George Wein, producer of the Kool festival and a veteran jazz pianist himself, who had visited his hospital bedside, "but you could see the agony on his face."

On one occasion, Mr. Davis says, Mr. Wein made him a gift of $10,000. "I asked, 'What's this for?' and George told me, 'You might need it for cigarette money.'"

"Santana gave me this," says Mr. Davis, proudly displaying a gold St. Christopher medal presented to him by the bandleader during his hospitalization. He then explains he wanted to refuse it, just out of graciousness, but a musician friend had told him such an act would be insulting.

Mr. Wein says that after Mr. Davis's release from the hospital he occasionally visited and played tapes of his trumpet work, but apparently, for a time, without the old brilliance. "Then one day he played something that gave me that old case of gooseflesh. I didn't want to push him. I waited for him to say when."

Mr. Wein says Mr. Davis waited until after the news conference announcing the talent lineup for the festival, then brought up how much money he ought to get for an appearance. Mr. Davis maintains he was promised $90,000 for two performances, a figure one knowledgeable observer said is not "unheard" of. But Mr. Wein denied the offer was actually that high. "I love Miles, we have a love-hate relationship," says Mr. Wein, "but I will not discuss the money issue except to say that $90,000 is not an accurate figure."

According to Columbia Records spokesmen, nearly all of Mr. Davis's recordings have remained in the active catalogue because of the musician's popularity. Almost since his arrival on the New York music scene in 1945, when he was first taken under the protective wing of Charlie "Yardbird" Parker, with whom he shared his first New York apartment, Mr. Davis has been a man of burgeoning influence in jazz, a term he never uses to describe his music.

"It's a nigger word," the trumpeter says, explaining that he believes the term "jazz" is used to set aside and diminish the importance of a contribution to the world's music primarily identified with blacks. While some might argue with Mr. Davis over that notion, few, indeed, would question the importance of his own contributions—vast contributions—to the idiom that is described by Mr. Wein as "hard to overestimate."

To John Hammond, the authoritative critic and jazz patron credited with the "discovery" of such greats as Bessie Smith and Louis "Satchmo" Armstrong, Mr. Davis is the only major performer of his generation who broadened rather than contracted the appeal of jazz music.

In his autobiography, a chronicle of music dating back to the early 1900's, Mr. Hammond writes of the generation preceding Mr. Davis and the "cool" jazz school he is credited with founding: "The Boppers gave a nod to Lester Young, to Charlie Christian and other real innovators, without absorbing what they had to give. Instead of expanding the form, they contracted it, made it their private language. I extend this critical judgment even to such giants as Bird Parker, Thelonious Monk and John Coltrane," Mr. Hammond wrote. "The superlative Miles Davis is exempted."

Ralph Gleason, another prominent critic, wrote that the trumpeter has "played the role in his generation that Louis Armstrong played in his." He has been the supreme influence within his peer group, reaching a "lay audience of greater proportion than any pure, undiluted jazz-for-its-own sake player."

Musicians who have worked for Mr. Davis during his career comprise a "Who's Who," and a partial listing includes among the saxophonists John Coltrane and Julian "Cannonball" Adderly, both of whom are deceased; Sonny Rollins, George Coleman and Wayne Shorter, co-leader with Joe Zawinul of the group Weather Report.

Among his better known piano alumni are Keith Jarrett, Herbie Hancock, Chick Corea, Red Garland and the late Bill Evans. Although Mr. Davis's impact on each was varied, it centered mostly on the expression of an emotional intensity in their music. He encouraged them to be individualistic, always under control but paradoxically spontaneous. Mr. Hancock says he remembers what Mr. Shorter related: "He told us he was the only bandleader who paid his personnel not to practice their solos at home so as to avoid the polish that makes even some improvised music sound boring. He always wanted it fresh."

While Miles Davis's flamboyant personal style has had a strong effect on many jazz players, his chief influence has come from his approach to music. Miles Davis, in the words of Gil Evans, the arranger who collaborated in the creation of five important recordings, "was the first man to change the sound of the trumpet since Louis Armstrong." As early as the 1950's, critics vied among themselves on his album liners and in magazine articles for the *mots juste* to describe the Davis sound.

Accordingly, it was said that Barry Ulanov, an editor of *Metronome*, the now defunct jazz periodical, insured a place for himself when he characterized the sound of Miles Davis as "the sound of a man walking on egg shells." In answer to that description, the jazz writer Ira Gitler came up with his own quotable comment: "Miles may be a man walking on eggshells," Mr. Gitler wrote in attempting to capture the essence of Mr. Davis's playing, "but he is also a diamond cutting into opaque glass."

By the late 1950's and early 1960's, when Mr. Davis's sound had reached maturity, the musician could bring his listeners to the verge of tears, wrenching the most melancholy qualities from a song without falling into sentimentality. Concentrating on the middle register of the horn where, as the critics noted, his technical prowess was strongest, Mr. Davis played with an emphasis on lyrical voice-like simplicity. To many, he seemed to streamline the more complicated earlier approach of his mentors—Mr. Parker and Dizzy Gillespie—who was still considered the reigning master of trumpet technique.

To worshipful fans, from Hollywood to Antibes, the sound of Mr. Davis became the perfect signature for his personality, the style and substance of the new archetypical man of jazz. The trumpeter added a quality of elegance to "Bird's" image of raw authenticity, and it was embodied in the sound that fit him as perfectly as his finely tailored clothes that caught the eye of *Esquire* and

Gentleman's Quarterly magazines, which chose Mr. Davis as one of the nation's 10 best dressed men. There were other notably contrasting features between Mr. Davis and the older Mr. Gillespie that illustrate attitudinal differences as much as differences in their ideas about music.

While much of Mr. Gillespie's forté lies in his easy mastery of dazzling technique—a characteristic feature of the be-bop school, in which musicians sometimes employed comic antics that established a warm personal rapport with the audiences they entertained, Mr. Davis and his younger followers never made an effort to entertain his listeners and has been roundly criticized by reviewers for sometimes turning his back during a performance or walking off stage or refusing to smile or to announce his personnel or the selections they play. Among his peers, his attitude of casually shrugging off his critics is just as much the substance of "cool" as the sound of his horn. "I'm not being vain or anything, but that's the way I am," says Mr. Davis. "I play for myself and I play for musicians."

Mr. Davis says people he doesn't know approach him on the streets with an easy familiarity he finds offensive. Mimicking the exchange, Mr. Davis relates the following: "I drive a $56,000 car," a yellow Ferrari, he says, "and white people look at me like I'm crazy. You must be an entertainer. I say no," says Mr. Davis, with a wide-eyed glare. "Are you Miles Davis?" "No," he says he answers, "I'm a janitor."

Miles Dewey Davis 3d is the son of a dental surgeon who raised champion pedigreed pigs as a hobby. His mother was a music teacher in East St. Louis, Ill., where the family moved shortly after Miles was born in Alton, Ill. According to his sister, Dorothy Wilburn, a teacher in the Chicago public schools, Miles was always independent, but especially so because the family, which included Miles, herself, and their brother, Vernon, was financially comfortable. Unlike many black musicians of his generation, he could "turn his back on people he didn't like and did so frequently whenever he sensed a racial snub. He always spoke his mind," she added.

Though his father wanted Miles to pursue a career in medicine, Mrs. Wilburn continues, "at about the age of 12," Miles picked up a trumpet "and that was it." Upon his graduation from the all-black Lincoln High School, Mr. Davis set out for New York City, accepting an invitation from Mr. Parker and Mr. Gillespie, whom he met when they passed through town.

At his mother's insistence, Mr. Davis enrolled in Juilliard, but his real music education began in the nightclubs, then the thriving centers along 52nd Street for a new music called "be-bop."

"Up at Juilliard," Mr. Davis says, "I played in the symphony, two notes, 'bop-bop,' every 90 bars, so I said let me out of here and then I left."

In a career whose development is well documented on records, Mr. Davis first went into the studio with the tenor saxophonist Coleman Hawkins who, he says, hired him to listen for mistakes in bands for which the saxophonist wrote parts. Mr. Davis says Mr. Hawkins also looked after his money and helped him assemble a quality wardrobe. "He would buy a coat for $300 and sell it to me for $15," he says. During this period Mr. Davis worked in the bands of Benny Carter and Billy Eckstine, and later with Mr. Parker.

Sometime during the late 1940's Mr. Davis succumbed to heroin addiction, which initiated a gradual period of physical decline, finally forcing his absence from the music scene by the early 1950's. Mrs. Wilburn says the addiction came as a bitter shock to the family, "and up to this very day, none of us discuss it publicly."

Hired by producer George Wein in the summer of 1954, however, Mr. Davis made a smashing return with a quintet featuring John Coltrane, then an unknown.

By the end of the decade, Mr. Davis had once again become bored with his music and, perhaps, with his personal life. A nine-year marriage to the former Frances Taylor was on the rocks. The trumpeter has three children born of an earlier relationship—Miles, Gregory and Cheryl. A second marriage, to the singer Betty Davis, was of brief duration.

Exceptionally busy during the 1960's with a band the record industry categorized as a jazz group, Mr. Davis had begun to push against the boundaries of that designation. By the spring of 1970, the trumpeter's biggest-selling release, "Bitches Brew," signaled his success in extending jazz to a new realm.

The album sold 500,000 copies, which was considered a "phenomenal success" at Columbia Records. While rock groups sold larger numbers of albums, Mr. Davis's achievement was regarded as particularly noteworthy, considering he was an artist so deeply associated with jazz.

From an artistic standpoint, the album initiated what is still a controversial and not always successful effort among a legion of younger musicians to blend elements of rock with those of jazz. To a band that included the bassist Ron

Carter, pianist Chick Corea, the saxophonist Wayne Shorter and the drummer Jack DeJohnette, Mr. Davis added the fiery Brazilian percussionist Airto Moreira and John McLaughlin, a facile and imaginative guitarist.

The trumpeter wired them all for sound then amplified the results against a volatile hotbed of tribal rhythms. Though Mr. Davis alienated many of his old fans, he was not concerned. The older fans he had replaced with a younger, record-buying public.

In the words of the musicologist Michael Budds, what the trumpeter did was find a "solution to the integration of rock features in jazz [that] included the adoption of electronic instruments and devices, the underlying presence of complex multilayered rhythmic ostinatos, solo improvisation as well as group interaction and use of modal scales. The single most constructive achievement," he said, "is devising a system in which rhythmic structure would not be locked into literal repetition of rhythmic patterns . . . "

Mr. Davis says he has no interest in such music today. "My ideas about music have changed," he says. "I only listen to Stockhausen. New York is great. I've got so much noise. Subways. Horns. I can't stand nothing quiet. I go nuts." But concerning his own creative gifts in music, Mr. Davis says they are best described as a curse.

"I can't stop once I start thinking about it," he says, rapping his knuckles on his circular coffee table in an unrelenting beat. "My mind is like this. I can't sleep for three days, four days at a time."

Was there ever a time during his absence when he thought he would lose his ability to play? "It doesn't go like that with me," the trumpeter says. "I never think about not being able to do anything. I just pick up my horn and play the hell out of it."

THE MAN WITH THE HORN

Interviewer: Cheryl McCall
Musician, March 1982

Cheryl McCall, a gifted journalist and jazz tyro, worked at *Life* magazine and later for a nascent publication called *People*. She interviewed thousands of subjects "from fascist dictators to sports stars to mass murderers to supercelebrities." She spent a weekend with Miles, Cicely Tyson, and members of his entourage at his home in Montauk on the far end of Long Island. Instead of the allegedly angry, surly, profane, reticent trumpeter, Miles Davis, "an unforgettable figure on the landscape," was gracious, sensitive, and helpful (even if he did palm her wristwatch).

McCall was also an anti-war activist blacklisted by the FBI; an Oscar-nominated producer of *Streetwise* (about Seattle street kids); and a champion of the impoverished and powerless, especially children. She left journalism to become a lawyer and children's rights advocate. In November 2005 lung cancer snatched her at age fifty-five.

One hot midnight last July, two friends took me to New York's Savoy to hear Miles Davis play. I could dismiss Mark Rothbaum's evangelism because he manages Miles but my other friend, Bob Neuwirth, a songwriter and musician whom I greatly respect, had no vested interest except to expand my horizons. Or something like that. There was a palpable, contagious excitement in the hardened cynic Neuwirth, and I noticed folks like Rickie Lee Jones, Mick Jagger and Charlie Watts in the audience.

The concert was sensational. Miles took more chances than he had a couple of weeks earlier at

the Kool Jazz Festival. He pushed his reviving chops to their limit, freely mix-
ing tunes like "All of You" with his contemporary material and even, during a
long exploration of "My Man's Gone Now" that used three tempi (slow funk,
mid-walk, fast four), took an extended solo on Fender piano that had a wealth
of imagination in it and more than enough technique. If Herbie Hancock ever
needs to hire a piano player, he might be the man.

Miles' band, which had taken unprecedented flak from the press of three
cities, had begun to metamorphose into a flexible and free-associative performing unit. Saxophonist Bill Evans soloed more comfortably than he had either
at Avery Fisher or on record, and the much-maligned guitarist Mike "Fat Time"
Stern finally had a chance to show how much he loved bebop.

Miles was full of energy and uncommonly extroverted onstage, and acknowledged the existence of the audience to the extent of French-kissing a blonde
in the front row in the middle of one of his *moments musicaux*. When I went
backstage, I was shocked to find Miles Davis in a state of collapse, sweating like a
prizefighter between rounds and similarly attended by men with towels, drink,
encouragement and aid. A while later I found my way back to the street, dazed,
went home and listened to his albums until long after dawn had broken on the
Hudson and the adrenalin had stopped flowing. Next midnight we returned to
the Savoy and sat transfixed again until the final abrupt note.

For weeks, Mark Rothbaum had been trying to convince me to write an
article for *People* magazine about Miles—who wouldn't talk to the jazz critics—
and Neuwirth had urged me to do it, but I had resisted on the legitimate grounds
that I'm not a jazz buff and did not know enough about the man or his music.
That night, still apprehensive but thoroughly intrigued, I told Mark I'd do an
interview if Miles agreed.

Before meeting him, I read reams of clippings and articles dating back to
the late 1940s and was left with the impression that Miles Davis' influence as
a stylist and composer exceeded even his immense talent as a musician. He is
an unforgettable figure on the landscape. The way critics fumbled for adjec-
tives and exhausted their store of superlatives to describe his live music and
sixty recordings convinced me that my own visceral and enthusiastic reaction
to the Savoy dates had been the appropriate response. He is still a looming, if
reluctant, presence on the cutting edge of jazz, capable of boosting his music
over the hump of public indifference and winning popularity polls without

losing serious critical acclaim. Canonized by the press and respected by his peers, Miles had sounded the clarion calls to new eras in jazz for decades, from bebop to the cool to third stream to fusion. He was never known to make a foolish move.

But the compelling myth surrounding Miles made him appear, in print at least, a fearsome, blunt man of few words, most of them hostile epithets. Even though he'd been cordial backstage at the Savoy, I didn't know what to expect the weekend we drove to the Montauk cottage where he and Cicely Tyson were relaxing while his New York brownstone was being renovated. Of the thousands of people I've interviewed over the years, from fascist dictators to sports stars to mass murderers to supercelebrities, I'd never felt the trepidation gnawing at my insides that I felt that day. With Mark and Bill Evans, I entered a house that was already full of people—Miles, Cicely, his road managers Jim Rose and Chris Murphy—all watching boxing on TV. Miles said "Hi," and when I didn't know what to say, he picked up on it with a degree of sensitivity that my researches had not led me to expect. He did everything to put me at my ease. "Can I get you a beer, Cheryl?" he asked me, using my name to include me in the family unit. He walked by me, brushed my wrist in passing, continued for five paces, then turned around to show me my wristwatch in the palm of his hand. "That's one of the tricks I picked up in the old days," he said in his hoarse whisper of a voice, and it was impossible not to laugh and begin to relax. Usually when I do an interview I spend some time getting to know the person first, but Miles quickly said, "Let's do it," gave me a beer and led me to a screened-in porch overlooking the ocean. As we talked he waved to people outside, leered extravagantly at passing women, clowned.

When the interview was done, I spent that weekend with the Davis entourage in Montauk, where he continued to disregard his sullen stereotype. I had expected to see everyone waiting on him and found the reverse: Miles the host, providing food, beer, conversation and humor; Miles the joker, sparring with everyone who passed, sneaking Bill Evans' ring off his finger, palming my lighter, engaging in conversation with his invisible alter ego Leroy: "Hey Leroy, what's happening?" and clown Leroy answering back, Interlocutor and Mr. Bones.

When I went on tour with Miles and the band, the enveloping warmth of the home situation continued. He could not have been more affectionate with his band, hugging them, reassuring them, defending them fiercely from the bad reviews. He taught Bill Evans how to dress for the stage, how to tap his foot heel first—"Now *that's* cool"—instead of leading with the toe. He always made a point of including me, introducing me to his sister Dorothy Wilburn, his daughter Cheryl and his brother Vernon at the family reunion in Chicago, playing me tapes after the concert, telling me to notice this, listen to that. I've traveled with a lot of bands in my time, but I've never encountered anything like the atmosphere of reciprocity and love that Miles Davis brings with him. Cicely Tyson says he's always been like that and that the toughness is all façade.

His health was not good. Sometimes he was so stiff he was not able to bend sufficiently to put on his pants; the band had to help him. Concerts often exhausted him, but he had made a real commitment to working, his band, and even the audience. In Chicago and Detroit, Miles had to take oxygen from a portable tank in order to get through his concerts. He contracted pneumonia after a date in Ann Arbor, and although he's been a famous no-show in the past, got out of a hospital bed to make a gig in L.A.

For all the warmth of his presence, and for all his humor—he does not stop inventing little bits of business with whatever props come to hand—there is still an air of inconsolable grief about him, which I think Cicely has finally touched. People see it in him and want to protect him; because he trusts them, he gives it back redoubled. At the Chicago reunion, where he introduced Cicely to his family, I spoke with childhood friends of his from St. Louis, who were familiar with his loneliness from way back. He was so shy in those days, they told me, you almost never heard him talk. "I didn't have anything to say," he said. When he's happy about something he smiles like a child, and lights up, if not the world, the room. The single time he was angry with me his face shut like a steel door. After the tour I was no longer afraid of him but I still found the mystery impenetrable. I doubt that I'll ever encounter anyone as complicated, mercurial, quixotic, enigmatic and hip.

After the American tour, he took off on his seven-dates-for-$700,000 tour of Japan, from which he returned in shocking health to play a set on *Saturday Night Live*. In November, 'round midnight of a Wednesday fading into Thanksgiving, at Bill Cosby's house, in a ceremony presided over by the Reverend Andrew Young and attended by a few friends like Max Roach and Dick Gregory, Miles Davis and Cicely Tyson were married.

The day we did this interview, I admitted up front that I was a jazz *naïf*, afraid of him and worried about his famous temper. He never raised it. When he realized that I was worried that his voice was not being picked up by the recorder, he picked it up and held it to his mouth while he paced back and forth. Chain-smoking and talking for two hours, he discussed his seclusion, his motivations for coming back, his friends, his loves, and his early life. His talk was full of Geminian mindplay: if I'd say he was like this, he'd say no, I'm like *that*. I incorporated the interview into my article for *People*; here it is in more nearly complete form. I'm still no authority on Miles Davis and I certainly don't pretend to be his good friend (like dozens of people I've met who exchanged words with him once) but I came away understanding as much of him as he allows. It was a privilege.

For full effect, the interview should be read in a hoarse whisper.

MUSICIAN: After five years, what made you start playing again?

MILES: Bill Evans, Al Foster, Dizzy and them gettin' on my ass talkin', "Man why don't you play this trumpet?" That didn't really make me play, I just felt like playing now.

MUSICIAN: What were you doing those five years?

MILES: Nothin'. Gettin' high.

MUSICIAN: But you had some medical problems and operations, didn't you?

MILES: One leg operation . . . two, yeah. That's what stopped me. That operation, man, I was so *disgusted* I just said fuck it for a while. I needed the operation. I was in Japan, and I was taking this codeine and morphine and didn't even know it. They gave it to me to help my leg.

MUSICIAN: What happened to your leg?

MILES: It's just a black disease where your bones get so brittle that they break off. Broke off, yeah, in the hip. Which is very painful, you know. It just chips.

First they did a bone graft and then they put a cap on it. Dr. Wilson did it, my doctor Philip Wilson, he's great. . . . A doctor told me in Sweden—*he shot me right in the leg*—he said I know how many girls want to come over here and give you a *shot*. I said fuck that if I don't feel better. He said tomorrow you'll feel better, or the next day. But I didn't know I was sick from this morphine and codeine until I got to St. Louis and I started throwing up blood, and my *boys*, Dr. Weathers and a few friends of mine, they run the hospital, and they said, "Come on," and put me in the hospital.

MUSICIAN: What made you throw up blood, the morphine?

MILES: No. You see, your liver gets fucked up, plus drinking, plus the pills . . . you throw up. And that blood, it just sits in those little blood vessels down there . . .

MUSICIAN: You were in bad shape for five years?

MILES: No, I was all right. It was just that I took so much medicine I didn't *feel* like playing the trumpet, didn't *feel* like listening to music. Didn't want to hear it, see it, smell it, nothin' about it.

MUSICIAN: Was that tough? Music is your whole life, isn't it?

MILES: That's not my whole life. Music is three-quarters of my life . . . ninety percent.

MUSICIAN: You must have gotten really depressed.

MILES: *Bored* is the word. So bored that you can't realize what boredom *is*. I didn't come out of the house for about four years.

MUSICIAN: That would drive me crazy.

MILES: I *was* nuts.

MUSICIAN: What did you do for four years in your house?

MILES: Nothing! Everything would come to my house. You know, anything you want you can get. All you have to do is ask for it. I didn't go to the store, I didn't go anywhere. . . . Try it sometime.

MUSICIAN: So how did you get the band together? You must have gone out to listen a little bit.

MILES: You can get a band together. Just ask somebody, "Who can play?" I asked Dave Liebman, he's a good friend of mine, who would you get if you wanted a saxophone player? He said Bill Evans. So I asked Bill, who would you get if you wanted a guy to play the guitar? He said there's a guy named Mike Stern, he's excellent. I said okay. Now, if Bill plays that good, he's got it all, and Mike plays that good, I'm goin' to play. Yeah, we played downstairs, and it was *nice.*

MUSICIAN: And that got you excited about playing, or did they get on your case?

MILES: . . . Nobody gets on my case. *Mark* [Rothbaum, his manager] gets on my fucking case, that I can stand. Nobody else can tell me *shit*—except the musicians in my band. But Mark—the reason I did it really was just because Mark didn't think I was gonna do it. Smartass motherfucker.

MUSICIAN: You must have been writing pieces.

MILES: Yeah. I can write when I hear what's happening. Then I can write.

MUSICIAN: How do songs come to you?

MILES: *In tens.* . . . Actually, see, you never retire from an instrument if you've been playing it since you were 12 because it's always in your head. I wasn't hearing any melodies or anything, 'cause I wouldn't let myself hear anything, and all of a sudden these melodies started coming back to me. I just wrote one on a piece of paper bag, called "Love without Time." Different types. It was good to lay off.

MUSICIAN: Do you think laying off made a big difference to your music?

MILES: Yeah.

MUSICIAN: When do you find music coming to you? In the night, or—when?

MILES: Anytime. Mostly at night. I write it down on anything if I have a pencil. I could write it down on your hand. Also, I do like Gil Evans told me to do, years ago, say "Always keep the tape recorder on." Yeah, I'm never gonna turn it off. You don't know what you might stumble upon and you can't—on the gig, you really can't go back to it because you don't know what it is.

MUSICIAN: And if it's on tape—

MILES: It's like a mind bank. Music bank. I could write a piece on what I just wrote down here.

MUSICIAN: I see. . . . You don't draw the bar lines.

MILES: No. I don't know what tempo I'm gonna write it in.

MUSICIAN: It must be a heavy burden to be the guy that's supposed to lead everybody else.

MILES: Who? *Me?*

MUSICIAN: People look to you to be in the front, the avant-garde, to take a new direction and they'll follow it.

MILES: I don't know what people think and I don't care. Especially that phrase avant-garde—you can look to so many people for that. Just certain people I care what they think.

MUSICIAN: But you're aware that with your comeback, all the critics are waiting to see what you're going to do, and you're either going to get shot down or praised for something new. That must be tough on a musician.

MILES: I don't know what to say to that because I don't look at critics. I don't say hello to 'em, I don't know what they're gonna write, I don't care what they're gonna write because I can only do what I can do and that's it. I'm not gonna tell them anything . . .

MUSICIAN: When you read bad reviews, doesn't it bother you?

MILES: No. You know why? I don't read them. I know what they're going to say.

MUSICIAN: And when they knock your band for no reason?

MILES: One guy did it 'cause I wouldn't do an interview with him. He kind of upset my guitar player. I said, man, look at me, I've been called a black motherfucker, and black this and that, some this here and that there. . . . Man, you just ignore it. The best thing is not to say anything at all.

MUSICIAN: I don't know how you see yourself, but you must realize that in some ways you're in a class by yourself.

MILES: I am. It's no burden, it's just that I can't play like anyone else, I can't fight like anyone else, I can't do *anything* like anybody else. I'm just myself. And I don't fuck around with music because I love music. That takes up ninety percent of my life. The other part is Cicely and some more people I know. Mark, Bill, all of my guys. Fat Time, Al Foster. I stay in constant touch with Al no matter where he is. Santana. I *try* to see what they're doing and what it's like. Al called me up from France and said you should see the hotel I'm staying in. I said I told you about that. Why would you stay in a bad hotel, you don't live in a bad house? You lose half your money just trying to find a bed. He said, It's not like when we're traveling with you, chief, 'cause you had us the best food and rooms. I said, when you're with the best you get the best.

MUSICIAN: Let me see if the tape is picking up your voice.

MILES: (*picks up machine and talks directly into it*) Can you hear me *nowwwww-www*? Do you want me to say *green beans* like Bill Cosby?

MUSICIAN: Is that your phone ringing?

MILES: I don't answer the phone. I never answer the phone.

MUSICIAN: You've taken some flak in the past for hiring white musicians. Is it the same now?

MILES: Just a few musicians who can't play ask me why do I hire this guy and this guy and he's white? I say he's white but he can play, just listen to him. What difference does it make what color he is, he's black.

MUSICIAN: What do you look for in a person to play with you?

MILES: His carriage . . . first. His carriage of the instrument. You can tell whether he plays or not by the way he carries the instrument, whether it *means* something to him or not. Then the way they talk and act. If they act too hip you know they can't play shit. So you don't bother with them. Can you hear me now on that thing? (*He picks up the tape recorder, puts it under his mouth and begins walking around with it.*)

MUSICIAN: You like to move around a lot, don't you?

MILES: Yeah, I can't be still. It's a trait I've had since I was a kid. Since I was a chi-yi-yild.

MUSICIAN: Mark told me you went out to see Willie Nelson in Vegas.

MILES: Yes. It was nice. I *love* the way Willie sings, the way he phrases is great. He phrases sometimes like I do.

MUSICIAN: Yeah, I've always thought he had some kind of jazz phrasing.

MILES: Don't say *jazz*. Jazz is like saying nigger phrasing. If you say jazz, automatically you think of what? You think of a black person, right?

MUSICIAN: No I don't. I think of music.

MILES: *Come on now, come on.*

MUSICIAN: I think of New York City, dawn on the Hudson, the sound of a saxophone . . .

MILES: Well then you're not the average person. Too bad you can't play an instrument or you'd be hired.

MUSICIAN: What kind of music do you listen to? You seem to incorporate a lot of different elements.

MILES: Gil Evans is my favorite. Anything he does, writes . . . He's also one of my best friends. . . . He also guides me when I ask him what I should do. He's a nice guy to ask a question 'cause he'll say, "I don't know." (*laughs*) His favorite answer. He's all right. He's some person, he's quite a man. There's no words to describe *Mr. Evans.*

MUSICIAN: How much practicing did you guys do before you cut *The Man with the Horn*?

MILES: Me? None.

MUSICIAN: You just went right into the studio?

MILES: I did.

MUSICIAN: And the chops came back, just like that?

MILES: They don't leave. Feel that? (*Presses my hand to his lips.*) Keep feeling it. It took me thirty or forty years to build that. When you practice you take the edge off something. We don't practice, we *rehearse*, there's a difference. We rehearse and throw things around. After a couple of times they get the idea. And that's it.

MUSICIAN: You played quite a bit of piano at the Savoy, and you also use the piano to cue the band.

MILES: That's right. Because all the guys I have play the piano.

MUSICIAN: You had Bill Evans play some piano at the Savoy too. You pushed him over to the piano and he looked like, Does he really mean it?

MILES: Bill Evans plays great piano, he used to play classical piano and give concerts of Rachmaninoff and stuff like that when he was 16. People don't know that. I wouldn't ask him to sit down if he couldn't play. He's one of the greatest musicians I've ever come upon. He and Gil Evans. There must be something with those Evanses. Must be a breed.

MUSICIAN: Isn't it uncanny that his name is Bill Evans, the same. I thought they were related or something.

MILES: It's too painful for me to think of *Bill* Evans and his piano. He's one of my favorite pianists. Or he was. But . . . that's the way it goes.

MUSICIAN: Could you have ended up like Charlie Parker, dead that prematurely?

MILES: I'm not as selfish as he was.

MUSICIAN: Or you don't have that self-destructiveness.

MILES: Some people say I do, but I'm not that selfish. Bird was really selfish. If you had some dope he'd want all of it. If you had some food, he'd want all of *that*.

MUSICIAN: There had to be a real self-hatred or—

MILES: I don't think so. People just say that kind of thing. He loved life, you know. He had a lot of fun. If people had left him alone, he would have been all right.

MUSICIAN: If who had left him alone?

MILES: People saying you can't use this dope and to keep from getting busted you have to use all of it. You have to use all of it because if somebody catches you they'll put you in jail. What could be any worse than whiskey? It's got my liver all fucked up.

MUSICIAN: How is your health generally?

MILES: All right, because I didn't eat meat for seven years and I box.

MUSICIAN: What got you off meat?

MILES: A doctor went to check my blood pressure and he said, Where is it? Do you *have* any blood? Really? (*laughs*) He told me to eat some bread so I could get my strength up and have my blood. I had to have a five-hour operation and I needed strength for that.

MUSICIAN: Do you think your health can withstand all this touring now?

MILES: No.

MUSICIAN: What about Japan? Will you be playing every night?

MILES: I can take it.

MUSICIAN: Are you happy to be touring again? Do you enjoy it?

MILES: Not really. It's just playing with Bill and these guys. It turns me on. It makes the adrenalin start flowing. It's such a great bunch of guys, they play so well, it's a pity to let them down, you know. And Randy Hall, and my nephew and little Bobby, they all write great music for me. I need a bubble-gum song, I just call up Randy and say, Randy send me a bubble-gum song. Like "Shout."

MUSICIAN: What's the jazz scene like in Japan?

MILES: I don't know anything about jazz! You keep asking me about jazz! I've been in Japan and most countries. Japanese people are funny. They like anything that's good. You can't bring no bullshit over there. They know you're not coming back so they're gonna listen. So they can *copy*. You know how Japanese people are. They *copy*. And when they copy, they copy the *best*. And they *want* the best. They don't settle for anything but the best.

MUSICIAN: You've said that you're not an entertainer. Is that still true?

MILES: Yeah, I'm an entertainer. I got a certain amount of ham in me. I don't know. I'm doin' what I'm doin' but I know I'm a big ham. It doesn't take away from the music, because I just enjoy what I'm doin' at that particular time, and now that I play so *different* you have to put in something for the rhythm that you don't play inside of. You know what I mean? It's like subtracting and puttin' in other beats. Because I play very strange. I've heard it from the band, I play—you know how I play, mostly like sanctified people will play in a church, or the way a hillbilly sings songs. They sing songs to please the lyrics, and not to people, or the rhythms. And the words fall on *funny beats*. So that's the reason I come in like old Bill Cosby with his *green beans*. I love to hear him say that.

MUSICIAN: Do these guys really work you? The guys in your present band?

MILES: Shit, I be wringing wet after I get through playing with them. Dirty motherfuckers. (*laughs*) I got to play all these notes on account of they did this, they did that.

MUSICIAN: I've seen you backstage afterwards. You're full of energy onstage and then two seconds later you look like you're going to pass out.

MILES: Well, you have to relax. You can't stay that tense, you know?

MUSICIAN: And you have to try to live up to yourself as an artist.

MILES: Well, I always try to have a good tone, 'cause I know if I don't it's gonna drag me, and it's gonna drag people I respect a lot, people like Dizzy and Freddie Hubbard and all the trumpet players.

MUSICIAN: But your first responsibility is to yourself.

MILES: Yeah, your first responsibility is to yourself (a *girl passes by outside*) and girls like that one right there. . . . (*laughs*) Ah, yeah.

MUSICIAN: You get these young guys in your band, and they go off in other directions.

MILES: I didn't know they were that young. I don't pick a guy because he's young.

MUSICIAN: You pick them because they're good.

MILES: Coleman Hawkins once told me not to play with anybody old because they'll be hard to bend to the way you want them to play.

MUSICIAN: So you do what then?

MILES: I don't do anything. I just keep 'em from goin' out the door.

MUSICIAN: But you lead them, right?

MILES: They pay attention. And they're all professionals, so professionally they know if they miss anything, it's gonna fall right back on them. Everybody in my band could have a band right now. I don't tell them what to do, I just *suggest* something and if they don't like it they'll suggest something else. Say, we can do this *and* this. Or they'll know what I mean and add something to it that makes it better.

MUSICIAN: Have you taken a lot of heat because you were the first, or one of the first, to be a superstar?

MILES: Am I a superstar? I don't know that.

MUSICIAN: Why do you think everyone's so excited that you're playing again?

MILES: I thought they liked the music.

MUSICIAN: You're one of the first to bring jazz to a lot of people.

MILES: Well, I don't know, see, 'cause Columbia is so *vague* and *cheap*. Now they're not cheap anymore, they think I'm a genius. They thought I was a genius before, but now they're *convinced*.

MUSICIAN: Because you're number one. You got on the pop charts.

MILES: AND I'M REALLY MILES DAVIS! They had me for three years. (*sings to the tune of "Bette Davis Eyes"*) 'Cause I got . . . Betty Grable's legs. . . . They wouldn't let me *sing*. Next album I'm singing. Sure. I'm going to siiiiinnng some soooulful ballads. "Love without Time." (*sings*) "Love without time. Just don't give me no limit. Don't need no limit." . . . I have it on tape.

MUSICIAN: Have you got any nagging regrets about things you've done or haven't done?

MILES: No. (*Pause.*) No. No. No. No. No. I'm happy now. I could have been happy years ago if I had married Cicely. But years ago . . . no. Time takes care of that, time takes care of everything. If I had married Cicely she wouldn't have been a star now.

MUSICIAN: Wasn't she a star then?

MILES: Yes, but she was too involved with me to be, you know, to keep her mind and body and work on it. And *I* work. And besides she's very smart. I know a couple women like that who are very smart and I try to stay out of their way—even if I do love them. Because they're living the way they want to live. If they love you, it's bad. You have to keep asking them, "Do you love me . . . today?" Tuesday the same thing. You have to ask. Well, that's the way people do. I'm thinking of in general. Not me. I don't go around asking anything. Or anyone.

MUSICIAN: Were you completely alone those five years?

MILES: *I'm never alone.* I was . . . yeah, I was alone. I was alone most of the time. But I hate to be alone. I call up some of my friends. Gil, Bill Evans. Dave Liebman, Al Foster used to come by all the time, telling me what's happening out on the street.

MUSICIAN: Did you feel you wouldn't play again?

MILES: No. I knew if I felt like playing I would play. Even if it was just once. I didn't go places and sit in. Nobody had anything I wanted to sit in *with*. I went down to the Vanguard once and sat in the brass section, played everybody's trumpet, just once. I knew what was happening out there. I didn't have to hear. I'd take their word for it. When Al Foster would tell me ain't nothin' happening, or Dave Liebman, or Gil Evans, I know it isn't nothing happening.

MUSICIAN: Did life turn out the way you thought it would?

MILES: *I never thought about life.*

MUSICIAN: When you were a kid, what did you think you were going to be?

MILES: I thought I was going to be the greatest thing I ever attempted, in whatever I attempted. I thought I was going to be one of the best.

MUSICIAN: Were you the oldest child?

MILES: I was the oldest *boy*. My sister was the oldest.

MUSICIAN: You were a middle child? Middle kids are always stuck in between.

MILES: Stuck where? I had my paper route, making money, doing everything.

MUSICIAN: Middle kids sometimes need to achieve more, I've heard.

MILES: Well, that's what they say. I don't know what *they* say, or who says it. Maybe now, but not then. I know whatever I did, if it wasn't any good, my father was gonna strangle me.

MUSICIAN: He was a real perfectionist?

MILES: Well, he was a professional surgeon. An oral surgeon. Yeah, it was strict. Not religion, but it was strict. I couldn't fuck around, but they never did stop me. Guys used to come over to my house, like Clark Terry—he's my favorite trumpet player. Clark Terry—and I was about 14. He used to come over and ask my father could I go out on a jam session with him. My father would say yes. We ran a jam session because the guys coming up on the riverboat from New Orleans would jam all night. I'd tell Clark, "Go and ask him." 'Cause I wasn't afraid of my father. He'd never spank me or nothin'.

MUSICIAN: You were lucky. A lot of kids get spanked.

MILES: For what? I never did do anything.

MUSICIAN: You were perfect.

MILES: I'm *always* perfect. I was buying his clothes and fixing his false plates and all that shit. In the lab. That's *tedious*. Then I had a paper route, and I was jamming. Making six dollars a night.

MUSICIAN: When you were fourteen?

MILES: Fourteen I was making three dollars a night. Fifteen I was making six. Sixteen I was making $100 a week. When the guys come off from the boat, we'd jam. Clark and I would go to a club called the Moonlight Inn. We'd be in there about ten minutes and the place'd get packed. They'd say come on, Miles and Clark are jamming—whee!—everybody would come.

MUSICIAN: Were you ever afraid that you weren't good enough?

MILES: Good enough for what? I was in a *band* [Eddie Randall's Blue Devils], paying me $100 a week to rehearse the band and to rehearse the show, 'cause all the guys had to go to the steel foundry so I was musical director. I didn't care what the guys off the boat thought.

MUSICIAN: You must have picked up the horn awful fast. You started at twelve? Thirteen?

MILES: Twelve. I knew I could play.

MUSICIAN: I've read about you spitting rice all the way to school and back to build up your lip. Did you think that up?

MILES: My instructor, Mr. Buchanan, Elwood Buchanan of East St. Louis, Illinois, he told me to do that. I had a mouth full of rice, or I'd take some beans and break them up in my mouth and spit out all the way to school. About a mile and a half.

MUSICIAN: So you did three miles a day of spitting. Was there a band in school? Did you play there too?

MILES: Marching band. We'd march and the trumpet would go all over my fucking lip. (*laughs*) Marching. Me and my brother got—I taught him how to play trumpet. He was in the band. He plays trumpet, piano. He went to the conservatory. My mother played piano, my sister played piano. I don't think my father did anything, but watched everybody. My father taught us all to draw. I always like to have a pencil and paper around. You look at a paper and see things in it and I just draw.

MUSICIAN: What was your mother's name?

MILES: Cleota. She was a very beautiful woman. My sister and brother used to give *shows* every night and I was the audience. They would sit me down and say, "You ready, Junior?" I said, "Yeah I'm ready." Here they come, dancin', comin' out, you know, like— (*makes tapping sound*). I said, "No, you'll have to do better than that shit, you'll have to get some better steps than that to come out here with." They say, "Don't you like that?" I said, "No, I paid my money, come on, give me something." (*laughs*) Then they'd do some steps again. They said, "How do you like that?" I said, "That was good." I'd applaud. That would go on every night. It was very funny.

MUSICIAN: You grew up with a lot of good influences, Miles.

MILES: We had the wrong books. We didn't have any Negro histories. We had a school teacher named Miss Wilson who used to slip in, teach us Negro history, Marcus Garvey and things like that. And my father ran for state representative, my father did, of Illinois.

MUSICIAN: Did he win?

MILES: Of course not. . . . My mother was pretty and very . . . blank-faced. Just like you're looking at me . . . *no expression.* She looked at me when I played the trumpet. She'd say *when are you gonna play something that I can understand?*

MUSICIAN: She didn't like it?

MILES: She didn't say that. If she didn't like it, she used to tell me to go down to the basement. And my big band would come, we would rehearse. I had a big band when I was about 15. With 18 musicians, and I had to pay 'em. It was the school band, swing band. The swing band was in the marching band.

MUSICIAN: And you organized it.

MILES: 'Cause I had the basement. My basement, my band. (*laughs*) And I used to copy the music off the records. I was the leader. We never did play *any* place but in the basement. We used to have some gigs, but it was only four of us would play.

MUSICIAN: So you knew pretty early in life what you wanted to do.

MILES: I couldn't help it, 'cause I played trumpet so bad, had to keep playing to clean it up. . . . My mother said, "He's crazy." My father told her, he say, "Remember that. Now leave him alone." My father was a riot, boy.

MUSICIAN: What was New York like when you first arrived?

MILES: *Oh man.* I was very excited when I first came. I used to walk in the rain. I'd never seen a place like that before. *Subways.* All sorts of pastry, until I tried all the pastry, and it tasted like shit. It wasn't scary, because I wasn't looking *up.* I had one thing to do, was go to Juilliard. I was getting an allowance. I'd get the bus and go to Juilliard. I'd get $40 a week . . . when I *got* it, I blew it, takin' care of Bird and Dex and all them guys. They didn't have any money, *I* had the money. Got so bad I used to call them, just keep some of it, 'cause those guys asked me for money.

MUSICIAN: You were rooming with Charlie Parker?

MILES: He roomed with *me.* And *please* put in that I was born May 26, 1926. Somebody tried to fuck that all up.

MUSICIAN: Bird and Dex were putting all their money in the arm? Is that how you got into it?

MILES: No. I just did that—Gene Ammons and I done that, we just started doin' it. First we started snorting it, then we started shooting it, and I didn't even know what was happening. I should have thought about it a little bit. I stopped after about three or four years. I stopped . . . *cold turkey.* My father bought me a new five-gaited pony. We had 500 acres near St. Louis, in Milstead, Illinois. I stayed out on the farm for about two and a half weeks until I was straight.

MUSICIAN: What made you finally decide to stop?

MILES: Max Roach gave me $200 and put it in my pocket, say I looked good. It drug me so much I went right to St. Louis. I said that motherfucker gave me $200, told me I looked good and I'm fucked up and he knows it. And he's my best friend, right? It just *embarrassed* me to death. I looked in the mirror and I said, Goddamn it Miles, come on. So I called my father to send me a ticket, and he sent me a ticket.

MUSICIAN: Did he know you were strung out?

MILES: My sister told him. *She tells him everything.* I said, You bitch, you fucking whore. She said, Well somebody had to tell him, and I just told him. I said, All right, all right, all right. . . . He asked me—we walked out in the pasture and he said, "If you were with a woman and the woman left you, I would know what to tell you, you could get another woman. But this you have to do by yourself, you know that, 'cause you been around drugs all your life. You know what you have to do . . ." So I said, "Do I look like I have a habit to you?" He said *yess*. He had a set of rooms like this and a big large farm house, colonial type farm house, and I went in there and shut the door and didn't come out. The maid said, "Junior you want some breakfast?" I said, "*Get* outta here." I did that for about two weeks.

MUSICIAN: Was that the worst you ever been through?

MILES: Yeah. Oh, it's terrible.

MUSICIAN: I had a friend who lived across the hall from me in Detroit who did that. He was screaming, begging . . .

MILES: I wasn't doin' none of that shit, 'cause my father was next door and I was sure not gonna let him hear me holler and scream. . . . Had a plan though, see, I'm gonna jump out this window, and luckily I'll break my leg and they'll give me something for my leg and I'll be cool, you know? Yeah, maybe I'll hit my head on something, knock me out for a while. . . . I said, No, I'm gonna break my right arm, can't play the trumpet, fuck that. I'll just stay here. (*laughs*) So each day it got better and better.

MUSICIAN: That's what I was asking before. Why did you end up not going the way Charlie Parker went?

MILES: 'Cause he didn't stop. I got tired of lookin' at myself. I was a pimp, I had a lot of girls, I was doin' this, doin' that. . . . I had more money then than I have now. Yeah, I had about seven girls, made a lot of money. Can't 'call the names, though.

MUSICIAN: I never understood why women would turn the money over to a pimp.

MILES: They wouldn't give me their money. They just give me money to take them out. They made a lot of money . . . screwin.' They didn't give all their money to me, they just said, "Miles, take me out. I don't like people I don't like, I like you, take me out . . ." That's like a family they like to be in. I know, I can understand that. Yeah, that's what it is. (*pause*) Question.

MUSICIAN: What makes you angry?

MILES: Everything.

MUSICIAN: What makes you mad?

MILES: Everything.

MUSICIAN: What makes you happy?

MILES: Little things, you know. Everything doesn't make me mad, angry. It takes a lot to make me angry enough. It's not that I'm angry, it's the way I speak. I don't *lie,* so it comes off like that. I ask people, when I say something, they think that my voice every time I'm straining to talk sounds like I'm drunk or high or something. So I just . . . When I get on the phone they say, "Yes ma'am, what did you say?" They think I'm a woman. (*laughs*)

MUSICIAN: There's a real reactionary swing right now with Reagan and the Moral Majority.

MILES: It's a swing, yes. But the people still, they test you and see how you are . . . and they let you know that they're not prejudiced. Which takes quite some time, it's like 15, 20 minutes. Then you know that they're all right.

MUSICIAN: You've been hassled by cops, been beaten up.

MILES: It's the way I talk to them. I gotta buy a Ferrari, it's red, right? They stop me and they say . . . I was standing outside Birdland once and a cop asked me to go *inside.* I said for what? He said, *for what*? I said, "That's what I said." He said, "Because I said so." I say, "I just got through doing a broadcast for the armed services, I'm trying to dry off, get some air, it's smokey down there. . . ." He said, "You're a wise guy, aren't you?" I said, "Yes, you know I'm wise because I don't have that funny looking blue suit you got on." He said, "Ohh here we go, you're under arrest." And two guys jumped out of the crowd and started beating on my head.

MUSICIAN: There's a picture of you all bandaged. You made a good remark. They asked you if the cop dropped his nightstick and did you pick it up, and you said, "If I picked it up I wouldn't look like this."

MILES: Right. They asked me did I hit him.

MUSICIAN: And once someone shot at you in Brooklyn.

MILES: I didn't know what that was all about. The agency knew, 'cause they were having an agency war. I didn't know it. I was talking to Marguerite. If she had gotten out of the car she'd have got killed. But I had just kissed her in the car, you know? And I looked around and this guy is staring at me— (*makes the sound of a gun firing*) and I said *shit*, this is . . .

MUSICIAN: Did you think it was her husband?

MILES: I don't mess with married women.

MUSICIAN: Was that the last major thing that happened to you of that kind?

MILES: Yeah, but I used to get arrested all the time. (*spars with Mark Rothbaum, who is passing through*) Violence gets you nowhere, Mark. Great guy, Mark. My managerrrrr.

MUSICIAN: Bill told me you're a good cook.

MILES: Very good. Because the women I had couldn't—bitches couldn't cook. I picked it up from my father actually, although my mother would cook. He would say, "Come on, go in there with me," and we'd go and he would cook something . . . else. I have a French cookbook and anything I taste, I could tell what's in it. I get a kick out of doing it, you know, for them [the band], 'cause I don't eat that much. I don't like a lot of food.

MUSICIAN: What do you do in your leisure time?

MILES: I haven't been to a movie in ten years. Maybe longer.

MUSICIAN: Do you read much?

MILES: No. But I can *sing*. I read music books. And, uh, different things. Dirt. Like in *People* magazine (*laughs*) and the *Enquirer*, stuff like that. I'm a real New Yorker, I want to know what's happening out there in Hollywood.

MUSICIAN: Well here's the *New York Post*'s big headline: SEX FIEND IS LOOSE!

MILES: That means all of us are loose.

MUSICIAN: Do you still box?

MILES: That's my pastime. Everybody comes to see me. All the ex-fighters are Moslems. I'm not Moslem, but I lean toward Islam. They're a great people, you know.

MUSICIAN: Do you know Ali?

MILES: Sure I know him. He's crazy. These guys in Islam, they say he and I act alike. I say nobody acts like me. I don't act like anyone—Hey, Jim! What happened to the hamburgers?

JIM: You ate the hamburgers. Or Chris ate them. I can put two more on.

MILES: No you know, just—I'd like to have a *thin* hamburger, not a thick one. And I want an onion. Hey, Marko, I want an onion, a thin slice of onion, and a tomato—piece of tomato, and mustard . . . and an old pickle. An old Jewish pickle. Not PLO . . . POL.

MUSICIAN: What are your plans now, Miles? Are you going to stay active, doing this gig?

MILES: I'll stay active till I die, now.

MUSICIAN: You're not going to go back into . . .

MILES: Seclusion? No, I had enough of that. I did what I wanted to do. Stopped for awhile, give the trumpet a rest, give my head a rest. Relax. That was it. Do I get paid for this [the interview]?

MUSICIAN: How does the world look to you?

MILES: I don't know about the world, you can see it's already fucked up. They still practicing genocide with the black people, nobody ever says anything about that, they always talk about the Jews. They never talk about the black people gettin' fucked up. Been that junk for years, starvin' and all that shit. That's one of the things you don't speak of, speak about.

MUSICIAN: Are you politically involved now? You gave a benefit concert or so back in the sixties?

MILES: CORE. For CORE I did it. For SNCC. I helped out the African Foundation. I just did one concert. It was a double concert, but I'm not going that way again. I think the government should take care of their own people. They took my son, fucked *him* up in the war. I don't even want to say which son.

MUSICIAN: Is there anything you want that you don't have?

MILES: You, Cheryl, I want you, but I know I can't have you.

MUSICIAN: Besides that.

MILES: I want a cigarette boat.

MUSICIAN: A cigarette *what*?

MILES: *Boat.* Speedboat. I want me a solar energy house.

MUSICIAN: You'd have to go someplace where there's more sun in the winter. Would you miss New York if you left it?

MILES: Sure. I'm not going too far from New York. I love it. I love New York. I love the noise. I can't sleep without noise. I can't sleep without lights. I can't sleep without New York. I would never leave New York. Never ever ever ever never never never never. (*sings*) "That's why New York's my home, da dela de dadah . . ." (*makes knocking sounds with mouth*)

MUSICIAN: Do you ever think about teaching people?

MILES: I teach people all the time. Don't I teach you, Bill Evans? Bill Evans, have I ever taught you anything?

EVANS: Everything.

MILES: Asshole. Fuck. (*laughing*) There's my favorite pupil. They're teaching me right back. Puts you right back on it. Bill's my *right hand man*, boy. Without him

I don't know what I'd do. Isn't that right, Bill? Without you I wouldn't know what I'm doing, would I? Without you and Leroy.

EVANS: No. Leroy does all our business.

MILES: If Leroy was out here today, what d'you think he'd say, Bill? What do you think Leroy would say about this place out here? *Where all the pictures at? There's no pictures? Let's go.* Want me to call up Leroy? (*horse passes by*) Hi, horse.

MUSICIAN: I don't have any more questions, Miles. Just tell me what you think you're about.

MILES: About WHAT?

MUSICIAN: You always sound like . . . do you feel you're misunderstood?

MILES: I didn't say that. It comes across like that because they're white and I'm black.

MUSICIAN: It even comes across like that when you're interviewed by a black man.

MILES: Well, it must be a guy who's trying to act black, guy trying to act black and he's really white and has a black face. Should we go into that?

MUSICIAN: I just want to know who you think *you* are.

MILES: My brother says I'm King Tut . . . reincarnated. That's what he calls me, King Tut.

MUSICIAN: Who do you think you are?

MILES: I don't know. I think I'm a fellow.

MUSICIAN: Well then, what moves or motivates you?

MILES: When I hear some good music, it motivates me to the . . . *nth* degree.

MUSICIAN: But you also create the music.

MILES: I know. I'm King Tut. I write the music and I create the music and I play the songs that I love. Can I go now?

EXCERPTS FROM THREE
ANONYMOUS INTERVIEWS

Interviewers: Unknown, c. mid-1980s

We have been unable to locate the precise sources of the following excerpts
from mid-1980s radio interviews.

How to Cope with Numb Lips

INTERVIEWER: You seem to be very busy playing and recording. How do you
manage to keep up that tempo?

MD: What tempo?

INTERVIEWER: Many musicians today maybe play like an hour show and then
leave, but I mean you're over sixty years old and still play for three hours.

MD: "How old you are" is what you're doing. If you're devoted to music like I am,
and it doesn't bother me to play that long. My mouth gets numb sometimes. I
just take my horn down. Dizzy told me that years ago. I said, "Why do I always
have to stop?" and I said, "Why do my lips get numb?" He said, "Because you
don't take it down." He's like my brother, right? Big brother. He said, "Just take
your horn down from your mouth and let the blood rush in." So if I'm playin'
and all of a sudden it gets numb from holding notes straight, I just take it down,
even if it's in the middle of a melody. My mouth gets dry.

On Fashion

MD: I like those Mexican colors, you know, the mustard and the red, red, red.
Earth colors. But this is nice, look at that. That's from drawing forty-five min-

utes. I also did some . . . where was I? In Germany. I did these faces. I'll show you some. These faces in bronze and iridescent white and you mix the colors and you get little vignettes all over like blue and brown and you have to know when not to touch it. It's the same way with music. You have to know when the composition is over. Or if you play too long, or if you play too loud, it won't balance it and people are used to being balanced. You know, breakfast, lunch, dinner. Supper. That carries over. It keeps you thinking all the time. How can I balance this? Even when you put on clothes: is there too much jewelry on this, too much black on this. *I'm* black, I don't *need* black. I can't wear brown. I have a brown shirt in there now, must be $1,200, it's like this. I can't wear it because you can't see me if I put it on. I'm the same color as my shirt. I did that once in New York. I had a brown suit, a brown shirt, and brown shoes, and I passed by a window and I didn't see nothin'. I just got me a new Ferrari. I got the Testarosa. I haven't driven it and I'm buying a new horse that I like. I like to go to California and, you know, just ride a little bit.

On Leaving Columbia Records

MD: (*Music*) They want to meet the man, the legend, jazz. When you go in a record store, you don't . . . people walk by something that's called lies—jazz. They don't look at it. It took them almost a year to release "Time After Time." And after that I decided to leave. Over incompetence like that, you know, they don't pay attention to you, what you're doing, and it's like, "Why should I do it when they bury it?" So I left. I told my manager, David Franken, to get me a little record contract. So he got one, because what culminated with that album was it was to be the last one for Columbia. They were gonna call it *Contemporary Jazz*, and I said, "No, you're not. I'm keepin' the master tape." Paulie wrote a masterpiece, it'll be here after we're all dead, but you know, I don't want Columbia to have it. I told them I don't figure they're gonna do justice to it. That masterpiece, they'll just take it and stick it in a corner somewhere. He wanted to call it *Contemporary Jazz*, which is a sad name for a work like that.

SEARCHING FOR MILES: THEME AND VARIATIONS ON THE LIFE OF A TRUMPETER

Interviewer: David Breskin
Rolling Stone, September 29, 1983

Poet, novelist, investigative journalist, record producer, and interviewer extraordinaire, David Breskin published regularly in the 1980s and early '90s in *GQ*, *Life*, and *Rolling Stone*, where this profile first appeared. His work includes the novel *The Real Life Diary of a Boomtown Girl* and novel-in-verse *Supermodel*; the poetry collections *Fresh Kills* and *Escape Velocity*; and the seminal *Inner Views: Filmmakers in Conversation*, which gathered together his dialogues with directors David Lynch, Francis Coppola, Robert Altman, Clint Eastwood, Spike Lee, Oliver Stone, Tim Burton, and David Cronenberg. His poems have appeared in *The New Yorker* and *The Paris Review*, among many other publications, and he has produced recordings for Bill Frisell, Ronald Shannon Jackson, John Zorn, Vernon Reid, Bobby Previte, Joey Baron, and Nels Cline. He lives in San Francisco.

March 2, 1983

Dear Sir:

I started Miles Davis out on trumpet in the sixth grade at the Crispus Attucks School about September 1937. He continued training with me at Lincoln Junior High School in 1938. He was playing good then. He remained with me through senior high school. He was one of my most progressive students in the Lincoln High School Band (and the instrumental program in Public School District 189 in East St. Louis, Illinois).

Miles Dewey Davis III was born on May 25th, 1926, in Alton, Illinois. Miles' father was not only a respected citizen

and dentist but a prosperous landowner. As the result of Miles'
outstanding ability, I got his father to get him a trumpet of
his own. After great success in the Lincoln High School Con-
cert and Marching Band, he graduated about 1943. He was one
of the best musicians I ever taught in instrumental music. He
received all first awards with my band groups that competed in
the Illinois State High School Music Association contests.

I had him try out with Eddie Randle's St. Louis "Blue Devils"
Jazz Band. Miles gained recognition and received a scholarship
to the Juilliard School of Music. His mother wanted him to go
to Fisk University, in Nashville, Tennessee. It took Miles almost
a year to convince his father to allow him to go to New York,
but he finally relented, much to the dismay of his mother, Mrs.
Davis. When Miles was nineteen, still naive but strong-willed,
he arrived in New York City.

Miles had mixed feelings about Juilliard. He really had gone
to New York to try to hook up with Charlie Parker and his
band. He met Charlie Parker in St. Louis at the Riveria Nite
Club on Delmar at Taylor Avenue. (Big Bands played there—
Duke Ellington, Billy Eckstine, Jimmy Lunceford, Count Basie
and others.) I think one semester was enough for Miles at Juil-
liard. He caught up with Charlie Parker and Dizzy Gillespie.
After a while in New York, Miles lived with Parker one year. On
Parker's first record as a leader, he decided to take Miles. From
then until present, Miles Dewey Davis III has been one of the
top jazz musicians.

Sincerely,

Elwood C. Buchanon Sr.

P.S. Send me about six copies of the article or magazine.

———

"I drive my yellow one in New York. Police don't bother me 'cause it looks like
a cab. *Wsssshhhhtt!* They figure, Oh shit, that's just a taxi. I did that shit once
in front of a brother, I did one of those funny things that only a Ferrari can do.

He stopped me and said, 'God*damn*, Miles, why you do that shit?' I said, 'What would *you* do if you had this motherfucker?' And he said, 'Okay, go ahead.' The shit was outrageous, though. Only a Ferrari would do that shit. I love a Ferrari, man. The white cops, they all know me by now. Motherfuckers say, 'Oh, that's just *him*.'"

———

Laughter cracks the scorched whisper of his voice. He slouches over a sketch pad on his Houston hotel-suite bed, drawing a woman with slashing jaw, electrocuted hair, ballerina legs. *Damn, this bitch is fine.* His teeth battle with a wad of gum, and his eyes swing up from the fine bitch to college hoops on the tube and then back again. Anticipating a rubdown from his trainer and gofer, Zeke, he wears only a jockstrap and open robe. Sweat rolls down the balding head he doesn't let his audiences see (his splendid haberdashery), and he rasps, with splendid irritation and amusement, "Better ask me some questions, 'cause your time is runnin' out *fasssst*."

Though Miles rarely cooperates with the press, for some reason known only to himself, he's consented to an interview. Over the next weeks, there are several. I travel with his band in Texas, and they talk, mostly off-the-record. I speak with sister, brother, daughter, nephew, teachers, students, producers, managers, collaborators. Yellowed clips of exploits, both with and without horn, crinkle back to the Forties, and I'm buried, searching for the key. After Miles wins his latest Grammy, he calls me from the Ritz-Carlton in Chicago. When I answer the phone, he whines, "You again?" and hangs up. Calls right back, and charmingly asks what more I'd like to know. That's just *him*. We all know him by now.

———

"White people do that, man. They say, 'He does this and he don't do that, and he fucks five girls a night and he makes $10,000 a second, but he's a nice guy and his mother threw him out when he was two.' Fuck that! Why do they ask all those rock stars that shit? 'She wears her hair like this, and he has fifty dozen girls, her life is an open book, *but* she's misunderstood.' Who they fuck and why they fuck and this song has a message. White people do that shit. What does it mean? I don't like that. It's all just music."

———

Miles Davis is arguably the most important of all living American musicians. His music stands with the greatest of the century. It begins with him spitting rice and beans to build up his lip as he walks to school. His mother wants him to play violin, his father overrules with the trumpet. Mother wants him to be a dentist like father, father wants him to be the best at whatever he chooses. Father wins that argument. *If you're a thief, don't be no jive thief.*

In between school, a paper route, work in dad's lab and weekend jam sessions paying three dollars a night, young Miles hangs out at his father's farm. "Not a bullshit farm, a gentleman's farm," says brother Vernon. "Two hundred acres with a lake and one of those Southern colonial homes and a Jaguar in the driveway." Miles fishes, hunts, rides one of thirteen horses. At sixteen, Miles marries Irene—the first of four wives. Baby Cheryl is already on the way. *Picking cotton does not teach anyone how to play the blues.*

———

"If I was black for sixteen years and I turned white—I mean my insides and everything—shit, I'd commit suicide. 'Cause whites have knowledge but no rhythm. Classical music was invented 'cause white people didn't have no rhythm, and they could *write* it and *plan* it and all. Once you have a *taste* of rhythm—say, for sixteen years—and someone say, 'Do you want to be white, with all the trimmings?' Shit no. Brooks Brothers suit is all right, but I'm talking about the *feeling.*

"Now, did you see last night, I was playing a blues and I go over and bend down and play to that fat woman in the second row. She says, 'That's right, Miles, come on over here, you can *stay* over here.' So then I play something real fast, and she says, 'Not like *that*, though. Go back over there if you're gonna play that shit.' Now, do you think a white person would tell me that? They don't even know what she's talking about. She's talking about . . . she's talking about the *bluuueesss*. In my hometown, if you don't play the blues, shit, them motherfuckers go to ordering drinks, but if you play the blues, they'll stay right there. That fat bitch, she'd have me blowing all night."

———

All night, 1945, swinging on 52nd Street, blowing his allowance and horn, Miles slips into the ferocious lives of Charlie "Bird" Parker and Dizzy Gillespie and up onto the bandstand of the be-bop revolution. His tone is pure, round, without vibrato. On his first recordings with Bird, he shows technical limitations but also the first signs of lyrical brilliance. He can't play as high or as fast as Dizzy; he sticks to the middle registers. He makes less mean more. Bird and Miles have a stormy love-hate relationship, and Bird humiliates him with games on the bandstand. *Makes you feel one foot tall.* They split in '48.

Be-bop is only the first of many movements Miles will either captain or observe from the crow's nest. Soon he's in arranger Gil Evans' one-room basement apartment behind a Chinese laundry, working on a way to calm the frenetic and scalding turbulence of be-bop without chilling the passion. It's called "cool jazz," and until Evans orchestrates it and Miles plays it, the trumpet is but half a horn; then it's capable of introspection, light and shadows, restraint, repose. Miles quickly develops an economy of expression unmatched in American improvisation.

He travels to Paris, where the French lionize him. He hangs out with Jean-Paul Sartre on the Left Bank. Miles doesn't understand Sartre, but Sartre knows existentialist trumpet when he hears it. When Miles comes back to the States, he finds heroin and checks out for four years. He lies, steals, cheats, pimps. His trumpet turns to metal.

———

"Max Roach walked up to me one day on the street, we were real tight, and said, 'Damn man, you sure do look good, what's happening?' But I could tell he was looking at me. And as he left, he touched me in my pocket, put a hundred dollars in my pocket. And I didn't dig it until he left—telling me I looked good and then giving me a hundred dollars like I'm a fucking bum. And that's all you are when you use that shit. I went right to St. Louis and kicked."

———

Cold turkey on the farm, followed by a triumphant return at the 1955 Newport Jazz Festival. This time it's called "hard bop," and it reenergizes the blues with elegant modernity and streamlined muscle. For the next twenty years, Miles doesn't play music so much as invent it. With the help of those in his employ—always the best and the brightest—his career becomes a rich quarrel between tradition and innovation. He collaborates with Gil Evans on a stunning series of orchestral recordings—*Sketches of Spain, Porgy & Bess, Miles Ahead*—that blend classical, ethnic, and African-American idioms. He gives ballads and standards a new emotional depth through his use of the Harmon mute. He junks chord changes and soars off with John Coltrane on modal excursions. He writes and plays with increasing abstraction and freedom while leading (and following) a band of Young Turks—Wayne Shorter, Tony Williams, Ron Carter, Herbie Hancock. Finally, he sums up the electric spirit of the late Sixties and early Seventies by supervising the birth and development of jazz-rock fusion. Restless, relentless, he synergizes new vocabularies, masters the language, then moves on with another generation in tow. He's the Picasso of Invisible Art.

By September 1975, in New York's Central Park, he's playing an excoriating version of heavy metal funk 'n' roll—full of dark distortion, demonic intensity, tortured guitars, screeching trumpet. Then he stops. Pulls away, retires to a dark space on Manhattan's Upper West Side. Leaves behind over fifty albums, no clues.

> *I loved it when he used to dress so cute in those suits. When I was a teenager. Those Italian suits. Polka-dot ties. Those cute suits. Oh, he was so cute. I used to love it when he put on those cute suits.*
>
> —Cheryl Davis

> *I call him King Tut because King Tut was a black king in his time and Miles is the black prince from this time. So I call him King Tut. I couldn't call him Prince Charles, could I?*
>
> —Vernon Davis

Miles Davis has an image. Nasty and notorious, arrogant and whimsical, he does nothing he doesn't want to do, and he makes a point of it. When he feels like biting his producer's ear, he bites. *That's a nice WHITE ear.* When he decides he doesn't want to speak to this same producer for three years, he doesn't. When the producer, Teo Macero, calls every so often, Miles shouts, "So what?" and hangs up. Irascible and insolent, he's the Evil Genius, the Sorcerer, the Prince of Darkness. He won't bow to his audience for the same reason doctors don't bow to their patients, won't face his audience for the same reason conductors don't face theirs. He doesn't speak to his audience, because he plays the trumpet for a living.

Miles is only five foot four, but he can look down on whomever he sees. His *attitude* is in his heels: boxer's stance, his high-profile mystery and intrigue, his proud pose as the anti-Tom. He may arrive late, walk offstage after his solos, sneer superciliously from behind his shades. Despite some superficial complaints, all this secretly delights his audience. They wouldn't want him any other way.

Miles Davis is aware of his image and knows how to use it. He knows there are women in Sweden in love with his photograph and young men in Japan wearing his glasses and babies in Nigeria with his name. Whether it be with polka-dot tie, dashiki, or Japanese jumpsuit, gangster cool or green trumpet, his ascent to the peak of Bad Motherfuckerdom ensures his currency even among people who don't make a steady diet of jazz. It's not just the music that puts him—and who else among instrumentalists?—on the society and gossip pages. It's his magnetism, his sexuality, his hubris.

And his talent for trouble: cops arrest him for narcotics and brass knuckles and .25-caliber automatics, beat him over the head outside Birdland. Racketeers shoot through the door of his Ferrari and he breaks both legs smashing up his Lambourghini. A woman sues him for unlawful imprisonment and menacing in his apartment, a man for being thrown down the stairs. Miles Davis is a pop star.

But while most pop stars' music only confirms and bolsters their public image, Miles' art always strips bare the pretense of his facade. Behind the veil of his rancorous public profile, the music reveals the person: romantic, lonely, vulnerable, full of pain and pathos and humor and joy, all the recombinant powers of the heart. Even the world's largest corporation recognizes his potent emotional pull when, in the late Fifties, it runs a magazine ad showing a man talking to a woman on the phone (their product), saying, "I was listening to Miles playing 'My Funny Valentine,' and I started thinking of you." Miles Davis is a funny valentine.

———

"If I didn't play trumpet, I don't know what I would have done. I couldn't stay in an office. I'd do some kind of research. That W-H-Y is always my first word, you know. I'd do research, 'cause I like to see why things are, how they are, the shape and flesh and everything. I'm one of them motherfuckers. I'll never have an easy life. I'll always be in trouble because my nature is to say 'why?' to things I don't know anything about. And get in 'em and find out myself."

———

For six years, Miles researches pain and pleasure at his Upper West Side townhouse. He doesn't play trumpet, doesn't perform or record. There is no music in his head, and it's killing him, if his illnesses aren't already: arthritis, bursitis, stomach ulcers, throat polyps, pneumonia, infections, repeated operations on a disintegrated hip. The doctors move around the bones in his body. Miles moves around the pain with booze, barbiturates, and cocaine.

He cooks his famous bouillabaisse. He doesn't sleep. He calls his sister in Chicago to ask her what time it is. It's an excuse for contact. He goes to after-hours joints and provokes bar fights, throwing tantrums and ashtrays. He gets carried out, piggyback, by one of his right-hand men. Always, he's with one of his revolving platoon of right-hand men. He can't stand to be alone. He lives on the telephone and with the television on. His apartment looks bombed out.

———

> Many times he'd say, "Go to Leo's Liquor Store and get jugs of Mateus wine." And I'd go hang out with him at some girl's place. He'd say, "Here's your bottle of wine and your stash of coke," and then he'd go into the bedroom with his bottle of wine and his coke, and we'd sit there and wait for him to finish up whatever he was up to. It was weird. Calls at 5:30 in the morning, he says, "Get up here and keep me from killing Loretta." That was one of his girlfriends.
>
> I'd get up there, and Loretta and him would be going at each other with these huge scissors that you could just put through somebody. I'd have to break the fight up and hide the scissors, and he'd punch her out and I'd cool him out and he'd cool the police out to keep him from being arrested.
>
> —a right-hand man

———

Miles chases a man out of his townhouse. The man runs through his backyard and climbs over a wall. Miles tries to follow him over the wall but loses his grip. To break his fall, he puts out his hands, but his wrists are brittle with bursitis. He's in agony, stretched out on his stomach, screaming. A woman from a neighboring building leans out her window and shouts, "What's going on out here?" Miles shoots back, "I'm fucking your mother." Through all his pain, humor is his only home.

The backyard is about as far as Miles will go. He almost never leaves the apartment. He brags about being the best at whatever he chooses, and now he proves best at doing nothing. He's bored. He's rich. Under a special deal, CBS sends him an allowance whether he records or not. (Only he and Vladimir Horowitz have this arrangement.) A local pharmacy sends him drugs without a doctor's prescription. The press dubs him "the Howard Hughes of Jazz."

He stands on his sunken porch, drooling from a Heineken bottle, and introduces himself to a female passerby with a squeeze of her tit. Mick Jagger comes by to genuflect. It's been arranged. Miles keeps him waiting in his limo for hours and then decides he doesn't want to meet him. Sends the little limey away. He shoots happiness into his leg with a dirty needle and pays no mind until one day he can't walk. The infection is severe; Miles faces amputation. Another huge scar, and it's saved. CBS tries to interest him in recording projects, but his mind is divorced from his fingers. Doctors ask him if he wants to live. Friends expect a funeral.

———

When Miles plays, it takes a tremendous amount of aggression, because everything he plays is so hard. Well, if he doesn't use aggression on the horn, he gets it out with people. Chasing people, fighting, with guns, all sorts of things were happening up there: kicking people down the stairs, falling down the stairs himself. One time he was wrestling with one of his kids and broke his leg. He had to find an outlet for some of those emotions he uses in his work. And I wouldn't say Miles never turned his anger against himself. He's dabbled in everything not good for you. And I think some of his illnesses were his way of turning against himself, his masochism.

—Gil Evans

———

"I was just having myself a good time. But I don't like to lay back. I don't like to relax. Show me a motherfucker that's relaxed, and I'll show you a motherfucker that's afraid of success. When I was out, when I didn't work, Dizzy came by and said, 'Man get the *fuck in* trumpet and play it, motherfucker.' I said, 'Man, if you don't get out of my house, I'll break your fucking neck.' He said, 'No, you won't.' He's a funny motherfucker, boy. Dizzy say, 'Man, you're supposed to play *music.*' I said I didn't feel like it. But you know, he was right."

———

Finally, Miles feels like it. Though still phlegmatic and drunk, he's at long last bored with boredom. He's also not as wealthy as he once was. CBS cut him off his steady stream of advances in an effort to cut potential losses (if he never records again) and lure him back into the studio. Miles is still comfortable, but he needs to be more than comfy, and he'll have to work some to keep himself in limo trunkloads of new Italian shoes. Besides, this will be a challenge for a man who thrives on proving things—mostly to himself.

To assist him, he recruits a young, unknown, white, straight-arrow saxophonist named Bill Evans. Evans visits Miles every day during one of his hospital gigs, protects him during his late-night perambulations, runs his errands. Miles calls him at all hours, and Evans helps him form a new band. They have a sick father / healthy son relationship. Evans idolizes Miles, gives him energy and ideas, and Miles gives him his first gig out of college. He feels like it.

In the summer of 1981, at the Kix nightclub in Boston, Miles Davis makes his comeback appearance. He uses a battery-pack microphone on his trumpet, which gives him all the mobility his shaky legs will allow. He moves to the front of the stage for his solos, bends his legs into a squat, and hunches over the horn until the bell is inches from the ground. It's a protected fetuslike position. Spotting a kid in a wheelchair, he limps into the audience. The kid has no legs. Miles leans over the paraplegic, puts the trumpet right up to his torso, and plays a long, beautiful solo.

———

Cicely Tyson and Miles Davis are skinny and gorgeous after
going vegetarian for eight days at the upstate Pawling Health

Manor. *Their limo carted home cases of kiwi and papaya, bush-*
els of corn and apples, sacks of cukes, carrots, broccoli, pine-
apples, a tub of home-grown lettuce, and an encyclopedia of
carrot-cutlet recipes.

—New York Post, *November 4, 1982*

————

Cicely Tyson and Miles Davis have a love affair from 1966 to 1969. She wants to marry him, and he puts her on the cover of an album, *Sorcerer*. After they split, she calls him on New Year's Eve. He is not having particularly happy new years. She tells him to play his trumpet. He hangs up on her. She calls right back. Cicely Tyson will not take no for an answer. She calls all his bluffs, defuses all his games; she knows the hurting, shy little boy behind his gruff facade. One night she calls, and for the first time in years, he plays to her over the phone. As he falls back in love with the horn, he falls back in love with Cicely. In a midnight ceremony on Thanksgiving Day 1981, at best man Bill Cosby's Massachusetts estate, the honorable Andrew Young, mayor of Atlanta and former ambassador to the United Nations, marries Cicely Tyson and Miles Davis.

————

"Cicely was in Africa, I was in New York. Shit, I woke up one morning, I couldn't even move my fingers. It stayed like that for a month. I go to the doctor and he says you got the Honeymoon Paralysis. Honeymoon Paralysis, that's when guys get so tired from fucking so much that they go to sleep on their hand, and it wakes up numb. It was a stroke. And he told Cicely that I would never use this hand again, this one I'm drawing with here."

————

After his stroke and her return, Cicely takes Miles to her Chinese doctor for acupuncture. He responds well to treatment. He quits smoking, drinking, snorting, pill popping, replacing those old habits with new daily dependencies: Chinese herbs, mineral water, swimming, sketching, working out. (His doctor also tells him to cut down on fucking, but Miles has his limits.) Cicely takes Miles out to benefits, dinners, balls. Cicely goes on tour with Miles, lugging her food processor from hotel suite to hotel suite, carrying it on the plane from gig to gig. Cicely Tyson is giving Miles Davis a personality lift.

When heavy rains threaten to dislodge Southern California from the mainland, Cicely leaves the tour to attend to their Malibu house—one of five shared residences. This upsets Miles, breaks his rhythm. But Cicely will be in his hotel room shortly. A Houston TV station is showing her portrayal of Harriet Tubman in *A Woman Called Moses*. Miles tells his guest to turn on the set. He's speaking on the phone to his veteran drummer Al Foster, who's staying across town at the Holiday Inn. Miles stays in a different—better—hotel than the rest of the band. "Just turn the channel till you see black people. . . . No, man, not the basketball game. . . . there." A few minutes of Grandma Moses and he orders, "Man, I don't want to see that shit, turn that off. Fuck that, man, Zeke told me they're gonna hook her up to a wagon and all that shit. I can't watch that, hitching her up to a wagon. Make me mad. I'll go off, laying here by myself. Make me break some glasses." The guest says it's nice she's on TV, wagon or no. "Yeah," croaks Miles, "it means I'm gonna get a raise."

———

Miles saunters onstage in Texas in a black fedora, sunglasses, black shirt, a red leather fringed jacket, black pants, and bright red high-heeled boots. He fiddles with his synthesizer, which he's taken to playing concurrently with the trumpet—one with each hand. He does this because "synthesizers are programmed to sound white—that's how prejudiced white people are—so if I don't play over it, it will sound mechanical." Onstage, among Miles' six musicians, are three whites: Bill Evans and guitarists Mike Stern and John Scofield. Among his loves are Sinatra and Stockhausen. Miles Davis is no racist.

The music he now plays is conservative. In the absence of a new conceptual statement, Miles curates his career during each performance, presenting a collage of up-tempo funk, oddly strolling blues and singsong ballads haunted with Spanish and bop motifs. His trumpet playing is extravagant, by turns dramatic and desultory. He is healthy enough now to play anything he wants on the horn, but seems unsure where to take the music as a whole—and so he toys with it.

He walks forward and backward across the front of the stage. He stops to stick out his tongue, show a lady his wedding band, count the photographers, with whom he plays cat-and-mouse. He attempts to empty his spit valve on one, puts the bell of the horn over the camera of another. Laughter from the audience. Night after night, in the middle of a solo, he hitches up his pants to expose his fire-engine-red boots. Much applause. Then he engages saxist Evans in a humiliating little game of call-and-response, in which Evans inevitably fails to mimic exactly the master's lines. Shouts of "School him, Miles" and "That's not what he told you" come from the crowd. Miles then directs Evans over to the electric piano—sometimes by the elbow—as if to suggest a new instrument. When he tires of Evans' piano solo, he points him back to the saxophone. It's a denigrating display of a "good-natured joke," and it makes Evans feel about one foot tall.

This transformation of Miles from a forbiddingly serious artist to a showbiz ham is an unexpected joy for some concertgoers, a depressing experience for others. As for the band, they're in a different hotel even on the same stage. No matter. Miles is having fun cashing in on his comeback. He commands top dollar in the States, an eighty-dollar ticket in Paris, and receives nearly $100,000 a night in Japan.

He also now insists, "I don't like to record at all, live or studio. I just do it to make money." He releases three post-comeback records that seem to prove his point: 1981's tepid warm-up *The Man with the Horn*, '82's live hit-and-miss *We Want Miles*, and the new *Star People*, with its wandering blues and fragmented funk. Still, he wins a Grammy for *We Want Miles*, though he insists he doesn't know why. He wins it for that red leather fringed jacket.

When he goes to Los Angeles to perform on the show, he stays at Beverly Hills's sumptuous L'Ermitage Hotel. While there, he orders his white Ferrari airlifted from New York to L.A., towed from the airport, and parked in front of the hotel. The Ferrari can't be driven—it's had a mechanical problem for some time—but it's a stage prop that makes him feel good. Miles Davis feels good these days.

———

Miles Davis comes off the plane last in Austin, Texas. An airport employee waits to drive him to his limo in an electric cart. It's too long a walk to the terminal. Miles eases up onto his seat. Shrouded by his fedora and shades, he listens to last night's concert on his Walkman. He wears his headphones upside down, under his chin, and presses them to his ears to block out the spastic beeping of the cart, warning all that King Tut is coming. Travelers headed for their gates part to let him pass. They all stare. Those that know nudge each other, and a middle-aged woman drawls, "It's that Davis man." A few heads tilt under cowboy hats, like dogs' heads do when they're puzzled, as if to ask: who could this man possibly be?

MILES DAVIS

Interviewer: Ben Sidran, January 1986
from *Talking Jazz: An Oral History—43 Jazz Conversations*
(Expanded Edition, 1995)

Ben Sidran is truly a musical renaissance man: a pianist who tours regularly in Europe and Asia; a producer of recordings for Van Morrison, Diana Ross, Mose Allison, and Jon Hendricks; a singer with twenty-five solo albums, including the Grammy-nominated *Concert for Garcia Lorca,* under his belt; a composer (the scores for *Hoop Dreams* and *Vietnam: Long Time Coming*); host of National Public Radio's landmark Peabody Award–winning series "Jazz Alive"; and author of the cultural history of jazz *Black Talk*, his memoir *A Life in The Music,* and *Talking Jazz: An Oral History*, from which the Miles conversation is taken.

The following interview was held on a warm January afternoon on the terrace of Miles Davis' beach house in Malibu, California. I had gone to the house with Miles' record producer, Tommy LiPuma, who had told me that Miles' reputation for being a difficult man to talk to was not necessarily true. From the minute Miles opened the large wooden front door to his house and invited us inside, it was obvious that Tommy was right. In fact, when Tommy introduced us, Miles inexplicably gave me a hug. Throughout the interview, which took place during the afternoon and, informally, continued well into the evening, Miles was gracious, humorous and extremely generous with himself and his time. The interview began with us sitting across from each other at a table, with a bowl of potato chips in-between. Miles had a sketch pad in his lap and was drawing with a large magenta felt-tip pen.

BEN: As we're talking, you're starting to do some drawing. I know that drawing has been a big part of how you've been spending your time for the last several years. Have you always been involved in drawing?

MILES: Yeah, my father taught me and my brother. Actually, I showed my brother how to sketch. My brother can see anything and draw it right off, you know. But he doesn't have any imagination like I have.

BEN: So imagination is . . .

MILES: That's it. In everything. Imagination.

BEN: My impression is that your drawings are related to your playing in some ways, the gestures . . .

MILES: What it is is balance. If you make a drawing on a page, you have to balance it, you know. And that's the way most everything is. Art, music, composition, solos, clothes, you know, when you dress up . . .

BEN: Balance.

MILES: Yeah, a little over *here*, a little *there*, a little *there*.

BEN: I first noticed your sketches on the cover of one of your record albums a few years ago. Is drawing something you've always done, has it always been part of your artistic process, or did you become interested in it again later in life?

MILES: Yeah, you know, I stopped for a while. I really started to sketch again after I married Cicely. Because she takes so long. You know how actresses are. They take so long to get ready for anything, you know. Rather than scream at her, I just started sketching. Especially on planes. After we had a close call going to Peru for the Miss Universe Contest. The plane dropped about 2500 feet and then dropped another 1000 feet. And you know everybody was . . . some people were crying. A lot of celebrities were on that flight. And then I started sketching, you know, cause it really scared me. That's really a trip to do that, to go through that.

So now when I fly from New York to California, sometimes I sketch. Most *all* the time I sketch. If I don't go to sleep, I'm sketching. And I've done sketches that took me five hours, you know, to finish. But it relaxes you, you know?

BEN: Are you spending most of your time in California these days?

MILES: Most of the time I try to. I try to stay here because of my circulation. It's good for my circulation. The cold weather really does a number on my skin in New York, and the air's dirty, the streets are dirty. But that pace in New York, I love that pace. I would never live out here all seasons. Just in the winter time. Either here or the south of France.

BEN: You really are a part of the greater art community, not just the music community. You're one of the few American jazz musicians to have made that transition.

MILES: From what to what?

BEN: From being thought of as a *player* to being thought of as an *artist*.

MILES: Oh, yeah. Well you know, if I was thought of any way else than that, I wouldn't want to be here. If I couldn't contribute. You know, I was telling some friends in Sweden if I couldn't do anything to help, even if I was in some other form of art, if I couldn't discover something or help the art, or find a new way to do it, you know, I wouldn't want to be here. I would just want to be dead. If I couldn't create. There would be nothing for me to live for. If I couldn't maybe write a composition that I like. Not somebody else; that *I* would like, and my *friends* would like. And they say "Yeah, Miles, that sounds good." If I couldn't do that, I wouldn't want to be here. It's selfish, I know. But geniuses are selfish. *[Laughs.]*

BEN: Part of your genius it seems has been to take groups of musicians and put them in challenging situations. Looking back over the output of your recorded work, the "newness" a lot of times stands out as much as anything. You're creating situations that force musicians to rely on their instincts rather than their habits.

MILES: That's right. It's the groups of people that you associate with, you know. It's not all *me*. It's them. People like Herbie Hancock, Chick Corea, those people that I work with. They're talented people. Especially when they get in their creative period. People have creative periods, periods where they *[snaps his fingers three times]*, like that, you know? And then if they could just *wait* on that, or recognize it when it's there. *I* recognize it in other people. I recognized it in Wayne Shorter and Herbie and Chick, Keith Jarrett, Sonny Rollins, different people, you know, Philly Joe, Red Garland, George Duke. He is something else, man. See, I saw that. I heard that. You know, he reminds me so much of Herbie. If Herbie would just slow down a little bit. George has great talent. Have a potato chip.

BEN: Thanks. *[Eating sounds.]* Again, part of the message of your music seems to be "be yourself," and you use minimalism to achieve this. Like those pretty notes you play, as opposed to a lot of notes.

MILES: Pretty notes! If you play a sound you have to pick it out . . . it's like the eye of the hurricane, you know? You have to pick out the most important note that fertilizes the sound. You know what I mean? It makes the sound grow, and then it makes it definite so your other colleagues can hear and *react* to it. You know what I mean? If you play what's already there, *they* know it's there. The thing is to bring it out. It's like putting lemon on fish. Or vegetables. You know, it brings out the flavor. That's what they call pretty notes. Just major notes that *should* be played.

And rhythms. I used to, a lot of times, I would tell Herbie to lay out. He wrote a couple of pieces that were up in tempo, and rather than have him play the sound for me, I played the sound for him to listen to, you know? The sound of the composition he wrote. Because if you have too much background, you can't play an up tempo and really do what the composer tries to give . . . to me. And I try to give to the fans and music lovers.

BEN: You talk about the "sound" of the composition, as if a song has a central "sound" to it, a sound source.

MILES: I try to get *his* sound, whoever is writing the composition. If I'm going to play something against that, I have to get the sound that *he* wants in there, without destroying and blowing over it, so as not to bury it. You know what I mean? So it takes a lot . . . it really takes a long time to do that, you know. But if you're leaning that way, it doesn't. But if you aren't, and somebody tells you?

When I was about fifteen, a drummer I was playing a number with at the Castle Ballroom in Saint Louis . . . we had a ten piece band, three trumpets, four saxophones, you know . . . and he asked me, "Little Davis, why don't you play what you played last night?" I said, "What, what do you mean?" He said, "You don't know what it is?" I said, "No, what is it?" He said, "You were playing something coming out of the middle of the tune, and play it again." I said, "I don't know what I played." He said, "If you don't know what you're playing, then you ain't doing nothing."

Well that hit me. Like *bammm*. So I went and got everything, every book that I could get. To learn about theory. To this day, I know what he's talking about. I know what note he was talking about.

BEN: What note was it?

MILES: It was a raised ninth. I mean a flatted ninth. *[Laughs.]*

BEN: This conversation about the "sound" of the composition brings to mind the recording *Kind of Blue*. As you know, *Kind of Blue* is probably the number one jazz record on virtually all the jazz critics' lists.

MILES: Isn't that something.

BEN: Does the success of that record surprise you, Miles? It seems to have been such a simple record in a lot of ways.

MILES: Not back then. Because Bill Evans, his approach to the piano brought that piece out. He used to bring me pieces by Ravel. Like the Concerto for Left Hand and Orchestra. Have you heard that? It's a piece Ravel wrote for his friend who went to the army. He came back, but he was a pianist and he lost his right hand. So Ravel wrote a piece for Left Hand and Orchestra, for piano.

And Bill used to tell me about different modes, which I already knew. And we just agreed on something and that's the way that album *went*. We were just *leaning* toward . . . like Ravel, playing a sound with only the white keys . . . and it just came out. It was like the thing to do. You know what I mean? Like an architect, all of a sudden *all* of the architects in the world start making circles, you know, like Frank Lloyd Wright. All his colleagues are leaning the *same* way at the *same* time, you know?

So it was Bill, and it was *made* for Coltrane, you know, that kind of thing. Because I used to give him a lot of chords. I would give him five chords to play in one chord, and I would tell him that he could play either way. He was the only one who could do that. But I got it from Rachmaninoff, modulating from key to key. Bill and I used to listen to Bartok and, ah, what's his name, who wrote "The Fire Dance"?

BEN: Khachaturian?

MILES: Yeah, Khachaturian. I would give Coltrane little chords like that to play, you know, against one "sound." You know, instead of saying like "D dominant seventh," or something like that, you could play under the chord, over the chord, or a minor third up from the fifth of the chord, you know?

But it has to be a dramatic player like Trane was, who can just turn you on with the sound of one note, and a group of notes. The only two people I ever heard doing that was Charlie Parker and Coltrane. You know, that's the only two I ever heard in my life do that.

BEN: You mean the rhythmic freedom in the way they run changes?

MILES: Coltrane didn't start playing like that until . . . a girlfriend of mine in France, one day she said, "Miles, these guys want to talk to you; they want to give you a trumpet or something." So I said, "I don't want to talk to anybody." She said, "They just want to talk to you and maybe you can pick out a couple of trumpets that you want." So I said, "OK." So I also got a soprano sax for Trane. And he never put it down. It was on a tour with Norman Granz. He played soprano sax in the bus, in the hotel, every day, all day, 24 hours a day. And he got that "sound." And then I gave him those chords and he just *went*, you know? Because he wasn't playing like that before. Sometimes a player plays so *loud* that it locks in with the sound that he *left*. You know, like *bammm*. It blocks out everything else. So I gave him all these options. I mean, it sounds technical, but you have to think like that if you're an artist, you know. You have to know how to do different things.

BEN: Hearing you talk about this session, I am struck by the fact that like Duke Ellington you would prepare music for your players, rather than bring music to them and say "play this." Your music really does come out of the people you are hanging out with and recording with.

MILES: Yeah, that's right. Duke is one of my favorite composers. Just lately, I have been hearing in my head "Rain Check," that he wrote.

BEN: You mentioned Coltrane's sound on the soprano saxophone. At one point, Coltrane said that he had been hearing a higher sound in his head, but that it wasn't until he got his hands on the soprano that he was actually able to realize what he had been hearing internally all along.

MILES: Right. See, it takes a long time for guys to develop. You know what I mean?

BEN: How come nobody else can get *your* sound? It's a simple thing, a gesture almost, but it is very difficult.

MILES: I have my own sound, because when I was like this [*gestures with his hand low to the floor*] my trumpet instructor, I loved the way he sounded. He was black and he used to play with Andy Kirk, and the low register like Harold Baker. And you know, I just leaned toward that cornet sound, you know, like Nat Adderley plays cornet? But it's just a "sound." And it's popular. [*Laughs.*] You know, like years ago, composers . . . the reason you read about Beethoven was because he was the one they could understand. The other ones, you know, that they couldn't understand, they didn't get mentioned. So my tone must be the easiest for somebody to hear. You know, like Louis Armstrong, that kind of sound.

But you see, your sound is like your, it's your sweat. You know, it's your "sound." Lester Young had his sound. Coleman Hawkins, Clifford Brown, Fats. You know, there's no more "sound" today. Freddie [Hubbard] has a sound but it's . . . during those days when you didn't hear anybody to copy, guys got their *own* sound. But now that you have so many records and cassettes, it's not about sound, you know what I mean? That's the reason they can put the sound in a keyboard [a digital sampling device]. But it's the white sound in the keyboard. It's the white trumpet player's sound in the keyboard.

BEN: You can't put the black sound in a digital sampling keyboard?

MILES: Nobody's done it yet.

BEN: That's an interesting point, that before there was such a wide recording distribution, people were forced to develop their own sounds.

MILES: Forced to play without . . . they didn't have anything to listen to, you know? But you *would* watch guys play an instrument and you would like the attitude, the concept, the way it *looks*, the way they hold it, the way they dress. But nowadays, they have . . . I saw maybe three trumpet players in Lionel Hampton's band, and they were white, right? They all sound alike. Wynton [Marsalis]. He doesn't have a distinctive sound. But Freddie almost has. Woody Shaw is a real creative trumpet player. He's like Dizzy. They might do anything. I mean you can still get a good solo out of Dizzy 'cause he's . . . he really turned my brain. And Charlie Parker. You know those guys, they did a number on my head. As far as me learning.

BEN: How did they do it?

MILES: They just opened it up.

BEN: You mean just hearing and watching them?

MILES: See, what they were thinking, it put a stamp on what I was thinking, that it was OK to go like that.

BEN: You mentioned people getting excited just watching a player. I remember you said one time that we could know everything there was to know about your playing by watching how you stand.

MILES: It's a certain way, like when I play, sometimes if I play about that high from the floor *[holds his hand out three feet above the floor]* it's another sound that you can get . . . there might be one over there *[raises his hand higher]*, maybe be one up there, but I never go higher than that. Standing straight up maybe.

But I found out in Juilliard that if I stayed any longer, you know, I was going to have to play like a white man. I was going to have to *act* like a white man toward music. The direction, you know what I mean, so I left. Because there was certain things you had to do, or a certain way you had to play top get in there, to be with them. And I didn't come all the way from St. Louis just to be with a white orchestra. You know, I turned down a lot of those.

But I found that I could go my own way. I said to my friend Freddie Webster, I said, "Freddie, I'm going back to St. Louis . . ." And he was one of those who said, "Man, you know if you go to St. Louis, back to St. Louis and them hooges and crackers there, you're going to get mad and blah blah blah . . . you know, you might get killed." So I said, "No, I have to go tell my father that I'm gonna leave Juilliard." He said, "Why don't you call him up?" I said, "Uh uh, not my father. I can't call him up and say I'm going with Bird and they do *this* and Dizzy is *this*." You know, my father was a professional man. He was a surgeon. So I caught the train, I went in his office, he looked up and said, "What the fuck are you doing here?" I said, "As soon as you get through." He was working on a patient. He's a dentist. So when he got through I said, "This music is happening. I'm learning more down there, what *I* want to do, than at Juilliard." My trumpet instructor at Juilliard is *still* in the Philharmonic Orchestra, New York. But I couldn't do that, you know? So he said, "OK." So I said, "Save your money." So that was it. But I couldn't stay. I couldn't stay.

[He looks at the sketch he's making.] Damn, am I messing up something right now?

I couldn't phone my father from New York and tell him that. Duke Ellington he knew, but not Dizzy and Bird and Monk and Coleman Hawkins. Although we did have a record of "Body and Soul." And Art Tatum. That's the only records we had in our house.

BEN: Those two records?

MILES: Art Tatum and Duke with Jimmy Blanton. Blanton is from St. Louis, from my home town. Oh yeah, I had Bird with Jay McShann, "Hootie Blues." And Basie. Yeah, we had a few, but that was after I knew what I wanted to hear. Cause those bands, those days, Earl Hines and Jimmy Lunceford . . . Sonny Stitt was with the McKinney Cotton Pickers, and they heard about me in St. Louis and they wanted me to go with them, and my mother wouldn't let me go. And I said, "Ah, shit!"

BEN: You got there by going to Juilliard instead.

MILES: Right.

BEN: These days [what] you're talking about seems so far away from today. The times, the way music was treated by the players . . .

MILES: Yeah, I know. Something else gets in your mind, in my head, but those are good memories for me, you know.

BEN: It seems people today, even musicians, do have difficulty keeping interested in the music, when in the past, it was everything.

MILES: You know, it's because they don't take the time out to learn different things. They wouldn't take time out to do that. A jazz musician that you call a jazz musician . . . I was reading this damn thing in *The Times* about jazz legends. These legends shouldn't have to call people and ask them, can we play here and stuff like that. I don't do that. I would *never* do that, you know. I didn't get into music just to make money. If I wanted to make money, I know what to do.

BEN: It seems a major thing has happened to all music, not just jazz, and that is it's moved from music that was *captured* in a recording studio to music that was *manufactured* in a recording studio. It's a whole different premise now, the way music is being made. How was recording your latest album, which is done with drum machines and sequencers, different from the way you used to make a record, where you came in with some tunes, did them and left? Do you approach it a lot differently or does it feel the same to you?

MILES: It's easier.

BEN: Really?

MILES: Um hum. Because I show the guys I'm working with what I want. I write it out or play it. And then by the time I get to the studio, it's all on tape. You feed it right into the board. And all I have to do is play over it. It's easier like that. I like to went crazy trying to make *Decoy*. I mean I threw everything out. Now, I just take a studio, we use a drum machine to keep it in, 'cause I tried to put things together in *Decoy*, and they, you know, the ones that didn't have a drum machine, the tempo was doing this and doing that. Musicians feel sad, they have personalities. Like Al Foster, and like some of them want to play and there's no part for them anymore. I can see they don't feel it. But rather than wait for two and three sessions for them to feel like it and learn the composition, they add to the composition, rather than playing over it. Like a lot of guys do, they play too many fucking notes. Like Mike Stern. I tell him all the time, I said, "Mike, you need to go to Notes Anonymous." You know, like Alcoholics Anonymous? I mean, it's much easier now for me.

Because, you know, like a guy like George Duke, he writes a composition, it's all there, all you have to do is play on it, and respect that man's composition. But you have to pick the people that you want.

You see, my voice is changing, because this is very touchy with me. I don't want to fire him, I don't want to fire these guys. But I do want, when a person writes a composition, you have to let that composition *soak* in. You know what I mean? You have to try to *see* or *hear* what the composer wanted, you know, and you have to play that *style*. Not that you're just gonna play *your* style in somebody else's music. If they composed it, they didn't want that kind of thing in there. And you gonna do it on every number?

So we don't need that. Or if you're in the rhythm section and the tempo drops, you get mad 'cause somebody tells you the tempo dropped. We don't need *that*. We have time and it's right there. As long as electricity is *on*, the tempo is like *that*. And you don't have to use an excuse like I can't play with the drum machine, you know, there's no excuse. If you're a musician, if you love music, you would want "Body and Soul" to sound like "Body and Soul."

BEN: Well, what about "Body and Soul," and what about those classic songs?

MILES: Those songs to me don't exist, you know? I'm not gonna play that shit. We don't have time for "Body and Soul," and "I Got Rhythm," you know? Or "So What," or "Kind of Blue." Those things are *there*. They were done in that era, the right hour, the right day, and it happened. It's over, it's on the record. People ask me why don't you play this. Go buy the record. It's still there. What you like is on the record. You don't like *me*, and I don't want you to like me, because of "Kind of Blue." Like me for what we're doing now, you know?

I was put here to play music, and interpret music. That's what I do. No attitude, nothing. That's *all* I want to do. And I do it good. 'Cause my colleagues say "Yeah," you know what I mean, and that's enough for me to keep doing what I do.

I stopped playing the trumpet. Dizzy came over to my house. He said, "What the fuck is wrong with you? Are you crazy or something?" I say "Man, you better get out of here." He said, "No, I'm not either." He's like my brother, you know? But that's it for me. All the rest, people think I do *this*, I do *that*. Yeah, I do *that* and *this*. I might do a lot of things, but the main thing that I *love*, that comes before everything, even breathing, is music. That's it, you know. Nothing. I buy Ferraris, yeah, but music is always there. Right here.

BEN: And that means that you're going to have to keep hanging out with musicians . . .

MILES: That's right.

BEN: And you're going to have to keep your ear tuned to the radio, and you're going to have to plug in all the latest equipment?

MILES: Right.

BEN: Because you can't go back.

MILES: Uh uh. I can't.

BEN: As we've been sitting here talking, you've been drawing. And it's almost been one gesture, drawing and talking . . .

MILES: Right, it's the same thing.

BEN: I got one more question for you. The song "Nardis." How did you happen to name it "Nardis."

MILES: I can't remember. It might have had something to do with nuclear power. I wrote it for Cannonball [Adderley]. I think I just liked the name. What does it mean?

BEN: I don't know, but it's my last name backwards.

MILES: No kidding? No kidding. I don't know, but that's a nice name, man.

LIGHTENING UP WITH THE PRINCE OF DARKNESS

Interviewer: Nick Kent, May 1986
from *The Dark Stuff: Selected Writings on Rock Music*

Over the course of his thirty-year career, veteran music journalist Nick Kent has written for *New Musical Express*, *Spin*, *Details*, *GQ*, *Mojo*, *The Sunday Times*, *The Guardian*, and *The Face*, for which he originally wrote the following piece (included in *The Dark Stuff*). A musician as well, he played guitar with the Sex Pistols in 1975 and later fronted his own band, the Subterraneans. He lives in Paris.

In this interview Miles discusses his contentious relationship with Wynton Marsalis, his unreleased collaboration with Prince, and his views on Mick Jagger, Sade, and Sting.

It was a priceless photograph. Not a classic because of the technique involved, or the lighting, but just because the cameraman had been lucky enough to be there, backstage at Carnegie Hall, and was able to capture a vision of magical confrontation in jazz history. He got to shoot together, face to face, an aging, ornery Miles Davis and a young, earnest Wynton Marsalis.

The new star trumpeter Marsalis was the one in the business suit while Miles, for this particular shot, looked disconcerting, like some hack SF moviemaker's vision of a species of ebony mutant lizard. "Macabre" might be an apt description of Miles's strained put-on of a half-smile over the usual backdrop of cat black. It's an effect he's the undisputed master of, even now, with his receding hairline and shoulder-length curls.

Still in his mid-twenties and clearly a novice next to Miles's propensity for achieving the look of perfect disdain, one still has to admire Marsalis for having the brass balls to get involved in a heart-stopping eyeball-to-eyeball encounter like this. Both are seated, their shoulders hunched, squaring off like boxers trading looks instead of punches, seemingly lost in a contest over who can outglare the other. Marsalis's stance is tense. It's as if he's facing off the once-great Miles Davis who, as far as he, Marsalis, is concerned, has opted to become a buffoon: a role his flinty visage may refute but one which his garish pop star clothing (not to mention the music he's been playing for some time now) cannot deny.

Davis, however, looks barely phased by Marsalis's scrutinizing eyes. His expression, furrowed but adamant, seems to be sizing up this gifted young big-mouth, whose work so clearly apes his earlier idioms, adding considerable polish and an undeniably brilliant technique, but not taking these reference points anywhere further. In short, Miles seems to be drinking him in and spitting him out.

Marsalis came away from the encounter with his suspicions confirmed, or so he later claimed. He and Miles had spoken and, according to the former, Miles was more than ready to acknowledge the younger man's challenge.

"Miles just stated outright that what he does now is a joke," claimed the 23-year-old prodigy.

"Hell, you know, I believe music—just about everything—*sounds* better these days. Even a car crash sounds better!"

Everything, that is, except the voice of Miles Davis, a charred husk of sound, hoarse and cancerous. He is talking about whether today's computerized recording studio techniques have benefited or damaged the musical process as he, a forty-year veteran of performing and recording, conceives it.

"It's never been better! Damn right! Are there drawbacks? *None whatsoever!* Hell, some damn *critic*"—the word is spat out—"might disagree but, you see, he don't know! All this shit about me bein' better in the old days . . . Music bein' better. That's reactionary thinking from pitiful motherfuckers who weren't even there. The old days . . . shit! In the old days, when it was alive and happening, jazz was made by this breed of musicians; I'm talking here about creative guys but they were also weird, idiosyncratic cats! Strictly night people, y'see? Somethin' about that night time made it real conducive to playin' blues. . . . You know, 'Blues After Midnight'?" He gives a parched chuckle. "Oh yes! Attitude shit.

"Now these cats," the bone-scraping croak continues, "they always had their problems. I mean, I'd book a session, let 'em know where and when . . . Hell, half the cats wouldn't be there! I don't *need* that kind of mess! Runnin' around these fuckin' dives lookin' for the drummer, say, 'cos he's probably off somewhere scorin' dope! Bass player's a goddamned lush, always goin' too far at the bar. Trying to get him sober enough to stand up! Meanwhile, the sax player, he's pawned his goddamned horn! *That's* the old days, far as I can recall! Nobody needs that shit! It's demoralizing! Critics say, 'Oh, Miles and Bird . . . the golden days!' What's *golden* about a cat all strung out on dope playin' a goddamned instrument with half the keys mashed up? Hell, you tell me 'cos I'm damned if I know!

"But, see, nowadays, you walk in the studio, there's these machines that'll do it all for you. Drum machines—hell, you just program the motherfucker, press a button, you got that 'bim, bam, boom' twenty-four hours a day if you want it. You want it to stop? Press another button! Synthesizers too. I love 'em! I mean, say you want something with a little Brazilian sound, a Samba-type groove, then add in a little English-type music, plus a little bit of that Parisian sound—you can mix 'em all together. Get a whole new hybrid! Break down those frontiers! I love the textures you can get from those things. You don't have to be coppin' for no drum machine either. Don't have to wait till midnight to get the stuff down. *That's* how I like to work now. That's how it should be."

The above is stated absolutely deadpan, with no room for any kind of rebuttal. Nor is one forthcoming because—Good God almighty—this is after all *Miles Davis*. The *legendary* Miles Davis. The *indefatigable* Miles Davis. The *wickedest, canniest, deepest, slickest, baddest* musician this century will ever see. Miles Motherfucking Davis, three months from his sixtieth birthday, forty-seven of those years spent as a card-carrying professional musician. Miles has decided to open up a little. That's why he's talking down, and I am listening up.

Maybe it's that voice, emanating from a veritable graveyard of a larynx, a voice variously described as "demonic" and "chilling," that's keeping me in my place. And those descriptions were made seventeen years ago, before thirty more nodes were surgically removed from Davis's larynx, so that now the sound is quite other-worldly: at its most vitriolic, he spits out his syllables like a coiled snake dispensing some deadly poison.

Still, in the "old days" he disdainfully refers to, Davis was a man of few words. In the fifties, having tossed aside the Juilliard School of Music's academic straitjacket to become sorcerer's apprentice at Charlie Parker's mercurial creation of bebop, finally usurping his master's role as kingpin of jazz attitude (four years of heroin addiction having further distanced his bourgeois origins), Miles invented a whole new concept of "cool."

Ross Russell's *Bird Lives!* captures the Miles persona of that era better than any other account:

> *Aloof and disengaged, Miles turned his back on the audience, walked off the bandstand to sit alone, indolently smoking a cigarette and staring with stony contempt at the customers. Outwardly, he seemed unemotional, unconcerned and indifferent. Inwardly, he seethed with hostility. One of his favorite ploys was to shake hands with an old colleague, applying an excruciating jujitsu grip, and, as the other writhed in his grasp, hiss "I never liked you!" Or comment in a snaky voice, "Man, you're getting old."*

When Davis was approached by fans simply wishing to express their love of his music, he would stonily respond, "So what?" *Then* he could afford to behave with such imperious disdain. The Miles Davis enigma has been shaped in the balance between knowing when to react and when to stay silent. In the twilight sixties Davis, notorious for not giving interviews, suddenly granted youth-oriented periodicals considerable access, spending inordinate time discussing his new attitudes, his reasoning, allowing young scribes lavish insights into the thought process of jazz's most controversial figure.

Then, just as the seventies began, his guard once more shot up. Having been lauded as "the Picasso of invisible art" (a term coined by Duke Ellington), he was dubbed "the Howard Hughes of jazz." By the mid-seventies his enigma level was unsurpassed. This stemmed more from his bizarre nocturnal forays, however, than the quality of his music, which at that time sounded morose, directionless, perplexingly impotent. Between 1975 and 1980 he refused to enter a recording-studio, maintaining an ominous silence as rumors of illness and drug dependency persisted.

Yet Miles has never been short of *direction*. Trace his progress: early years as Parker's oft-humiliated protégé/errand-boy; the recording of *Birth of the Cool* in 1949; the four years as a heroin addict and pimp; the formidable comeback in late '54 through '57 and the seminal modal excursions with John Coltrane (best exemplified in *Kind of Blue*); then, the equally historic Gil Evans collaborations (*Sketches of Spain* and *Porgy and Bess*) of the early sixties. In 1968 Davis opted to work with electric backing creating more seminal music; *In a Silent Way* witnessed Davis's tonal transformation from the elegant blue melancholia of before to the fire-red extrapolations that reflected a mood of vehement black militancy then gripping America.

Commencing with the electric church tonalities and brooding spiritual interludes that made 1969's *In a Silent Way* one of the last albums to break new ground while still affording Miles the total reverence of his hard-line critics, he became immersed, more and more disdainfully rejecting Western concepts of structure, harmony and texture in favor of other idioms. The hypnotic drone imperative to Indian music was fused with an ever-increasing fascination with interplay around the repetition that has always been at the heart of Afro-American music.

At first, Davis worked at a furious rate, clearly elated by the sense of "command" and "possession" that the music summoned forth. *Bitches Brew*, his new recording, became the seminal work around which that dubious collation, jazz rock, was finally established, not to mention reaping sales that transcended the quantities sold by all other "jazz" records. Gigs were obsessively taped, Miles often performing to predominantly white, young rock audiences as a support act to the likes of Steve Miller, Neil Young and the Grateful Dead. Although there were many formidable moments of supreme ferocity and excitement (the most sustained example being Davis's soundtrack to the movie *Jack Johnson*), the odyssey from 1970 through to 1975 was one that that clearly showed signs of taking a down-bound curve both aesthetically *and* commercially. Miles's "African Bag" —with track titles culled from the names of African guerrilla movements—had begun to exclude other existing textures and juxtapositions. One was suddenly presented with the albums such as *On the Corner*, with its upmarket cocaine dynamic and up-front "street black culture" attitude. Two live albums from a Japanese tour, conducted some four months before his retirement, show just how lamentable Miles's focus on his music had in fact become.

Davis's retirement at this point has been explained by many factors. He had suffered from bursitis in his wrists and shoulders, a hip joint seemed to be disintegrating, insomnia was wasting him as much as the plethora of pain-killing drugs—codeine and morphine-based medications—which were helping to inflame several stomach ulcers. Probably worst of all, his muse wasn't functioning (his greatest periods of creativity have tended to always correspond to his having attained a condition of excellent physical fitness) and the sound emanating from his horn, bereft of its former spitfire alacrity, sounded incredibly weary and mournful, almost bordering on an aural evocation of cancer of the soul.

For Miles Davis the years between 1975 and 1980 were ones shrouded in mystery, intense rumor and speculation. Davis's numerous ailments—arthritis, bursitis, stomach ulcers, throat polyps, pneumonia, infections, repeated operations on the disintegrated hip—weren't helped by their victim's own attempts to stave off the pain and boredom by means of ingesting formidable supplies of alcohol, barbiturates and cocaine. Injecting various chemicals into his leg with a dirty needle, he suddenly found one day that he was unable to walk and was told he had to face up to the possibility of having his leg amputated. There was another operation and it was mercifully saved, but Davis continues to skin his teeth at fate.

"I was just having myself a good time," recalled Miles to writer David Breskin two years ago.

Miles's eighties recordings have been greeted to date with a bemusement that he himself has done little to dispel. In 1983, having recorded and released three albums since his return to the studio in 1980—*Man with the Horn*, the live *We Want Miles* and a Gil Evans collaboration, *Star People*—he brushed them all off, baldly stating, "I don't like to record at all, live or in the studio, I just do it to make money."

Ironically, it was 1985's *You're Under Arrest* that caused him to change his tune. It was to be Miles performing contemporary AOR numbers: pop songs he'd heard on the radio in his Maserati, taped and arranged with his trumpet as the lead instrument. Having noticed how well received his poignant live version of Cyndi Lauper's "Time After Time" had been with audiences, he went on to record, according to guitarist John Scofield, some forty songs, including several Toto compositions, Tina Turner's "What's Love Got to Do with It," Dionne Warwick's "Déjà Vu," even Lionel Richie songs and Kenny Loggins's "This Is It."

Ultimately, Davis included only the Lauper tune, the Toto-penned Michael Jackson opus "Human Nature" and D-Train's "Something on Your Mind," opting instead to toss in some original material composed by group members and arranged by himself. This gave the finished product a schizophrenic quality symptomatic of artistic tunnel vision, but Miles didn't care. He claimed *You're Under Arrest* to be his all-time favorite recording. "The best album I've ever made!"

That album's executive producer, Dr. George Butler, is not one of Miles Davis's favorite people. Since the abdication of Teo Macero, Miles's producer since 1959's historic *Porgy and Bess*, Butler became the key figure in playing midwife to the final recordings Davis did for Columbia/CBS. He considers Miles somewhat unpredictable:

"I think that sometimes his whims can get a little out of control. They're in his head, these little gems, so to speak, but the problems arise when it comes to translating them into a reality. He tends to need someone to pull them all together. Even when I worked with him, I often didn't know how it would work out as a complete project. I was usually always pleased with the results. He's still very clever. One of the very, very few."

Dr. Butler is of course a diplomat. He refers to Miles Davis as "unpredictable" in the same way an adversary might refer to his opponent as a hell of a guy. Miles, never renowned for being pragmatic about discussing those he dislikes, doesn't lay the blame for his problems with Columbia, the label he has been with for thirty years, solely at Butler's door, but he does get rather testy whenever the name is brought up:

"He [Butler] came up to me, this is a year and a half ago, and said, 'Miles, you should really put that version you do of "Time After Time" out. It could really take off, be a smash.' I said, 'George, I told you that six motherfuckin' months ago!' But he hadn't heard me then, he wasn't listenin'! He just don't know! See, I can't stand a black man who wants to be bourgeois! That's a pitiful condition to be in.

"Another time"—Miles is getting warmed up, that demonic croak lubricated by cantankerous phlegm—"that George, he phones my house. My daughter takes the call. She comes to me later, tells me he rang, right? I ask her what he wanted. She says, 'George wants you to phone and say happy birthday to Wynton!'" His voice registers a sound of exasperated contempt. "Happy birthday to Wynton! Shit on *that*! Who does he think I am? See, George, he reckoned it would make a nice gesture! He don't understand me, never did!"

Wynton Marsalis, whose virtuoso prowess as a trumpet-player is coupled with his controversial and reactionary views on staying true to the fifties spirit of jazz, has provided the media with their most recent opponent to Miles Davis. Dr. George Butler signed Marsalis to Columbia, and when the latter, at the precocious age of nineteen, successfully fronted Miles's classic sixties quintet— Herbie Hancock, Wayne Shorter, Ron Carter and Tony Williams—when Davis himself refused at the last minute to take part in a one-off reunion gig, a confrontation was inevitable.

"Wynton . . . well, he's a good player," mutters Miles reasonably. "No two ways around that. But see, I don't want to get caught up in some jive feud thing here. That may be *his* style but it's not mine! He's good but his whole style of presentation, his look, his manner—it's dumb! *Plus* he could do with a few lessons in couth! What's he doin', messin' with the past? A player of his caliber should just wise up and realize it's over. The past is dead. *Jazz is dead!* The whole context has changed and people gotta . . . Why get caught up in that 'old' shit? Music shouldn't be this stuff you play to kid your audience into thinkin' that's the way it was. Don't no one start telling me the way it was. Hell, I was there! *They* weren't!

"Some people, whatever is happening *now*, either they can't handle it or they don't want to know. They'll be messed up on that bogus nostalgia thing. Nostalgia, shit! That's a pitiful concept. Because it's dead, it's safe—that's what that shit's about! Hell, no one wanted to hear us when we were playin' jazz. Those days with Bird, Dizz, 'Trane—some were good, some were miserable. But, see, people don't understand why I get so touchy sometimes. I just don't want to talk about that stuff. People didn't like that stuff then. Hell, why you think we were playin' clubs? No one wanted us on prime-time TV. The music wasn't getting across, you dig! Jazz is dead. Goddammit. That's it. Finito! It's over and there is no point aping the shit."

Miles isn't angry, just adamant. His rationale is often wrought from a logic that is genuinely ingenious. At other times his philosophy is shaped from one overall point of view that he is Miles Davis and you're not. Musing over the previous outburst, he settles back to consider the simple fact that, *finally*, black music has overtaken the white folks' watered-down approximation of same in the market-place.

"Hell, y'know, Lionel, Quincy, Michael, Prince and me together . . . Now wouldn't that make for one hell of a movie?"

This is where Miles Davis chooses to pitch his tent in 1986. After thirty years as a Columbia recording artist, Miles Davis is releasing his first Warner Bros. album. Initially entitled *The Perfect Way*, after the Scritti Politti number on side two, it has since been renamed *Tutu* after one of five Marcus Miller originals that predominate among the product's contents. Speaking to Warners' A&R kingpin, Tommy LiPuma, late last year, little was forthcoming with regard to how much cash the label had spent on procuring Miles. "It's standard practice not to divulge such matters," said LiPuma, another good-natured pragmatist. It was, of course, "a great honor to have Miles Davis on the roster. He seemed to like our way of thinking. He felt that his association with Columbia had gone as far as it could. He was looking for a change." Not that LiPuma and Warners had any grand schemes for Miles. "Let's just say that, when you come to work with a musician of Miles's pedigree, it's not fitting to try and tell him what to do."

This, of course, was early in the relationship, before LiPuma would become executive producer of the first WB release, at that point tentatively penciled in for a late spring 1986 release. LiPuma had definite ideas about suitable collaborators: Thomas Dolby, for one, was high on the agenda; and Lyle Mays, the young keyboard player best known for his collaborations with guitarist Pat Metheny. It was then that Prince's name came up. LiPuma reacted immediately. "I felt that Prince might not be too conversant with certain idioms pertaining to Miles's playing. But his work on the *Family* album displayed a keen awareness of the dynamics inherent in be-bop so, yes, indeed, Prince was ideal." Miles refers to Prince excitedly as "that funky little dude." By the time of the release of *Around the World in a Day* in 1985, the aging trumpet legend had become totally smitten with pop music's most audaciously resourceful stylist:

"Prince wrote me a letter and along with the letter he enclosed a tape of instrumental tracks he'd recorded by himself in his studio. And in this letter he wrote, 'Miles, even though we have never met, I can tell just from listening to your music that you and I are so exactly alike that I know whatever you play would be what I'd do. So if this tape is of any use to you, please go ahead and play whatever you feel over it. Because I trust what you hear and play.' I mean, now here's a dude . . . Hell, he's got it *all*! Multi-musician with a damned vengeance! As a drummer he can hold it down, you know what I'm sayin'? There's not many cats can nail it tight what with current technology makin' most drummers damn near obsolete. As a guitar player . . . he puts *out*! Plus, he's a goddamn great piano player. Matter of fact, he's about as good as they get, and I've worked with the best, I should know!"

Did anyone say Wynton Marsalis? Prince is who Miles Davis checks out now. The way he works in the studio—"sheer genius," reckons Miles. Hell, it didn't even drag Miles's bag one bit when the boy genius suddenly called through for some typically enigmatic reason requesting Miles *not* to release the tracks he'd sent him. "I don't know exactly why he decided not to let 'em come out but I respect the boy.

"Do you know who Prince kinda reminds me of, particularly as a piano player? Duke! Yeah, he's the Duke Ellington of the eighties to my way of thinking. Only, back in them old days you couldn't get a man like Duke on primetime. No, white audiences didn't want to see that elegance, that attitude, 'cos it was too intimidatin'."

This leads Miles straight into another of his harangues:

"See, this is the thing you got to take into consideration here. Time and again, the black man has fucked up. He starts out with his shit together, then he gets damn side-tracked by white folks, y'know, whisperin' in his ear, 'Hey, son, you should do this. Clean it up. Tone it down. Get smart. Get jive. Get yourself a goddamn monkey-suit or somethin'.' The white man, see, he's always out to mess with our thing, packaging it, strapping some jive label on it. And the black man, he's fallen for it mostly every damn time. Why? 'Cos he's greedy, that's why! Hell, it's shameful what I'm sayin' here but it's the truth. White man starts talkin', the black man, he listens up, starts seeing dollar signs flashin' and the next thing you know he's sellin' himself out everywhere. See, *attitude*—that's what the black man's got. Attitude! The white man wants it so bad, he can't help but be jealous. So, over and over, the black man's music gets fucked with. But he don't see it happening 'cos greed is motivatin' him more than his better instincts."

That deadly voice, shorn of any pitch beyond a gravel-toned whisper, rarely registers an emotional counterpoint to these tenacious accusations. He does sound particularly melancholy, however, when I query him about the absence of Darryl Jones, the young bass-player featured in last year's ensemble. Davis, during 1985's European gig, had tended to behave somewhat mischievously towards his fellow musicians. At London's Festival Hall he kept resetting keyboard player Robert Irving III's synth patterns to no appreciable avail, while in Paris he brought on John McLaughlin in what could only be interpreted as a bid to upstage guitarist John Scofield. Only Jones was left unscathed by such questionable antics. At Montreux, Miles had even sidled up to the bassist and, his arm around his shoulder, gently coaxed him to the lip of the stage for an ovation. This occurred, mark you, just before young Darryl passed an audition to work with Sting on his *Dream of Blue Turtles* record and tour.

"Darryl? I had to let him go. Same shit as I've been relatin' to you. That boy . . . I liked him too. He could play so good and, hell, I felt kind of paternalistic toward him in a way. But then Sting comes along, offers him more money, high-class accommodation and all that stuff. And Darryl, he got so damn confused, I just said to him, real diplomatic and cordial like, 'Man, what do *you* really want?' You know what he said to me? Darryl said, 'Miles, I wanna do *cross-over*.' God, I almost threw up! Here's a boy with real potential and yet here he is falling for that white man's corporate bullshit. Cross-over my black ass! Don't *mean* nothing! . . . Anyway, the boy has made his choice."

Curiously, Miles then goes straight on to praise Sting's music.

"See, I like Sting! Yes, indeed! He's good and I like his songs—some of 'em—and his voice. He ain't like Mick Jagger rippin' off Wynonie Harris, shakin' his goddamn skinny white ass and pretendin' to sing the blues. You can take that shit, toss it in the river, watch it sink. Fuck that shit!

"Sade—her too, y'know. I think she's interestin' right now 'cos, see, if she works on her attitude she could shape up to be something good. Like, when she comes on the radio, I keep hearing intimations of Lena Horne comin' through.

Now, she ain't that good—yet. But, like Lena singin' 'Stormy Weather'—hell, it's something and God knows I love her but, damn, that 'my man is gone' shit . . . Women ain't like that *now*! Like, Billie [Holiday] singin' about 'her man' and how she ain't worth shit without him. That was real but that was *then*. It would be a lie to do that shit now though, 'cos women have changed. They don't need no pimp! They don't stand for that shit and that's how it should be. I know 'cos I used to be one myself! Had me seven women when I was strung out back in them old days [*mordant chuckle*]. And I'll be damned if I can remember their names . . .

"I don't like to think back to that. Women nowadays are into control. Like that song by Michael's sister, Janet [Jackson]. That's what's happenin'! Anyone who wants to go back to the past, they're too scared to live in the present."

Miles Davis at sixty years of age is one funny motherfucker. Almost garrulous, when once he was prone to the absolute minimum of verbal expression, the hostility that seethed within him seems now to have dissipated, leaving only the ghost he chooses to inhabit when his pride is threatened.

What remains is indeed complex, hard to pin down. His rhetoric is loaded with odd contradictions yet he remains consistent in more crucial areas than many of his most zealous followers seem able to fully comprehend. He has been criticized for playing at being a pop star but, first, he's not playing and, second, he's always been a pop star: a larger-than-life luminary whose name is recognized by multitudes of people to whom the medium of jazz expression is as alien as the ancient Greek alphabet.

Those millions may know of him because of his notorious past: getting busted for narcotics and a heavy-duty arsenal of weaponry in '52; getting savagely beaten by white cops outside Birdland; having New York mobsters in late '69 riddle his red Ferrari with bullets—the fact that Miles later would boast that both his adversaries (cops and mobsters) had been "dealt with." Even the plethora of decidedly chilling rumors regarding his imprisonment of women for days on end during the dark endless nights of the seventies. Maybe they know him because of his single-handed elevation of the fifties black hipster to a realm of treacherous grace which, through his sartorial elegance, his fat, bright sports cars, his beautiful statuesque ebony-skinned women friends, his feisty hyperactive persona, spelt out to all and sundry, *I'm not as good as you are. I'm better.*

And even if they may have only glimpsed one of the five separate periods of extraordinary creativity his muse has been responsible for setting into motion, they recognize that Miles Davis is *great* in a way that defies placing him in an immediate peer group.

Now, after six years of shaping himself up for that sixth shot at further greatness, Miles feels that he is ready. His divorce from Columbia is indeed a brave move, mainly because in so doing he has granted the label the right to release any number of extracts from what John Scofield claims to be some 300 hours of unreleased material; music, moreover, made by a younger, considerably more tenacious personality, whose artistic temperament—the depthless blue pools of longing that lurk alongside the shanty-town flame-thrower and the blood-red splashes of tension—has set aesthetic standards his Warner Bros. product is going to be hard pressed to keep pace with. Teo Macero hinted at the extent of an extraordinary mother-lode lurking in the vaults when he referred to late-sixties sessions alone:

"Everything that was done in the studio was recorded. Miles is probably the only artist in the world where everything is intact. I just edited out what I wanted, then the original went back into the vaults, untouched. Whoever doesn't like what I picked twenty years ago, they can go back and re-do it."

The very idea of a man as prodigiously talented as our subject having to do battle with his own past triumphs at the age of sixty seems one that would cause even the most self-assured egocentric sleepless nights. Miles, however, *seemed* totally unnonplussed by the concept:

"Did I relinquish the rights to my unreleased stuff on CBS? Well, yeah, but it don't scare me, hell no! 'Cos even if they want to release 'em they wouldn't know where to find 'em! Teo, I don't reckon he knows either. And what if they did? Hell, they put the shit out, it won't sell. There's enough old shit of mine bein' issued as it is. I never seen any of it toppin' no charts. No one wants to buy it. Why should they?"

Again, that overwhelming adamancy, that patented *I'm Miles Davis and you're not* vehemence. His past, those gone-dead decades he refuses to contemplate affectionately, filter through, but he looks back only in disgruntled sideways glances. Those damn critics, the same plebeians who used to bug him when he was *DownBeat*'s pet king-pin—they're the ones who fucked with his music:

"It's like Duke [Ellington], he said it first and he said it best: 'If it sounds good, it is good.' But them damn critics, they always had to complicate matters. Pigeonholing my music, they turned off my potential audience. First they said, 'Ah, well, this is Cool,' or 'This is space music.' Voodoo? Teo, he came up with that label for *Bitches Brew*! There wasn't no damn voodoo goin' on, it just sounded good to Teo and, hell, I wasn't in no mood to argue with him! There's more 'bottom' to that stuff. More rhythms.

"*Now* they say *Bitches Brew* is a goddamned masterpiece but, hell, those critics hated it. Jazz-rock, my ass! They couldn't see that I was hip to the way black folks were hearing *their* music. I wanted to play for *my* people! I was listenin' to James Brown 'cos James was the Man—still is—where rhythm is concerned. That's what all the stuff I put out from *Bitches* on out was based on."

Like the Janet Jackson record he admires so much, Miles Davis has always understood the need for control: to possess a firm grip on his life and his artistic destiny. The son of a bourgeois black family, he has succeeded in transcending the values of his upbringing, thwarting a debilitating drug habit, leading numerous formidable ensembles, controlling the music to suit his mercurial personality while, as Herbie Hancock once observed, keeping his musicians intimately involved. He has succeeded, above all, in both understanding and manipulating the key forces at work controlling a vicious business: the power of money, the power of image and taking hold of the power of mystique as a means to an end. As an artist, his role as catalyst is one that has involved an incredible facility for controlling often ridiculously opposed forces, harnessing a tenacious, fiery temperament to front music that has been mostly defined as "the sound of sadness and resignation." Similarly he has controlled his music's progression while rarely, if ever, turning his back on "tradition," always aiming for the "sophistication of simplicity."

This year has seen a number of interesting developments. Duke Ellington, Miles Davis's beloved predecessor, twelve years after dying of pneumonia in a New York hospital, has had his profile embossed on a postage stamp. Bill Cosby, the black American comedian who was best man at Miles's wedding to actress Cicely Tyson five years ago, boasts the most popular prime-time TV sitcom in the U.S. And Quincy Jones, Miles's old running buddy, with his Grammy nomination for *The Color Purple*, the movie he co-produced, has been putting Michael Jackson through his paces in the recording studio for another billion-dollar disc. Miles is ready to ascend from the comfy confines of prestigeville. America's TV heartland has already witnessed this curious image of a man, a skinny figure with gleaming skin and what remains of his hair curling all over his shoulders: his hands grip (what else?) a trumpet, his lithe form is slouched against a small Japanese scooter, his eyes stare out at the viewer with imperious disdain. Then the voice, emanating from that shredded, node-less killing-floor of a larynx, mutters, "I ain't here to talk about this thing, I'm here to ride it." Miles Davis, renowned for his taste in the slickest, fastest sports cars, has followed Lou Reed, Grace Jones and Adam Ant into advertising Honda scooters. The money helps but it's exposure he wants. And is getting, if the role of a pimp in a recent *Miami Vice* episode is any indication.

Amazingly, at sixty Davis looks better than he has in over fifteen years. At a diminutive 5 feet 4 inches, he nonetheless looks formidably exotic, in fact nothing short of stunning. In 1981 he looked awful—overweight and obviously very, very ill. Today he looks like a male Grace Jones—rail thin, his attitude in his heels, his eyes torching with a gleam that can turn from depthless calm to deadly volatility.

"Yeah, I'm lookin' good, ain't I! I swim every day when I'm touring, have acupuncture, stick to these special herbal diets. Don't fool around anymore. Dope is *out*! Used to get through maybe a third of an ounce of cocaine a day, stay up forty-eight hours, smoke six packs of cigarettes in that time, drink spirits, take sleeping-pills. I was killin' myself. I was a hog and that's . . . See what I mean by black people bein' greedy?" He credits his wife, Cicely Tyson, for saving him from death when his body was racked with painful ailments. His currently gleaming skin and trim physique he attributes to a more unusual source:

"I went to the place called La Prairie. This fella I know took me there. They give you these shots: I got eleven of 'em so far! They consist of, well, basically, it's unborn sheep glands! Yeah, that's right. Goddamn *sheep*! These shots, they make your eyesight sharper, make your skin softer too. Make your sex organs much—[*he issues a low grunting sound*]. It's funny though!" he continues, clearly drawn to the subject. "I didn't feel that eleventh shot! The other ten—I felt them, no damn problem! But that last one . . . man, maybe those sons of bitches ripped me off! Y'know what I'm saying. . . . And this shit costs a hell of a lot for it to be pumped into you. OK! Anyway. [*He pauses.*] Y'know this stuff—when it's in your bloodstream, it's like you're high on cocaine or somethin'. But it's natural! I'll tell you the feeling this stuff gives you. Say, you're sitting in your living-room and suddenly you start feeling kind of hungry. Well, with this sheep-shit pumpin' through your veins, you don't ask nobody to go and fix you something to eat! Hell, no, you get off your ass, go in the kitchen and go fix it yourself!"

Miles is clearly getting quite lively in his old age. With *Tutu* already long completed and down at the pressing-plant, Miles casually states that its successor has already been recorded:

"It sounds hot. Y'know, this new stuff I'm comin' out with is better than anythin' I've recorded in the past. Hell, I don't *think* so I *know* so! I want this shit to get out to the people. That's why I left Columbia, see. I kept tellin' 'em, 'If you dumb motherfuckers keep puttin' labels like "Contemporary Jazz" on my damn records, you might as well stick them up next to beans and molasses!' Might as well throw 'em in the river! I had to leave. It was degrading! Now *they* say, 'Jazz is comin' back; there's a revival.' They don't know! Same people that think that, they'll say, 'Bird died for his art. He had a good ole' time doing it!' He died on his knees, man! Broke and broken! He wasn't in control of nothin'! People love that bullshit, though. See, death—it's safe. All those fuckers too scared to feel anything: they get into that 'mystique' bullshit.

"If I was dead now, they'd love me whatever shit came out with my name on it. Hell, if I was a recluse doin' nothin', it would be the same. Fuck 'em. I don't like to relax, lay back on my old stuff. Show me a motherfucker who's relaxed and I'll show you a motherfucker that's afraid of success."

I ask him about his renowned quote: "I've got to change. It's like a curse." Is it still a curse?

"Funnily enough, someone else asked me that question. That quote, maybe I said it once but now I believe, hell, I *know*, it's a blessing! My music is better than ever. To my ears, I check out the contemporary heavyweights. I'd like to work with Quincy. He understands, Prince, *he* understands. In fact, Prince said to me, 'You don't ask God for what you want, you thank him for what you've got already.' Now I'm not a particularly religious person, but, hell, I can empathize!"

Max Roach, the great jazz drummer, stated, weeks before the first clumsy return to the stage in 1981, "Miles is a champion. Champs always come back." With Muhammad Ali brain-damaged, James Brown an egomaniac bordering on lunacy, and most other "champs" burned out, the vision of Miles Davis at sixty, still fit and functioning with formidable élan, is one worth cherishing.

"Don't you ever count me out!" he muttered as we concluded our talk. I don't intend to. Neither should you. After all, he's Miles Davis and you're not.

———

Five years after this was written, Miles Davis died from complications arising from pneumonia at his home in Los Angeles. He had been musically active up until the very last days of his life.

MILES DAVIS: THE PICASSO OF INVISIBLE ART

Interviewer: Robert L. Doerschuk
Keyboard, October 1987

Keyboard, a music-related magazine covering electronic keyboard instruments, often goes beyond discussions of products, the industry, and innovations in technology to include revealing interviews such as the one that follows, one of the very few in which Miles discourses at length on the pros and cons of pianos and synthesizers, their influence on his music, and past keyboardists with whom he's worked.

Robert L. Doerschuk spent seventeen years on the staff of *Keyboard*, where he won two ASCAP–Deems Taylor Awards for excellence in music journalism, and later served as editor-in-chief of the now-defunct *Musician*. The coauthor (with Keith Jarrett) of *88: The Great Jazz Pianists* and editor of *Playing from the Heart: Great Musicians Talk About Their Craft*, he is not only a widely respected music journalist but also a noted jazz pianist who has sat in and jammed with Wynton Marsalis, B. B. King, Prince, Stevie Ray Vaughan, Jerry Garcia, and many others. He lives in Nashville.

Walk into Miles Davis' house, north of Los Angeles on the last lip of land overhanging the Pacific Ocean. The windows open toward the water, and icy air pours through the entryway. A living room opens before you, its ceiling lost somewhere high above, its walls adorned with handsome artworks, most of them moody African-influenced studies, probably by Miles himself. A couch runs along the rim of a sunken area, facing a giant screen on which the stars and starlets of *Porky's II* frolic with incongruous insouciance.

Though it's just a short stretch from the front door to the action inside, you have to make a detour to get there, around a Yamaha grand piano, whose silhouette carves a dark outline against the brightly lit interior. Miles' piano reminds us of the keyboard parts that have woven around his magic trumpet lines for more than forty years. And what a fabric these parts form! Thoughtful tapestries from Bill Evans, earthy textures from Horace Silver, mysterious empty space laid out by Thelonious Monk, spicy jagged patterns from Chick Corea, cool electric hues from Herbie Hancock, sonic rainbows from Josef Zawinul, one image after another, stretching from 52nd Street in New York to the pastel jungle of *Miami Vice*.

There is nobody like Miles. Sure, other musicians have transcended changes in music—Coleman Hawkins blowing bebop sax with kids half his age 35 years after touring with Ma Rainey. But no one has been as in control of the changes as Miles. The first real alternative to Dizzy Gillespie–style bop trumpet, the first to explore so-called cool bop, the first real master of electric jazz, the first jazzman to take rock seriously. As the years passed, Miles faded in and out of sight; just as macabre rumors began spreading, there he was again, his back to the audience, blowing his steamy muted horn and people's minds.

Today, Miles Davis is unique in the world of art. He has been through more than a few hard times. He has been playing professionally since the age of 15, and was rooming with the doomed saxophonist Charlie Parker in New York while a student at Juilliard just four years later. Drugs, death, and music have made him tough and tender. Shielded behind wrap-around shades, he has attained a guru-like status. Musicians hang on his approval, sometimes expressed in silence, sometimes in his chilling sepulchral rasp.

Contradictions abound in the Davis persona. He switches masks frequently, alternating between forbidding and playful. "I don't want to be compared to any white musician," he growled in a Dec. '84 *DownBeat* interview. Yet most of his bands have been salt-and-pepper, reflecting his desire to work only with the best available musicians. And Miles himself has voiced his admiration for such classically white players as Harry James, while excoriating Cecil Taylor and certain other black new music icons. Yet, on such albums as *Bitches Brew*, he broke ground himself in the realm of free-form improvisation—a triple play in the contradiction game.

At the heart of his art is another meeting of thesis and antithesis: "Less is more." Unlike most of his early colleagues in bebop, Miles seldom overplayed. His solos were short and clipped, usually restricted to the trumpet's midrange, and often riddled with broken notes. Whether this style grew out of a chops deficiency is beside the point. What matters is that even the very young Miles knew his limits. And as the years passed, he was able to build within and around those limits a musical edifice so complex and dynamic that it outshines the gaudier monuments erected by his flashier peers.

Knowing thyself and thy limits may seem easy on paper, but it's a hard lesson to master, in life as in music. Miles has managed to nail it down in both disciplines, and many of those who have worked with him now carry that idea with them in their musical endeavors. As Keith Jarrett put it to us, "My greatest tribute to Miles would just be to be aware."

For this reason, Miles' impact reverberates throughout the music world. Many of today's most influential keyboardists, in particular, are alumni of one Davis band or another. In everything from their solos to their synthesizer programs, his spirit lingers, perhaps most significantly in the more liberal role keyboard players now take within rhythm sections. As far back as *Kind of Blue*, on which Bill Evans' voicings moved beyond mere comping and defined the texture of the music, Davis encouraged his pianists and, later, synthesists to reconsider their accompanimental roles. Their function became more coloristic, and their work a complex mix of intuitive understanding of ensemble interaction and freedom from a set score. Chick Corea remembers being terrified on his first gig with Miles: "I was shaking in my boots," he recalls. "First of all, there was no rehearsal, and the music was very challenging. I didn't know any of the songs. Miles just said, 'Go up and play.' I did the best I could. I did a lot of improvising." The experience helped steer Corea toward the free style he would later explore in *Circle*.

The more latitude Miles allowed his band, the more he allowed himself to recede. Frequently he let his musicians contribute compositions to his albums; several Hancock pieces are on *Nefertiti* and *Sorcerer*, and almost all of *Water Babies* was written by saxophonist Wayne Shorter. For long stretches of *Bitches Brew* he even moved from the studio to the control booth, leaving Corea, Zawinul, and the band to cool along on their own. Miles encouraged his sidemen to think along similar lines. Shorter and Hancock remember him advising them *not* to practice their repertoire at home, in order to keep their performances fresh. Sometimes, before slipping from center stage, Miles would give cryptic instructions; guitarist John McLaughlin, on his first session with Miles, was asked to play as if he didn't know his instrument. Davis' influence on the guitarist had grown by the time they recorded *Jack Johnson*: McLaughlin's playing is less glossy and far more cocky than anything he would do after Miles. During this solo, Miles is absent—yet, as an extension of his "less is more" approach, his persona envelops the music.

Miles' fearlessness in the face of musical change is another important bequest to his sidemen. After hearing Zawinul play electric piano on saxophonist Cannonball Adderley's recording of "Mercy, Mercy, Mercy," he immediately grasped the significance of the new music technology. It was Miles who introduced Hancock and Corea to electric keyboards. In both cases, with Hancock on *Miles in the Sky* and Corea on *Filles De Kilimanjaro*, he simply pointed at the instrument and said, "Play that." For both keyboardists, it was the first step into a new musical era.

Over the past few years, Miles has returned to his earliest interest in pop repertoire. Cyndi Lauper's "Time After Time" and Michael Jackson's "Human Nature" now take the place of such earlier Miles staples as "Someday My Prince Will Come" and "My Funny Valentine." The marathon exercises of the *Bitches Brew* and *Live/Evil* period contrast now with his more recent albums, *Decoy*, *You're Under Arrest,* and *Tutu*, on which he offers concise performances spiced with rich sampler/synthesizer textures and street beats reflecting everything from reggae to go-go.

How does he keep so tuned in with what's happening in music, where so many other musicians ossify into styles of the past? "It happens gradually," he explained to writer Sergio Albonico in an unpublished *Keyboard* interview. "Like the sounds you hear on the radio—commercials and stuff like that. If you're a thinking musician, like I am, you're aware of your surroundings, like cars. The metal and plastic changes, [so] accidents don't sound the same. My music is influenced by today's sounds. With synthesizers, there's always something new. Keyboards have something added every year. Horns are being used less on dates. All this influences and changes your sound—the texture of the music and the arrangements."

Not that Miles is completely happy with synthesizers. In the Dec. '84 issue of *DownBeat*, he told Howard Mandel, "Hey, talk about prejudice, dig this: The synthesizer sound for trumpet is a white trumpet player's sound. Not my sound, not Louis' sound, or Dizzy's sound—a white trumpet sound. It is! And the only way I can play it is to play over it with my trumpet. . . . They have to get that sound together; you should have a choice on a synthesizer between a black and white sound." Perhaps this problem is solved, at least as far as Miles is concerned. This month he is scheduled to receive his Perkiphone, a MIDIed trumpet built by J. L. Cooper. With Miles blowing, it's hard to imagine any synth program sounding too WASPy.

Miles' current band is about as contemporary, in sound and feel, as a band can get in '87. The bassist, Darryl Jones, played in Sting's ultra-hip *Dream of the Blue Turtles* group. Percussionist Mino Cinelu, formerly of Weather Report and Miles' *Decoy* and *We Want Miles* projects, returns on electronic drums MIDIed to an Ensoniq Mirage. Drummer Ricky Weldman comes from Washington, D.C.'s go-go scene. Saxophonist Kenny Garrett's credits include a stint with progressive trumpeter Woody Shaw. The guitarist, who goes by the name of Foley, was recruited on the basis of a demo tape by Davis' friend and frequent collaborator Marcus Miller. Foley lays his groove down on a Steinberger bass strung with four guitar strings tuned up a seventh (*D, G, C,* and *F*) for maximum funky pop. The keyboardists, Adam Holzman and Robert "Bobby" Irving III, tell their stories on page 82 [of this issue of *Keyboard*].

But Irving and Holzman are not always the only keyboard players in the band. Occasionally Miles puts his horn down and adds a few synthesizer fills, usually as cues or adjustments to whatever is happening in the music. There are some more extended examples of his keyboard work on record too, including the thoughtful melodic musings on "Freaky Deaky," from *Decoy*. He has a DX1, a gift from Yamaha, as well as other Yamaha gear. Onstage, though, he often plays his Oberheim OBXa, relying especially on one of his favorite patches, A-1.

Miles dresses contemporary too, as we learn shortly after arriving for our interview. He greets us near midnight at his California home in silk harem pants, a flowing silk robe, no shirt, and shades. He sizes us up and laughs: "Man, you dress like Bobby Irving! What is it with you keyboard players, man?" We take a break from *Porky's* to watch his guest shot in Cameo's "Don't Be Lonely" video. A friend, guitarist John Bigham, drops by with a demo tape.

Miles listens, leaning back on his couch and playing along on his own guitar as the ocean roars outside.

In another day or so, he is to start a long Euro-Asian tour with his band. For the moment, though, he pauses somewhere between Birdland and the unfathomable future to focus on the meaning of keyboards in his music.

———

When did you hear an electronic keyboard for the first time?
I think the first time was when I heard Cannonball [Adderley, saxophonist] play "Mercy, Mercy, Mercy," with Joe Zawinul. I think Joe probably turned me onto that.

What impressed you about it?
Just the way he played. You know, I first heard Joe play "Mercy, Mercy" on the piano, but he adapts to anything new. He can always find something to do. So it's safe to say it was him.

Did you feel right away like there was something in electronic keyboards that you could use in your music?
No, I didn't think that way about the instrument. That came later, when you find that you can get different sounds as prominent as that sound on the Fender [Rhodes]. The Fender Rhodes has no other sound; it has that one sound itself. But then Herbie [Hancock] played so good on Rhodes. See, I didn't look at it like that. I mean, you know how crazy I am about [bandleader] Gil Evans' voicings and chords and stuff. I could hear that you could write a bass line with the voicings that Gil did; we could put a little harmony on top [with the synthesizer], and it sounds full. The Fender picked up the meat of the sound, and when you double the bass it worked better than the piano. The piano never did anything from there.

So when synthesizers came in, you related their potential to the kind of work Gil Evans had done.
That was the only thought I had: What can I get to give me a cheap Gil Evans sound in a small band? That's the way I look at it—not just because it's electric. I almost forgot all about that.

How did you get to know the synthesizers?
You listen, and you talk to people. I'd say, "How can I get a brass sound that I like if I'm playing with five pieces?" Then somebody would say, "Well, the [Oberheim] OB-X is good."

You've played the OB-Xa a bit.
Yeah, but I don't get out of it what it can do, because I don't know that much about it. Adam [Holzman] shows me. I hired Adam because I couldn't tell Bobby [Irving] how to get the sound that Adam got. So, I don't know. You'd have to ask Adam. I said, "Adam, come on. You can go with us." So he left his truck out at the airport, and he came on. Adam was working in a store, showing people how to work the keyboards.

So Adam's main thing is to get the sounds you need.
Yeah, but Adam's soloing his ass off *now*!

He told me the other day he brought out a Yamaha KX5 portable keyboard onstage without telling you, and caught you by surprise.
That's right. I just laughed, that's all. He seems to have a lot of fun with it. People love Adam, too. The black people went nuts; they said, "Yeah!" [*Laughs.*]

When you began working with electronic keyboards, did that change your feelings about the piano's role in your band?
No, it didn't change that. You know, the guys who can play piano that I like— Keith Jarrett, Chick Corea, Herbie—they get that sound out of the piano. If you don't have them, you can get synthesizers and do something else. I had two keyboards, and Keith Jarrett played both of them; he played the organ and the Fender Rhodes.

That's funny, since he's so much into acoustic music now.
You know, Keith can do anything he wants to do, or play any instrument he wants to play—guitar, drums, saxophone. [Trumpeter] Fats Navarro used to do that. He used to play saxophone. You'd go to a rehearsal with Fats, and he'd get tired of hearing [saxophonist] Allen Eager playing all fucked up. He'd yank that

thing away and say, "Gimme that saxophone! If you're not gonna play it, *I'll* play it!" And nobody knew he could play saxophone like that, but he could play his ass off. But if I didn't have Herbie . . . You know, I always talk about Herbie and Wayne [Shorter, saxophonist], because that's the band we made the most progress in. But I've been where you don't even think of the piano. I mean, where's the piano gonna fit? If you got an electric bass, the balance is off. The piano has got that sound; you gotta get the sound out of it that Keith Jarrett does. That's professional sound, like Herbie gets.

A lot of musicians are going for piano sounds from samplers and piano modules, though.
Well, when you play acoustic, man, you gotta hear that rosin sound in the bass. You can't substitute that. But you can get another feel if the electric bass walks for a minute before you realize that you don't get no rosin and gut string sound. I bet you can duplicate that.

So what was the first synthesizer you actually owned?
A Yamaha. They gave it to me. I don't know what that was. See, what a synthesizer does, it makes a soloist hear what to do better. You don't have to strain your ear to hear a piano player. And piano players usually get in the fucking way. If they can play, they usually overplay. They don't complement a soloist. There's very few piano players who can do that, but Joe Zawinul learned it from playing with [singer] Dinah Washington. Herbie learned it from playing with [saxophonist] Benny Carter. I used to tell Herbie, "You don't need all of those notes in a chord. If you got the bass playing bass, and your voicings are right, the bass is on the bottom. If you can play three notes in a chord with that, you can get that sound. I found out years ago when I took Hindemith's *Kleine Klaviermusik* [Op. 45/4] apart to see how much harmony you got.

What you're saying is that the nature of the piano is to tempt good players to overplay, while synthesizers naturally lead toward sparser thinking.
That's right. And you can hear that in the soloists, if you're playing right. Now, Adam and those guys are still learning how to play behind the soloist. I tell 'em all the time, "Shut up!" Men have the biggest egos! I used to think that women had the egos because the woman dresses up and the man follows her, but that's

just a male/female thing. But men, they're motherfuckers, man! If their wives get in there, they'll overplay. That's why [basketball star] Magic Johnson is so good, man. He's a team player! He doesn't start showing off because his girl-friend happens to be there. It has to be a team! I've seen musicians turn up their amps because they want to be heard when they're playing a certain part, but the part doesn't mean anything if you hear it that loud. I hate to say it, but that's what they do. They go nuts with all their equipment.

Do you think that has something to do with age? Maybe the young musicians are just trying to check themselves out.
How long does it take you to check yourself out? You hear that the first night you do it. I have tapes of everything we do. I must say that Adam listens, though. All of them will listen, but if they do it, they'll do it once. Then the ego comes back. A man's ego is something else.

Judging from your concert in Los Angeles last December, it seems like Adam's style does balance out Bobby Irving's approach on the keyboard. . . .
That shit ain't happening no more.

Well, it sounded like Adam was mainly doing the solos, while Bobby was much more present in the accompaniment.
If you can hear him, he was too loud. You're supposed to be able to feel him, not hear him. I'm always telling tenor players, "You ought to learn to play with people, man." I could have the technician turn my trumpet up to where I can blast out the whole place, but that would make me sick, and I don't want to go to the hospital and have them put me to sleep. I'm that sensitive about my sound. It's the sound that makes the night go faster, and makes everything work. Don't make it be loud every night; make it be a challenge every night. That's the only thing I see about egos and synthesizers. It's not the synthe-sizer's fault. It's the guys who play the synthesizers, man. Look at Joe Zawinul! Joe's head is as big as this whole place, but he does what he says he's gonna do. He will not get in your way, because he learned that from Dinah Washing-ton. *I* learned it from being in those bands in St. Louis. You don't play while the singer is singing; you play when they stop! That's the basic thing in play-ing with a singer or a soloist. Bobby plays the same way every time, but I'll

tell him, "Bobby, don't play the turn back to the blues. Don't play nothin'." It's driving me nuts.

If men have such ego problems, have you ever worked with a female musician?
Shit, yeah! A woman named Mabel showed me how to voice my first chords. [Singer] Sarah Vaughan showed me things like "Embraceable You" and the chords on the piano. Dizzy and Monk showed me stuff. I asked Dizzy and Monk so many questions. Dizzy used to show me those minor sixths in the bass. I'd write this shit out as fast as I could on match covers, napkins, any kind of paper I could get a hold of, and I'd say, "Monk, what is that chord?" And he would always tell me. I'd say, "Did I play "Round About Midnight' right?" Carmen [McCrae, singer] plays good piano too. That's why they can sing like that. All good singers know something about the keyboard.

Did you start playing piano about the same time you started on the trumpet?
I don't know. I was thinking about that the other day. I didn't take that many lessons, but my sister used to take lessons all the time. It just came to me. And my mother played piano, which I didn't know until I was in my twenties. I heard her play some funky blues one day. I said, "Where did you learn that?" She said, "You haven't heard everything I can do," and I said, "Okay, okay" [*laughs*].

Didn't you take up piano again as a kind of physical therapy when you had your stroke several years ago?
Hell, no! My hand was paralyzed. I couldn't play nothing until I got acupuncture.

When you're working out arrangements for your band, how much of the synthesizer sounds come from your supervision?
If I'm in the band, it's gonna be my suggestions. I'll make the suggestions, but they usually know the sounds I want them to do. When their wives and girlfriends come in, that shit goes out the window. You have to remember that they don't know what to play unless you tell them. I'm crazy about the way Prince sounds, and the way Jimmy Jam and Terry Lewis do things, and Cameo. Larry [Blackmon, Cameo's drummer and leader] wrote me a composition, and that

shit was nice! He writes his ass off, man! I saw him in the beauty parlor, and I said, "Larry, write me a reggae."

This is the story. Years ago, when I wanted to learn how to box like my friend, my father said, "You want to learn something? Get the best to teach you." Okay, I got the best. So this guy Lee Black showed me something slick. He showed me how to pull guys in when the referee isn't there [*Miles illustrates by wrapping an arm around the writer's neck and drawing his face an inch or so from Miles' nose*], and hit him with the elbow. Lee says, "I want you to hear my son. He wants to be a musician." I said, "Lee, just show me the hook."

So anyway, I did Cameo's video, so when they played Radio City I went over there to hear them. I went backstage, and Larry was getting a massage. The security was tight, but I see Lee Black up there. I said, "Lee, what the fuck are you doing up here, man?" I thought maybe he was one of the bodyguards. He said, "Larry's my son! Remember when I brought him up? You told him, 'Music is like dope. You use it 'til you get tired of it.' Well, Larry said he never forgot that."

You did a video for one of your own records too—Decoy.
That wasn't nothing. I didn't like that so much.

Do you like the idea of videos, though?
Yeah. They're a lot of fun. What you get in videos is what guys like Larry and Prince think, and who should know more than them?

When you compose something, do you imagine visual images that go with the music?
Not unless I want to. I don't even have a name for the things I write. When I want to do something—make a video, whatever—my head is where I want it to be at that time, so I can tell people what I want, like Larry does.

I'd like to find out a little more about the instruments you own. I've heard, for instance, that Willie Nelson gave you an E-mu Emulator.
He gave me an Emulator. Gil [Evans] and I were using it, but somebody broke into Gil's house and stole it. I bought Gil an [Oberheim] OB-X and a drum machine too, and they stole that.

What kind of things did you do with the Emulator?

Gil was showing me how to use it. The name itself tells you what it does. You know, synthesizers don't bother me like you think, from the questions you're asking me. If there's some sound I want, I'll ask Adam, "What makes this sound?" Like I just told him, "You play too much reverb." So Rod tells me, "Well, maybe it's me." I said, "Man, I'm 'bout to knock Bobby and Adam out, and you're telling me you're doing the reverb!" The thing is, when you're in a band like this, it's got to sound like this [*Miles snaps his fingers*]. You can't have chords laying over. I don't like that. I told Adam, "White guys play the notes too long. I don't know why." When [guitarist] John Scofield used to play with us, man, he would play so far behind the beat, I'd say, "John, goddamn!" So Adam knows how I feel; he plays on top of the beat all the time. When those chords lag over, if they're playing with a lot of reverb, that's hard for me to play. I'm playing a phrase and getting ready to go to another phrase, but if I'm finished with the phrase and the chord is still going, it drives me nuts! Then, talk about a man's ego, if you say something, they say, "I thought you liked the way I play!"

Who have you worked with over the years who didn't have that kind of ego problem?

Bill Evans is the first one I can think of. And Gil Evans. Gil tells me that all the time. He says guys make him so sick playing solos. He calls it "duty playing," like there's certain things you're supposed to do on a saxophone when you get a solo. That isn't respect for the composition at all! That's just shit that you play on the saxophone, so that all the other saxophone players know that you know this too. It drives Gil crazy. I tell him, "You should be in *my* band for a while" [*laughs*].

But Bill Evans was easy to work with.

Yeah. And John Coltrane. Coltrane never did say shit [i.e., anything negative]. Listen, I got [saxophonist] Gary Thomas from Baltimore, and [saxophonist] Bob Berg quit. I called Bob up and said, "Man, you don't like us anymore?" He said, "You got a saxophone player. He's playing my shit!" Goddamn, I didn't know Bob was like that. I had Cannonball and Coltrane, and Coltrane and Sonny Rollins; they worked together fine. But I knew where he was coming from; he wanted that all by himself. I told him, "Bob, you play too long. Why did you come in on this part, where you weren't supposed to play?" He said, "Well, it sounded so good, I had to come in." I said, "Bob, the reason it sounded good, was because you weren't playing! You were listening to it!"

You've worked with a lot of great drummers too in the past, and now you've got live drums and drum machines at the same time. How do you put the two together?
You use the drum machine like a metronome. When you put a drummer with it, it starts to breathe. But, you know, people are always talking about electric this and electric that. All those things are just instruments! No two pitchers throw alike, and no two people are alike. You can't play like another person. If I could play like another person, I'd be playing like Dizzy, when I first heard him. Or I'd be playing like Harry James, or Roy Eldridge.

I've heard that you've been experimenting with the Fairlight Voicetracker [pitch-to-MIDI converter].
That thing that [saxophonist] Mike Brecker is using? My other roadie, Jim Rose, said, "We're gonna run you through the synthesizers" and all this shit. I told him I didn't need that. I'm having enough problems playing with what I got [*laughs*]. Not that I would shy away from it, but I don't want to play with myself. I want to play with other people.

That's one change we've seen in how music technology has affected the way people play. More and more musicians are working by themselves in home studios, rather than onstage with bands.
There's nothing wrong with that.

You don't think that has any negative effect?
It's according to what you're playing. I told you about how the egos come up. They're wondering, "Well, why am I here if I'm not gonna play? Why does he have me playing this part when I could push up past it?" But what you do [in solo recording], you can put out anything you want. You can have someone come in and overdub, and then take the synthesizer out. But I'm through looking at guys and saying, "You play this, you play that," and they don't feel like it. I had a lot of trouble with [guitarist] Mike Stern. He played the same thing, whole-tone chords, and when you do that, when you play a chord that can cover the sound of what you're trying to do, you spoil the concept of the composition.

Thelonious Monk used to play whole-tone runs a lot.

Monk used to zip it in on the seventh and put the chord there. But if you just lay down a track and have him come in, like singers do—Johnny Mathis used to do that years and years ago. I was thinking, "Damn, why doesn't that take away [from the composition]?" But it doesn't. It doesn't do anything. If you want to put it out, if you want it to sound just like you want it to sound, you do that. You bring in a few people. The one thing a synthesizer will do is it will sound as long as you pay the electric bill. You can have one note all the way through the piece. That alters compositions now. You can play off of that one. Sometimes I want the saxophone to play something; I'll just change the notes that sustain, and he'll play around that.

You did that when I saw your L.A. concert last December, at the end of "Human Nature."

Yeah. We put up certain notes and played around them, then we went into "Milestones." But when the soloist starts playing straight, then runs out of straight shit to play—sometimes they do it quick, sometimes it takes a little time—I just drop things on 'em, because I keep hearing them trying to get out of the mode we're playing in. Say we're playing on all the white keys; when they start playing a few black keys, it sounds wrong. So I'll put a cluster of notes in there, and then they won't sound that wrong. Then it's time for it to go out like that, to put a little wrinkle in the mode.

So you play some keyboards onstage?

Well, what I play is just little accents. Adam's always watching me, and he plays a lot of things I show him. He loves 'em. If I play something, and he looks at me and hears it, he'll pick it up. If I motion to him to put an accent on something, maybe he'll play it in the low register, and I'll say, "No, put it in the high register." But he follows eye contact. Bobby's a little old-fashioned, but he will play what I tell him to.

You know, Keith Jarrett once said that Miles Davis will work with a musician even if that musician can only play two notes, as long as those two notes sound good to Miles.

That's right [laughs].

So I'd like to find out what it is that attracted you to some of the keyboard players you've worked with. Red Garland, for instance.
I like the way Red feeds the soloist. Also, I was in love with the way Ahmad Jamal plays, and Red used to play something like that.

The next pianist you worked with after Red was Bill Evans.
Well, Bill had this thing for Ravel. We were both crazy about Ravel. He used to show me different things that Ravel did. He'd play me that *Concerto for the Left Hand* and show me the modulations that Ravel did. Gradually we went into playing modal things, like *Kind of Blue*. Bill was something else. It's a drag he's dead, because you can't hear him. I can't hear him play "Alfie."

Evans was more of a chordal player than a single-line player, wasn't he?
Bill played lines, but they were different. He and Keith Jarrett were different. Chick Corea is different. Chick knocks me out at that tempo [*Miles taps out a medium up tempo*]. Then you get Herbie; Herbie can do anything. He and Keith, I think they must have drunk the same dye [*laughs*].

You've done some work with George Duke too.
George Duke is another. George, Herbie, all of 'em are good musicians, good keyboard players. George knows what he wants to hear, just like Herbie.

You get so many interesting sidemen in your band. How do you find these guys?
She found him! [*Miles gestures toward a guest waiting in his living room.*] Jillian went to hear this guy play guitar. He's cold-blooded. Then John brought some tapes up, and said, "Listen to the other side." I listened to the other side; it was Chuck Brown and the Solar Searchers. The drummer [Ricky Weldman] was a motherfucker! I said, "Man, who the fuck is this playing drums?" Chuck Brown is from Washington; Mike is from Washington. I went to Washington. Mike says, "My cousin knows where he is." I said, "Tell your cousin to come over." So he does. Anyway, that's how I meet musicians. I told Gary, "I need another saxophone player. Who should I get?" He says, "Get Kenny, from San Francisco." That was the guy I wanted to get in the first place. So other musicians pick the guys for me. I saw Mino [Cinelu], and I hadn't hired him.

He's your percussionist?

Yeah. When I first saw him, I was getting my band together, and I said, "I want you to play." And Marion, he's too much, man. I had Aaron, Steve, and Vince. I had to let one of them go. I was sick about it. Damn.

Over the years you've gone from acoustic bass to electronic and sequenced bass lines. How do you decide what kind of approach to use in putting down a bass line?

Well, all of my bass lines, the ones I like, come from Marcus [Miller], when he was with the band. It's just the way he plays. Marcus walks in rhythm. If you want a model of a musician, I would pick Marcus, and Herbie, and Wayne [Shorter]. Wayne knows a whole lot of stuff. He's real laid back, but he's an artist. He can write music. Did you read the shit he said in *Spin*?

No.

Shit, man, you gotta read that. Joe Zawinul plays good bass lines too. But you get a guy like Marcus or Darryl [Jones, Davis' bassist], and you don't need to write a bass line. They'll find something. Darryl's always looking for something. He's got all them fucking pedals. But it ain't in the pedals; it's in his head already. He's a hell of a musician! He don't need no fucking pedals—not all the time. You know, I tried to get [Charles] Mingus in the band when I was with Bird [saxophonist Charlie Parker] and Max [Roach, drummer], but we never could get it together.

Mingus played with Duke Ellington for a while, didn't he?

Mingus wrote just like Duke Ellington.

How do you decide which songs to add to your repertoire? For example, Ray Charles talks about how he loves the song "Stardust," but has no interest in singing it himself. Do you have similar feelings about certain songs?

Yeah. A lot of them. Usually, when I like a song, I can't remember it, because I just like the way it makes me *feel*. But when I play it, I remember it. It's like knowing a girl and not making love to her; when you make love to her, it's different shit. If I play it, I always have to give it the respect it deserves. "Human Nature" was like that. And I used to play "My Funny Valentine." If I play ballads like that, with straight melodies, I have to like 'em in the beginning from the way they make me feel. But when I play it, that means I can play it any time I want. I have to make it sound like I like it, from the feelings it gives me, like it sounds okay without me, but when I play it, I have to make you like it like I like it.

Does your choice of songs depend on what combination of musicians you're working with at that time?
Like I said, when I hear a song that I like, I have to make everybody in the band like it when I play it.

How much do you actually sit down and play the piano for your own pleasure?
You know, if I were to play the piano for two or three days, I'd sound like a piano player that I like. But I'm usually doing this [drawing or painting], and when I do this, I don't do anything else. I can hardly get to the horn.

Do you write tunes on the piano?
Well, my mind is so fast that by the time I listen to a melody I'm doing on the piano, it's gone. Gil Evans tells me, "Man, I told you years ago, when you sit down to play, put the tape on! You don't have to like it, just give it to me."

My last question. A bass player I frequently work with told me two nights ago that his four biggest influences were Debussy, Beethoven, Duke Ellington, and Miles Davis . . .
[*Pleased and surprised.*] Oh, yeah?

. . . and he asked me to ask you how you feel knowing that so many people have that kind of respect for the work you've done over the years.
Well, it means that he likes music the way I like it. There are certain things you like, and you end up being 61, like I am. He probably just likes the way I went into doing things in music, and making it work, which is your whole life. I don't take no feeling after that. It doesn't bother me at all, him saying that, because I know how he feels. He must feel like I feel about music. I can't wait to wake up the next morning to see what's happening.

EXCERPTS FROM VH1'S *VIDEO HITS 1: NEW VISIONS DISK JOCKEY SHOW*

Guest DJs: Miles Davis, David Sanborn, and
Joe "Foley" McCreary
VH1, December 20, 1987

New Visions Disk Jockey Show, airing on MTV's sister channel VH1, which had occasionally shown one of his videos, was a two-hour program that Miles co-hosted. Between videos the unusually garrulous trumpeter chatted about a variety of topics, most interestingly on his habit and technique of drawing, which he took up on doctor's orders following a severe stroke in February 1982 that had paralyzed his right arm.

Miles on the Video for "Tutu"

MILES DAVIS: This is *New Visions.* We're gonna play—what are we gonna play, David Sanborn?

DAVID SANBORN: Yeah, "Love and Happiness."

Video of "Love and Happiness" is followed by the 1986 video "Tutu Melody," directed by Spike Lee, from Miles Davis's 1990 release Tutu.

MD: That was "Tutu" by me. Foley was on it. It's a good way to relax. I told Tommy LiPuma, the producer, I said, "Tommy, on the video I know a way you can get four songs, because I used to listen to this particular piece—it's a play—you got all this music that sounds like Stravinsky, and all of a sudden the actor goes to the window, and they lift the window up and a marching band comes right through, so the music, like Stravinsky, all at once you hear ttt-ttt-ttt-ttt-ttt."

So I told Tommy LiPuma, "All you have to do is play one minute of each composition." So we played one minute and we got four compositions. And then I told him "put 'em all together," so he put 'em all together like a collage. So that's where you get four tunes.

FOLEY: I love that, you're beautiful.

MD: How you gonna mess with Spike Lee *and* me?

Miles on Herbie Hancock

FOLEY: And we just saw Herbie Hancock's "Chameleon," and it's about twelve or thirteen years old. I didn't know they had it on video, but it's nice. Hancock's familiar. Didn't he used to play with you?

MD: For a short time, maybe a week. He used to be in one of my best bands.

FOLEY: Yeah, that was the *Bitches Brew* period, yeah.

MD: No, it was later. It was later.

FOLEY: I was maybe six years old or something. I bought the album.

MD: Yeah, come *on*, Foley. What did you like about what Herbie did?

FOLEY: I like all of Herbie's stuff, so it's an opinion for me.

MD: What about his videos?

FOLEY: I like all his videos, "Rockit" . . . Did you like it?

MD: The one in the subway?

FOLEY: Yeah. I liked the girl in there, too.

MD: I know. He said he got in a lot of trouble with that there.

FOLEY: Really?

MD: See this photo right here? When the plane, it's when I'm on a plane, you know, I got this pad out and I take the pencil and when the plane's taking off, all those lumps on the runway, I take the pencil and the pencil shakes, right? And you just try to make her real fast and it gets like that, so these? They're round lines, not square, so you never take the pencil off the paper. See all these faces? One, two, three, four, five, six . . . there's about fifty faces in there, maybe more. So I took all the colors, this is the style, right, and I can't do that unless I start on a plane.

FOLEY: *You* are on a lot of flights.

Miles on Prince

MD: Hello, this is *New Visions* and we're gonna play "Shalamar."

FOLEY: Oh, I think we're going to.

MD: All right. Whatever.

FOLEY: Shalamar, "Circumstantial Evidence," it's a funky tune, he requested it, I'm gonna watch it.

MD: Look out, Prince.

FOLEY: Bad boy.

MD: Yeah. We are gonna do . . . you know the five songs that he sent? The one I am gonna ask you to do is to learn "Give Me Some Chocolate." *[Editors: The*

Prince-penned song "Chocolate" was later released on Pandemonium *in 1990.
On Prince's demo, he sings the song using an uncanny Miles Davis vocal imper-
sonation.]* All right?

FOLEY: All right, all right, I learned it. All of it.

MD: See if you learned it, we gonna play it, 'cause I asked him myself, I said, "I
never hear the bass on your albums or on the composition." He says, "Because
I double it an octave lower." Actually, they don't need no bass, because they use
drum patterns. First you've got the tik-tik-tatick and the cymbal in the song, and
then you have the tik, tik-tum, tik-tum, you know, whatever, so you don't hear
the bass. You know, you don't need one.

FOLEY: Yeah, everything is pretty well put together.

MD: It's covered, right? I think he sticks it in the piano, in the keyboard. You
know the drum, tik-tik-tik-tik-tik, it goes on, whatever happens. Anyway, I asked
him about that and he told me on the way out from where they rehearse. *[Edi-
tors: Paisley Park in Chanhassen, Minnesota. On New Year's Eve of 1987 Davis
joined Prince onstage during a charity concert given inside the soundstage of
Prince's recording studio.]*

FOLEY: Yeah, I heard about it.

MD: So he said, "Do you mind if my father comes to dinner?" and I said, "No."
He's real quiet, you know, and he reminds me of Charlie Chaplin. When I tell
him that, he just giggles. Sheila E. was there and that was it. *[Editors: Sheila
Escovedo, Prince's drummer and percussionist at the time.]*

FOLEY: Were they recording or just rehearsing when you were there?

MD: The last two he did he had to stop, because he had a cold. I asked him about
it, on how he was. Remember we were supposed to meet him in London.

FOLEY: Yeah, yeah, the weather was really bad. We had to cancel it. I think it was an outdoor date.

MD: But he has more stuff. He has the eight-track board—I don't know how many tracks he has on that board—but it's right in the middle of his house. He's also building this complex with video—he says he wants to make it like an old gym with a stage and some lots. It's the same color as my house, you know, gray wood, and he has apartments in there, so guys can stay over and get up and finish their video and rehearsal. A commissary. And they have a big stage, where you can make a video, have a rehearsal, take a shower. That should be open. *[Editors: The ten-million-dollar complex, Paisley Park, which Prince leased as well, also became Prince's personal toy. It boasted multiple resources for recording, band rehearsal, and filming. It officially opened its doors on September 11, 1987. Studio A boasted an eighty-track recording console, Studio B a forty-eight-track console and a 12,000-square-foot soundstage. Prince intentionally wired every room in Paisley Park to allow him to record wherever he wants.]*

FOLEY: That would work out pretty well for him, because he directs a lot of his videos, too, I understand.

MD: Yeah, he's one of America's greatest poets.

The Video for "Decoy"

MD: Evening. This is Miles Davis and Foley. We're on VH1, *New Visions*, and we're gonna watch "Decoy," from the album with the visual that I don't like. It's left my head. I can't remember what we were doin'. I was in a coma. I didn't like it because it didn't have the colors I wanted. Ever see a film called *Wolf*? Those colors, pastel colors, those were the colors that I wanted on the video. It was just one of those cheap things that Columbia did. They weren't even into it like they should have been into it. And shortly after that, I left and I hated it, the video.

On Fashion, Girls, and Advice to an Aspiring Musician

MD: Did you see me in "Cameo"? See what I had on?

FOLEY: Yeah.

MD: Did you see the gray tuxedo with the black trim?

FOLEY: Yeah.

MD: The pockets? Did you see the girls all over me? And then did you see the long white gloves?

FOLEY: Yeah!

MD: What else did I wear? And the red jacket? Did you see that? I changed three times. Girls were all over me. Did you see me talking to the girl on the steps?

FOLEY: Yeah, I follow you.

MD: Now, anyway, Larry is a good friend of mine. When I was learning to box, his father showed me a left hook, how they do it. So when I went backstage, to their party, I saw Lee back there and I said, "Lee, what are you doing back here?" Lee Black. He said, "Don't you remember when I brought my son up?" Well, he brought his son up. "My son wants to be a musician," and I said, "Lee, just show me the left hook 'cuz you know how everybody wants to be a musician." So anyway he says that he wants to be a musician. Lee said, "Just talk to him a little bit," and I said, "Okay." Now this is Larry and I didn't even know it. I said, "Music is like dope. You use it and you get tired of it."

Miles on Drawing the Female Form

MD: That's another example of what I was trying to explain. It's two faces goin' that way. And one, two, three faces going this way on the same body. And it's four on the other side, one, two, three, four, and it's another body with the . . . shoulders, where the shoulder is. This is an ass. You draw a circle. It's sex and means a woman in all the circles. See the derriere right here? I like a woman with long legs, with a short thigh. So I put this . . . the knee comes right here and the rest is legs. Anyway, I'm gonna draw a face here, and then I'm gonna put another face with a different color—not really another face—I'm just gonna color . . . and this is her hair. A multi-colored face. I've got these pens in my mouth and you can't hear what I'm sayin', but you can see what I'm doin', maybe. These pens dry up quick if you're impatient like me—see? It's dead. But the colors. You can see that's a nice color. The way you line up a body on a woman. . . . Lemme turn this page. You draw a straight line like that, see? A straight line and make a circle here, and a circle here and a half-circle here, then you make this V—all women have a little V when they turn around, right? They connect. Then you can make each cheek, right, and then you bring it up the back, and the shoulders up higher, but you leave the line like that. And then the legs. Thigh. Hip. Everything is round on the body. Everything! From your fingers, your shoulders, your back, your nose, your cheekbones, your lips—everything is round but your hair. This is where you line that up.

On the Band

MD: This is VH1, *New Visions*. My name is Miles Davis and I've been here for two hours, and I want you to know the name of the musicians in my band. There's Foley playing guitar over here. And Kenny, Kenny Garrett is on saxophone. They *looove* Foley and Kenny. My band, they love them and Darryl, Darryl Jones. The European teenagers love Foley and Darryl and Kenny, and Adam playing synthesizer, Bobby and Ricky playing drums, and Rudy's playing the hand drums. And me. And we sound good! All the time, right? I been here with Michael and . . . what's the director's name? Keogh? Yo, Keogh! What it is? We're gonna have coffee, you and me. We're going to Europe in February, and France, and we're gonna play all of George Wing's concerts here, this summer, and if the Beacon Theater doesn't pay me that money for it, we're not gonna play there. We'll play there in a month if they're gonna pay us the money, but I'd much rather work at the Bottom Line anyway. You've got that club atmosphere, you know what I mean, Foley? And I got a new tailor, Patrick. What's Patrick's last name?

FOLEY: Bushnell.

MD: What?

FOLEY: Pat Bushnell.

MD: Bushnell, Pat Bushnell, in Philadelphia. He made this jacket here. It's an African influence, you know what I mean? And, he's gonna make some for the band. And we might hook up with Prince.

MILES DAVIS: REBEL WITHOUT A PAUSE

Interviewer: Peter Watrous
Musician, May 1989

Peter Watrous, a longtime contributing writer and reviewer for the *New York Times*, is currently finishing his novel *This Time the Dream's on Me*.

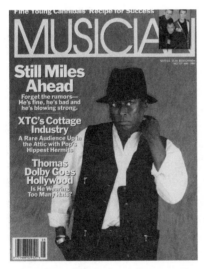

"What do you want?" asks Miles, like I'm wasting his time.

It's hard not to stare at him. Thin, with taut skin, he's immensely imposing, even though he's probably 5' 6". He looks fit, and handsome, and he stares at you when he speaks, waiting for you to respond, like a snake waiting for a mouse to move. His eyes have the milky white circles around the iris that old people often get. He walks with a bit of a limp.

I've been at his Malibu beach house, an hour away from Los Angeles, for forty-five minutes; Miles was in town getting acupuncture treatment for a crick in his neck. There is art all over the house. The tile porch overlooks impossibly beautiful ocean, strewn with rocks and clumps of seaweed that breaks the surface, causing ripples. A path wanders down to the beach; at the window in the living room a huge telescope stands silhouetted against the sky. It's just been reported in some seedy paper that Miles has AIDS; around New York rumors of his demise—bone cancer, lung cancer, anything else—float like trash on a wind down Broadway. He looks fine, even healthy, and the exercise cycle is prominently displayed near his piano and an oversized TV. He drives up to his house in his silver Ferrari.

"I want to ask you some questions," I say, playing the stare-back game. It's obvious he has no idea who I am. No response. He goes and talks to his assistant, Mike, who's gotten out of the car by now. Then he returns.

"Go make yourself at home, Peter. Go out on the porch. It's nice out there." Miles, it turns out, is a nice guy.

He's also a guy who, for all his musical movement and lip service to the present, is inexorably drawn to the ideas of his youth. He has taken the original tenets of the beboppers and lived them: change, elusiveness, a sense that art had radical imperatives. But still, this dates him both ideologically and as a memoirist. His comparisons are all to the great figures of his youth, before he became a great himself. Of his musical compatriots, Charlie Parker's name comes up over and over, not Wayne Shorter's. And although he has a paternal interest in his band, his new record, *Amandla*, isn't much on his mind. His autobiography is coming out soon, and Columbia Records' boxed-set summation of his Columbia career—instead of reissuing the records themselves—brings a frown to his face. When I ask him a question about it, he misunderstands and thinks that Columbia is doing another one. This genuinely shocks him.

"Yeah, I think people are trying to close the chapter of the book called Miles Davis. I know the nature of man, which is to do that. People don't like to talk about the same thing over and over again," he says. "You see this pin? It's from the Knights of Malta; I'm Sir Miles Davis. The guy who gave it to me said, 'We know style when we see it, but we don't know how to teach it. We can see a person and say, "They have style," but you can't take a person with non-style and teach him style.' That's what they told me when I got knighted: Keep on doing what I'm doing and not to discriminate. They said that I was the one they picked because I kept trying to keep the music going, change the colors. But that's my nature."

When did you start thinking about your sound?

"Forever."

But what were you thinking? Did you think that you had an individual sound?

"I just followed the sound that I liked. You just follow your body; I liked my instructor's sound when I was a kid in St. Louis."

What were you thinking about yourself, your playing, when you were a kid?

"Me? I didn't have time to think about myself! I was too busy playing."

But to get something distinct musically, you have to think.

"I was thinking about what chord Dizzy was playing. Sarah Vaughan and a woman named Mabel showed me major sevenths, what to do with them."

But you leave all this open space in your playing, I bludgeon.

"If you get a good rhythm section, why blow over it? It knocks me out when I hear it. I play against a rhythm section. They push you; that's what it's all about it. You have to fit in, not over, in, like you fit in a chord, not over a chord. You do all of that to goose a rhythm section, 'cause they get tired of playing like this [*imitates a drummer playing a ride cymbal*] if you don't do nothing. Tony Williams played with one of them trumpet players, it wasn't Freddie Hubbard, might have been Wynton. Put his sticks down. Tony's like that anyway. If he doesn't get a chance for interplay, he'll get fed up; if you're not going to play with the drummer, why not get a drum machine and hook it up?"

Very few people of his generation have changed contexts as readily as Miles—Max Roach is another, maybe Roy Haynes, but that pretty much sums it up. And of his generation, Davis is easily the most controversial. Bringing up his electric music in a room of the wrong jazz critics is like bringing up Salman Rushdie at an Ayatollah conference. Does he adapt his musical principles to his market, something which would be anathema to a hardcore be-bopper?

"Me? I know what you're saying, but I don't do that, I wouldn't change my style because that's the going thing. I make music that I like, but I found out that usually what I like, somebody else will like it, too. If you're sincere about it, somebody else can see it. But I have to change."

So what if the music doesn't change? Say if you said to yourself, "Well, I really like this group with Herbie and Wayne, I'm going to do it for the rest of my life and explore all the things that weren't explored." Why not? It's good music.

"It's good, but styles change. All cars look like Mercedes now. Corvettes look like Ferraris. Styles change, man, if you're not here to see it, say you're in jail and you've just come out, it becomes really obvious. Styles change subtly, words change their meanings."

But why do you have to change? Nobody *has* to change.

"Who? Me? I just have to play in different styles. Which doesn't mean that I'm not me. When your friend calls, you can tell it's them by the tone of their voice. It's not that you change, right? I can't say I'm going to change tomorrow. You've got to do it gradually, you change every day; last year was go-go music.

Now people have added something to it. Those that didn't hear it last year have to listen twice. I love the beat; we got it on the new record.

"Go-go is like Max used to play, the beat swings. I can tell you where it came from. Years ago when Art Blakey and Max and Kenny Clarke, Kenny Klook a mop we called him." [*Davis starts singing rhythms.*] "'Salt peanuts, salt peanuts.' See? That's the same thing."

When you heard go-go, you recognized it?

"Uh-uh. I felt it first. If I analyze something, I won't like it. But you can break it down, hear 'Salt Peanuts.'" He sings more rhythms. "I showed Vince, my cousin, that and he said, 'What!!!' What else you going to ask me? When can I be free?"

Even though you say your music hasn't really changed, it's become more pop than it was before.

"How so, what's pop?"

It's dealing with popular rhythms more than it did before. It's closer to dance music.

"For who? All people? Chinese people? Japanese people?"

We're talking about American people. If you play "Kind of Blue" or "'Round Midnight," that's not dance music.

"It was then."

People were dancing in the Blackhawk or at the Vanguard?

"Not in the Blackhawk, not the Vanguard. But Art Blakey, Kenny Clarke, and I would play the Audubon Ballroom and people would dance."

But the newer music sounds like dance music.

"How? It's the beat? Lionel Hampton had the same beat, and Mingus threw the drums off the stage, because Lionel liked the beat too much, which drove Mingus nuts." Miles laughs at the memory. "Anyway, I don't think if something is popular, it's bad."

But people say that, right?

"The only person I ever hear say that is Wynton Marsalis, and he doesn't think like that unless he's being interviewed. He wants to be an innovator, and he is, but he doesn't talk like that. Wynton plays perfect, like Fats and Brownie, he's a hell of a trumpet player. We're not talking about his mouth, his vocal cords, we're talking about his musicianship; he's a motherfucker. Maybe he has to talk to let off steam. I know some crazy bitches that made the best love.

"Crazy guys too, the tone that we all had in St. Louis, that we all got from listening to a guy called Levi. Levi was crazy. He'd start laughing and they had to take him back to the asylum. Clark Terry would call me and say [*Imitating Terry*], 'Levi just got out. And he's over at whatchamacallit. And he has his horn.' I'd say, 'Levi, just put your horn up to your mouth.' And he'd just smile.

"You look at Wynton's mouth. Wynton is a perfect trumpet player. It's just what he says . . . you have to let people think for themselves a little bit."

Davis' greatest influence has been his own unmistakable sound. He revolutionized mute playing. His broad, vibrato-less sound matched the plains around St. Louis, dry and unsentimental, but immensely romantic. And it's his sound that has wrecked generation after generation of trumpet players, as well, musicians who should have been finding their own way, instead of Davis'.

"Sound is the most important thing a musician can have," he says. "Because you can't do anything without a sound. If a musician is interested in his sound, then you can look for some good playing. Because if he doesn't find his sound, he can't play what he wants to play, can't do what he wants to do, can't play a good line. In the electric age, it works with the mix onstage, too. When I played out in Brooklyn, I told the promoters, 'If you don't get the sound together, I'm not going to be in the band.' If the sound ain't good, you want to kill yourself.

"The least little thing is exaggerated. Like the spit in your horn. With electronics it's like . . ." He makes a sound like an elephant dying. "If you don't hear your sound, you won't be able to play what you want to play, to connect phrases, you won't get nothing from it.

"Nobody can sound like Coltrane, for example. 'Cause it's Trane. First place, he had one tooth out. And it took Coltrane a long time to mature and ripen. Lucky Thompson and I used to talk about chords and shit, so I'd give Coltrane four or five chords to run on one chord, and he's the only one that can do it, he and Lucky and Bird and Coleman Hawkins. Nobody has that thing he had, which is from Eddie Davis and Sonny Stitt. Benny Carter [one of Davis' first employers] could do that too, if he chose to. He's real slick. He's always blinking his eyes and saying, 'Do I sound like Charlie Parker?' I'd say no. Because he knew that I used to play with Bird, and Bird was all the noise then. But Benny was a brave musician. Working with him, I learned a lot and so did J. J. Johnson. Look out, Vince!" he yells to his cousin, who's cooking barbecue. "What's happening over there? What else you want to know?"

What effect did living in New York have on your playing?

"New York is the place for me. You get that rush. You see so much art in New York, a guy can do something like that." He motions to the art work on his dining room table. "You can play like that. I think Charlie Christian had a big influence on me and Bird. Blanton, the Southwestern style, that's the way I play. I thought everyone was playing like Dizzy when I turned on the radio and it's the John Kirby band, and I hear this trumpet player that sounds like Dizzy. I say, 'Goddamn, I got to go to New York, because if all the trumpet players play like that I got to get up there.' So I asked Dizzy, 'Who's that playing with John Kirby that sounds like you?' He said, 'That was me! Charlie Shavers was sick.' Goddamn! That made me go to New York sooner. When I got to New York, nobody was playing. Dizzy, Bird, Vic Coulson had a nice tone.

"But back to Charlie Christian. He was one of the first be-boppers, 'Solo Flight.' We used to play like that. I was in school, and right across from school my friend Duke Brooks lived, and he'd get so high his mother put him on the porch and made a room for him. He was about four years older than me, but he played like Bud. He'd say, 'I got something to show you.' The piano was right there. He smoked so much reefer: reefer, piano and the bed, that's all he had in there. We played 'Airmail Special,' everything that the Benny Goodman sextet played. That was a good band. He and I, a bass player and a drummer. He'd play octaves, and we'd add a little bit to the arrangement. Ben Webster used that diminished chord in 'Cotton Tail,' stuff like that made my ear go west."

When you came out to Los Angeles in the '40s, what was the difference between New York and Central Avenue?

Davis rolls his eyes. "First place, they had two unions in Los Angeles. A black and white union; the black union, all the Tarzan movies—you saw the natives?— they just called up the black unions and got their extras. Central Avenue wasn't nothing like New York. New York was the best school you ever go to, 52nd Street, Ben Webster, Art Tatum, Charlie Parker, Dizzy, Sid Catlett, Earl Bostic, Savoy Ballroom, I got in on the tail end of that.

"All the musicians! You could take your pick for what you wanted to hear. For instance, Bird, you never heard anybody play as fast and loud as that, and with the long length of each note. That was the way I was taught. Don't sacrifice height for speed, if you play high; the only person I know who could play even in all the registers is Fats Navarro. He'd come and get me to jam. We'd go to

Minton's. Funny too, when we'd play together, we'd sound alike. When you do art with someone, whatever that style is, that's what you do. Even if you write together, 'What about this, how about this!' It's exciting to collaborate.

"52nd Street was much more progressive. They didn't even like us out here. I remember working with Benny Carter; I came out to see Bird, and they gave him shock treatments because he was . . . America should be ashamed of itself the way it treats artists. A guy doesn't have to be white to be a bad motherfucker. Somebody should recognize these people. If someone wants to use dope, let him use dope; it's his life. Bird scared a lot of people, especially white people. When they don't understand something, they put it down."

It wasn't just white people putting him down then. Black people didn't pay that much attention, either.

"That's true, but during that time, playing like we played, when we came out to L.A. we'd go to jam sessions, and people would want to hire us and the union would say, 'No, you have to wait three or six months.' That's not fair, to put you on ice. I'd go to the union hall and they'd whisper, 'There's Davis. He's playing that new stuff from the East.'

"I didn't give a fuck what they were saying, because I knew what I liked. I had gone out there—I had let Lucky Thompson stay with me in New York—and when I came out here, I said to him, 'I can't stand Benny Carter's band—Benny's all right, but his band. . . .' He said, 'Well, just leave, stay with me'; he'd bought a little house.

"I played with Mingus then, you know. Mingus is so funny; he likes the way Duke Ellington wrote. Myself, I like smooth voice leading and Mingus was a bad motherfucker, everybody can't do what he did. To me he was like a relative. He used to write things and we'd play them in the living room with six or seven people. And he'd order us to play them again, because he wanted to hear it. We'd argue a lot too, about chords. Bird and Dizzy, Bud Powell, the beauty in their playing is the way they add on to a chord. A chord is given, so add on to it, instead of changing it completely. Mingus would be walking along straight and all of a sudden he'd walk down five steps. I'd say, 'Mingus! How can you do that? You hear what the tune's doing.' But he was so stubborn. Then he wouldn't say anything. He gradually cleared it up.

"A lot of guys will do things like Sun Ra; you can't recognize the tune, it's destruction. Gil Evans and I had to re-write things like *Porgy and Bess* and *Miles*

Ahead. It sounds like a different thing; we had to write a whole other composition. So he stopped doing things like that.

"Gil's mind was like a computer. Because he stored everything he liked in his head. He'd call me up in the middle of the night and say, 'You know that part where Teddy Wilson did this, or Fletcher Henderson did this?' He called me up once and said, 'If you ever get unhappy or bored, listen to *Miles Ahead*, listen to the arrangements.' He was like that.

"If I took him to record a date of mine, and I'm playing and he has his legs crossed; he'd pull me over [*tugs my sleeve and whispers in my ear*]. 'Remember, you have a round tone. Remember that. And remember that they're white, and you have to put your sound on top of what they're doing, or it's nothing.' He's one of the few music lovers that I know. If I have to make a decision about something, I can always say, 'What would Gil say right here?'"

So you miss him?

"I don't miss him. Well, I miss him, you know. Other people missed him because they missed him when he was here. I don't really think about death. I don't think people die, you know what I mean? I don't believe their head stops. I don't know what happens; they have to come back and be around somewhere. I can't see where Gil Evans is dead at all. He's not dead to me. People like your mother and father, you can always tune into them. I get this kind of thing sometimes, like when a little breeze blows a door open in New York, in your apartment; things that old folks tell you, they have something. My sister said that she smelled my mother's perfume. I never smelled it because the perfume I bought her was from Paris, and she used to use it only at certain social functions; I bought it in 1949. I believe they communicate in different ways. I can see things I've never seen before, I really believe in that.

"I don't believe that thoughts get lost, you know what I'm saying? The thoughts are still there. I often think about—you can see TV, hear it—music on the radio; it must be going on all over the earth, music's floating around, and one day somebody's going to be able to pick it up. It's too much just to lose a night of playing like that. I was going to write a story like that, where all of a sudden you pick up a set you remember on 52nd Street and nobody remembers it, but you go around and find the people you were there with. And maybe someone remembers it. It's got to be somewhere, 'cause things like that are not going to be done again. The time, the humidity, everything comes together. It'll come back. I can pull in Gil or my parents whenever I want to. Gil knew he was going to die. He just didn't want to die around anybody he knew. That's why he went to Mexico. Around people, he'd get the routine: 'Hey man, you sure do look thin.'"

I guess you've been getting a lot of that recently?

"That thing came out [*referring to an article claiming Davis had AIDS*]. I didn't read it. I think an ex-wife must have had something to do with that. Sounds like some shit an ex-wife would do. Bitches are vicious. Maybe she thinks some girl will read it and won't want to fuck me. I got pneumonia in Europe, and I never did get rid of it. I never stayed in this house this long. I like it out here, I love it. Once you stay here for a few days, it gets better. I can't stand the city unless it's New York. So I stay here, exercise, and the other day the doctor told me the pneumonia was all gone. I don't have AIDS now. I don't think I'm going to sue. You have to say, "You already got mad at that, don't get mad again.' But women are bitches. It's just a way of thinking some women have. If they can't have it, nobody else will. They want to fix it like that. The only thing I can think of that I haven't done is to live to be ninety, and I'm not ninety yet. I'm going to do it, too."

Do you still like boxing?

"I like to watch Mike Tyson, yeah. Because he's a heavyweight. He's slipping. I look at him, pick things apart, every time he moves to the left he's coming. The best guy I've seen fight him was Bruno. Bruno let him off the hook. I saw him fight Green, too. All boxers play drums, there's a connection. You can see it in the ring. Timing, rhythm, I can tell from how a musician walks that he can play. They gave me an honorary doctorate in music in Boston, some university. So I went up there to get it, and every person who got their degree was like this." Miles walks crabbed. "You could tell that they were fucked with when they were kids. No balance, repressed, you can see it. They might have an umbrella, too."

Did you really tell Monk not to play on "Bags' Groove," behind you?

"Yeah! Because I can't play when he plays behind me like that. I just can't play; he knows that. The way he played, he played what he wanted. If we're going to play something other than ballads he wrote, the chords he would play behind you, you couldn't improve on. Flatted fifths, there's only one thing you can play, is to play that chord. I like Herbie's comping, he doesn't get in the way. Al Haig, Bill Evans, Red—they were all good at it."

Did you ever play with Ahmad Jamal?

"My sister called me once, she was in the Pershing Lounge. She said, 'Listen to this.' I said, 'Who the fuck is that?' She said his name is Ahmad Jamal. That's the same thing I got when I heard Art Blakey. You know that feeling when you're frightened, when you're out of breath, on coke, or when a pretty woman walks in and you just have to say, 'What the fuck is your name?' I got it from Ahmad, Art Blakey. The older you get, it comes in smaller doses. It wasn't the same thing I got watching Bird, or when I heard Bud. And I'd heard Art Tatum; my mother had his albums."

Davis' last engagement in New York had him playing with a new band, the best he's had since his comeback. The band thunders. It may not be art, but it is good entertainment, and Davis, when he wants, can be brilliant over the burly roadhouse underpinnings. That brilliance can be heard on *Amandla*, which like Davis said, has go-go beats on it. But the best parts about it are also the most tantalizing: among the funk grooves, which open up to let his trumpet shine through, like sun through clouds, are two ballads, which until they drown in saccharine electronics, offer proof that Davis could, if he wanted to, play up to his old standards.

"In a way, I can't throw all my ideas on my band, you know. All I can do is let them play what they do best. Kenny [Garrett, his saxophonist] is a motherfucker. He's improved a lot. Sometimes I give him things to play, like a long phrase like if you play 6/8 you have to play it, but you bust it up. And on the new album I heard him doing that. Marcus and myself and Kenny, that's the only thing I listen to in the arrangements. George Duke played a little bit, Joey De Francesco played about four bars. But Kenny and I do a lot of interplay, we're doing more and more. Sometimes he just looks me in the eyes to start with, and he and I just go; we do a lot of that. His mind is opening up, he doesn't sound like anybody else.

"Now, if we're playing and I hear something I don't like I'll just say, 'Play this, within the tunes' or 'Put a tag here' or 'Add chords, to sweeten it up a bit.' Every time somebody new joins the band, they change it. The personalities change it. With Joey in the band, he changed it, it was a lift. 'Cause he could do something that nobody else could do.

"And you have to organize everything. I told one guy in the band, 'You're no soloist, I got you to play the parts.' But you know, men are very vain. I thought women were vain, but women just dress like that. Men are the ones. Like a guy who can't solo, can't space a solo, some people can't just space things along, on the canvas, sometimes too it'll be too heavy here or there. Guys who go to be-bop school, forget it. I had to pull Joey out. I said, 'Joey, you're running this chord, but play half a step up, a diminished chord, or an augmented chord, play both of them!' That's why I said that about Coltrane. Gary and Kenny have this other style, which I like. Let's eat. You want some ribs? Damn, I shouldn't have asked you, now you'll say yes."

On the TV, Don Jackson, a black undercover policeman who was arrested and pushed through a plate glass window by white policemen for no reason, is on the news.

Think America's changed?

"No."

We hang out and by the time I leave, Miles is watching Geraldo Rivera take on teen lesbians, and the sun's setting.

THE PRINCE OF SILENCE

Interviewer: Mike Zwerin
International Herald Tribune, April 9, 1998

Paris-based Mike Zwerin has been contributing as a columnist and pop music critic to the *International Herald Times* since 1979, and for *Bloomberg News* since 2005, and in the process has forged a reputation as an insightful and personable music journalist. He has also written for the *Village Voice, Playboy, Esquire, Rolling Stone, Vogue, DownBeat,* and *Elle.* A gifted trombonist and bass trumpeter who has played with Miles Davis (as part of the *Birth of the Cool* band), Eric Dolphy, Earl Hines, and John Lewis, he is also author of *Swing Under the Nazis: Jazz as a Metaphor for Freedom* and *The Parisian Jazz Chronicles: An Improvisational Memoir.* His skills are amply evident in the three pieces that follow, in which Zwerin pays tribute to Miles, explores the trumpeter's passion for painting, and examines Davis's brief excursion into acting.

Miles Davis, "The Prince of Silence," was the last in the line of Kings, Dukes, Counts, and Lords who forged the basic vocabulary of jazz. He reigned with undisputed power, opening melodies like flowers, into the early '90s despite active nobles and young pretenders assaulting the throne.

He did not like to be called a "Legend." When he hit sixty, he told me: "A legend is an old man known for what he used to do. I'm still doing it. Just call me Miles."

Whatever you call him, his treasury was overflowing. Money was every bit as important to Prince Miles as creativity. Or rather they were inseparable. He related to money and superstardom as integral to his art. They were evidence of communication, arts in themselves. Making record companies and promoters pay maximum dollar for his services forced them to invest heavily in promotion to protect their investment, which inevitably improved business and they paid even more next time.

What separated this Prince from most of his subjects is that he made creativity pay royally. ("I do what I do good. Better than good.") He divided his time between five-star hotels, a large apartment overlooking Central Park in New York, and a million-dollar villa in Malibu, California. He drove expensive sports cars. Money was part of what made him—whether he liked it or not—legendary.

"Don't play what's there," he told his young musicians: "Play what's not there"; and "don't play what you know, play what you don't know." Legends say legendary things. "I have to change," he said: "It's like a curse." He played key roles in the birth of bebop (with Charlie Parker), cool jazz (*Birth of the Cool*), modal jazz (*Kind of Blue*), and jazz-rock fusion (*Bitches Brew*). "I can put together a better rock 'n' roll band than Jimi Hendrix," he bragged.

In the 1960s, John Coltrane (who would become a legend too) was a perfect musical foil for Miles. With Philly Joe Jones, drums, Paul Chambers, bass, and Red Garland on piano, this was one of the best jazz bands in history. Trane's streamlined, full-blooded goosebump-raising "sheets of sound" on the saxophone contrasted the eloquent serenity of Miles' courtly, special trumpet (audiences would applaud his silences)—twentieth-century speed and complexity in tandem with elegant nineteenth-century romanticism. Before leaving Miles to form his own band, Coltrane had been searching, a captive of his own intensity, playing forty-five-minute solos in the middle of what were supposed to be one hour sets.

"Can't you play twenty-seven choruses instead of twenty-eight?" Miles asked him.

"I know, I know," Coltrane replied: "I play too long. But I get so involved I don't know how to stop."

"Why don't you try taking the saxophone out of your mouth?" Miles advised. One legend to another. Twenty years later, Miles was still having trouble with saxophonists playing what he called "duty shit, all the things saxophone players think they are supposed to do." He asked tenorman Bob Berg why he had soloed in a place where he was not scheduled and had never before played.

"It sounded so good," Berg replied, "I just had to come in."

"Bob," said the Prince of Silence, "the reason it sounded good was because you *weren't* playing."

———

Miles was regally relaxing in one of the series of grandiose hotel suites in which I interviewed him over the years. People waited on him, a young woman usually sat by his side. He was obviously accustomed to luxury, looking like he expected and deserved it. He reminded me of an African Prince in his chambers.

We were in a penthouse atop the Concorde-Lafayette Hotel at Porte Maillot. Paris was at our feet. Drinking herbal tea, he had the world on a string. I thought of when, not all that long before, he had ingested more potent substances.

For many years, Miles had been famous, or infamous, for one negative habit often associated with those who are considered to be "hip"—drugs. The black creators of that revolutionary urban American improvised music which came to be called "bebop" endured critics who said that their jazz was not really "music." While the sounds they invented were adapted by so-called "serious" composers, who were acclaimed by these same critics (all white). The composers' jazz-influenced works were performed in prestigious halls and on the soundtracks of big-budget movies, while the creators worked in Mafia-controlled saloons and collected no royalties.

Bebop fathers fought alienation by constructing their own secret culture with its own style and language—"bad" meaning "good" is vintage bebop argot. Drugs were part of the huddle; they seemed to cure alienation for a minute. Not coincidentally, drugs disappeared when respect—and money—arrived. Jazz was presented in Carnegie Hall, Clint Eastwood made a movie about Charlie Parker, Miles became a pop star. When Miles cleaned up his habit, he made it "hip" to be "square."

"What do you want to know?" he asked me, in that legendary rasp which has become an emblem of "hip" to generations of hipsters and hippies.

Remembering that he had once said: "Music is like dope. You use it until you get tired of it," I asked him if he had tired of cocaine, heroin, and the rest.

He turned the pages of a large sketch pad, drawing flashy, fiery-haired bright-lipped women with an assortment of felt-tipped pens. Miles began to paint late in life. Since his death, neckties based on his paintings have become available in better stores everywhere, collectors pay high prices for his original works. He turned the pad around to show it to me:

"You like these chicks? These are Parisian women—sunken cheeks. Speaking French does that. They speak with their tongues out. Language forms your face."

Drawing more sunken cheeks, he began to answer my question: "I had to stop doing everything. . . ."

He was wearing rose-rimmed dark glasses and an understated expensive trim white shirt. His hairline had receded but what remained was curly and luxuriant. Miles Davis was the first jazz noble to have a hair transplant. There was some weight on his bones for a change. It was difficult to refrain from staring at his healthy velvety jet-black skin-tone. He was a beautiful-looking man who had affairs with Juliette Greco and Jeanne Moreau while in Paris recording the soundtrack for Louis Malle's film *Elevator to the Scaffold*. (The soundtrack holds up better than the movie).

"Everything," he repeated: "Listen." His hoarse whisper sounded like there was a mute in his throat. "I was snorting coke, right? Four, five grams a day. Go out drinking brandy and beer around the clock. Get up at midnight, stay out the rest of the night and half the day. Smoke four packs of cigarettes. Using sleeping pills too. One day I wake up I can't use my right hand. Can't straighten it out. Cicely panics. . . ."

Miles Dewey Davis III, son of a middle-class dentist from Alton, Illinois, was married to the actress Cicely Tyson, who won an Emmy Award (the American TV Oscar) for the title role in *The Autobiography of Miss Jane Pittman*. The marriage ceremony was performed by Andrew Young, mayor of Atlanta, Georgia, at the home of comedian Bill Cosby. This was the cream of the African-American aristocracy. Cicely and Miles were later divorced. In his autobiography, he accused her of trying to pull out his hair-weave.

"Cicely panics," he continued: "'Let's go see Dr. Shen,' she says. Acupuncture doctor. Dr. Shen gave me needles . . . here, here, here. He gave me herbs to clean my body out. Chinese medicine. I shed my skin. A whole layer of skin fell out. Weird stuff came out of my nose. I didn't know which drug was messing me up so I just decided to stop them all. Now I swim forty minutes every day. The only habit I got left is sweets.

"Cigarettes are the worst of all. You're better off snorting coke than smoking cigarettes. I saw Wayne [Shorter] stand there and light a cigarette. I said, 'Why you doing that?' He said, 'I need something to do with my hands.' I said, 'Why don't you put them in your pockets? You got four pockets.'"

I asked him what he would have done if Dr. Shen had told him to give up the trumpet too.

"Change doctors," he shot back without hesitation. "I was told that once, when I was, like, sixteen. Sonny Stitt came to St. Louis, right? And he had his hair straightened. He showed me how to do it, did it for me. My hair was wet. I was running around trying to be hip, right? So then I had to come back all across town to go home. I got sick. Went to the hospital. The doctor said, 'What, you play the trumpet? You can't do that any more.' If I'd listened to him, I'd be a dentist today. Isn't that a bitch?"

Miles was not exactly healthy to begin with, the rest was self-inflicted. He went in and out of surgery for sickle-cell anemia, banged up his Lamborghini ("Shit! Both ankles!"), had an ulcer, bouts of insomnia (the coke didn't help), polyps were removed from his vocal cords. After a hip operation (Miles was so hip, he even had hip operations) forced him into a wheelchair, he insisted on being wheeled from limousine to boarding ramp after he was loping around stages like a gazelle. "That's just Miles being princely," his guitar player explained.

Miles was famous for turning his back on the audience. I asked why he did that.

He lowered his head and stared up at me, glowering with narrowed menacing eyes, grinding his mouth like there was gum in it which there wasn't. Miles loved to play the devil, although I always thought it was just that—a game. When a woman once came up to him and said, "Mr. Davis, I love your music," he leered: "Wanna fuck?" (She did not think that was funny.) Now he hissed to me: "Nobody asks a symphony orchestra conductor why he turns his back on the audience." After 1970, when his "rock" period began with *Jack Johnson* and *Bitches Brew*, Miles took to standing in the middle of his bubbling cauldron of binary electronic avant-garde exploration on the cutting edge of distortion, signaling tempo and dynamic changes with an implied wave of his green trumpet or a pointed finger. At the same time, he denied the existence of signals: "The music just does what it's supposed to do."

His most musical as well as commercial collaboration was with the older white arranger/composer Gil Evans, a father figure to Miles. On their albums together—which were, well, symphonic—Miles was at the height of his power. He was like a violin soloist playing a concerto with Gil's big band. Their *Sketches of Spain* was a big hit. Gil said: "Miles is not afraid of what he likes. A lot of other musicians are constantly looking around to what the next person is doing, wondering what's in style. Miles goes his own way."

Now there was a silence in the suite on top of the Hotel Concorde-Lafayette. When you're with Miles Davis, silence is not exactly silent. There was a palpable vibe in the air. He went on happily drawing away. Miles taught me whatever I know about silence, apparently not enough. I grew paranoid. I blamed myself for the conversational stagnation. I was the journalist. I needed a question—fast. Make me sound intelligent. Whatever came to mind: "Do you still practice?"

He had finished another drawing. He drew the way he once smoked and snorted—compulsively. Perhaps it was drug-substitute gratification. He turned it around, showed it to me and said: "Yeah. Practice every day. People know me by my sound, like they know Frank Sinatra's sound. Got to keep my sound. I practice seventh chords. Practicing is like praying. You don't just pray once a week."

"Do you pray?"

"I was on a plane once and all of a sudden it dropped. I had this medal Carlos Santana gave me around my neck. It has a diamond and a ruby and a picture of some saint on it. I touched it. I think that thing saved me. Well, just say I pray in my way."

Jazz festivals will come to be divided into pre- and post-Miles Davis eras. For twenty years from 1971, Miles lent credibility to the rock backbeat. (He opened for the Grateful Dead and Jefferson Airplane at the Fillmore.) His presence continued to hover, providing a sort of tacit legitimacy for rock bands on jazz stages. After his death in the fall of 1991, it has become more difficult to rationalize. Miles did not play rock for the money. He was in search of communication, or, at worst, the fountain of youth. Sure, he wanted a large audience. He was no loser. But anything Miles touched can be defined as jazz, like Louis Armstrong. Now we're stuck with the youth without the fountain.

During the summer 1991 jazz festival season, Miles did something he said he would never do—look back. He led an all-star assortment of ex-employees— Herbie Hancock, Chick Corea, Joe Zawinul, Jackie McLean, John McLaughlin, etc.—in Paris. Quincy Jones conducted Miles soloing with a big band performing "Sketches of Spain" in Montreux. "I cannot help but wonder," I wrote on the front page of the *International Herald Tribune*, "if this unexpected flurry of nostalgia at the age of sixty-five is some sort of last roundup." That same summer, Jack Lang awarded him the Legion of Honor. I wrote: "It seems somehow like final punctuation." Later, I realized that I had written his obituary two months early, which really spooked me. Because I also wrote: "Miles Davis is playing the soundtrack for the movie of my life and when he stops, the movie's over."

Well, I'm still here. But life post-Miles is not easy. There is nobody to remind us of the importance of personal sound and silence. The silent sounds of *Tutu*, recorded in the late '80s, reflect the best of our contemporary urban experience—a peaceful garden in the middle of a polluted city, a warm café in winter, the metro when it is not on strike, walking streets, a friendly taxi driver, tree-lined empty boulevards at dawn. It has become much harder to ignore all the noise.

Miles was a regular at the "Grande Parade du Jazz" in Nice. Neighborly noise considerations forced a midnight curfew. When the stage manager waved off the band ten minutes early, Miles was furious. He wanted those ten minutes. He brought the band back until midnight on-the-nose. Money making as an art form involves doing what you want to do anyway even without the money.

Miles was also a master of the art of Good Publicity. His sparring with Wynton Marsalis in the press was a good example. Marsalis is the leader of the under-thirty generation of tradition and blues-oriented players which has installed itself as the immediate future. It can be called a movement. They build on the past and one day may leap into the future.

Right now, though, most of them sound like other, mostly dead, people. They are intelligent, clean-living, and highly specialized technocrats. Marsalis secured his influence on them through his post as director of the Lincoln Center jazz program at just about the time Miles Davis died. There was a void, although I beg to differ with those who consider Marsalis to be Miles' heir. Marsalis is not "cursed" by change, and he has yet to learn the value of silence.

Marsalis accused Miles of deserting "true" jazz by playing rock. Miles accused Marsalis of ditto for playing European classical music. Back and forth, taking one to know one, Miles said: "Wynton is just doing a press number, which he is always doing. Music shouldn't be like two gladiators fighting."

Which of course made a great press number. Miles was photographed giving Wynton one of his drawings. They were both smiling like two heavyweights promoting a championship match.

So as we ride away into the sunset towards the future of jazz, we remember the words of the Prince of Silence: "When I'm not playing music, I'm thinking about it. I think about it all the time, when I'm eating, swimming, drawing, there's music in my head right now talking to you. I don't like the word 'jazz' which white folks dropped on us. And I don't play rock. I make the kind of music the day recommends."

MILES THE PAINTER: COLORFUL FLOWING LINES

Interviewer: Mike Zwerin
International Herald Tribune, July 23, 1998

NEW YORK—Ask Miles Davis how he began to paint and you would get just the answer you'd expect from someone who has been called the "Prince of Silence":

"I used to draw Mickey Mouse and that airplane of his. Dick Tracy, he was easy, all I had to do was draw his nose. And Flash Gordon, I could do him. I did a drawing of Gerry Mulligan, that was in the '40s, looked exactly like him."

Arnold Schoenberg began to paint after he had made his musical name; as did John Lennon, Charlie Parker, Joni Mitchell, Tony Bennett, and Chick Corea. Miles started serious—some say compulsive—sketching in the early 1980s, about the same time he came off drugs, which may be no coincidence. His first formal exhibit—a total of thirty oils and pen-and-ink drawings—was in Munich in 1988 at the Mosel und Tschechow Gallery.

It is not unusual for musicians to come to painting. This private and silent work can be a relief for someone who makes his living in a collective endeavor which demands applause and bothers neighbors. It requires some degree of natural ability to begin with, but no formal training is necessary for immediate ego gratification. And you don't have to worry about the drummer showing up late.

It rarely happens in the opposite direction—imagine the complaints if a painter suddenly began to practice the trumpet in his Central Park South apartment. Of course, like any art, at some point you must decide on the degree of investment. Do you want to remain a dilettante for the rest of your life? Do you want to look like a fool? Or is it time to get serious? And if so is there enough energy in your fifties for two serious endeavors?

After looking at color photographs of more than a hundred of his works—signed "Miles"—and seeing the pile of canvases in various stages of completion spread over the floor of his Central Park South apartment, it was obvious that this was no mere "celebrity" painter.

There was an electric piano in a corner, a synthesizer in another, a trumpet on an easy chair, cassettes piled against a wall, and the latest Prince album playing on a professional sound system. It was not surprising that this man who had never been able to stick to one style of music ("I have to change, it's like a curse") and was now involved with the visual arts on top of it all had trouble sticking to the subject.

"You've been quoted as saying that musical training is important in order to learn what rules to break," I said. "Is that true for painting as well?"

"The first piano music Art Tatum ever heard was two boogie-woogie piano players on a cylinder," Miles replied in his trademark rasp. "He didn't know there were two of them. He thought that's the way a piano should sound and he learned how to play like two piano players at the same time. Some guys don't have to know anything about theory because they have something better you can't learn in a book."

This was a classic enigmatic answer from a man whose legend had been built on an enigmatic image he went to some length to encourage. We might assume that he considered himself to be one of those painters with too much good instinct and talent to be in need of perspective classes. Then again, he might just have been being enigmatic. In any case, his early sketches were of thin women with colorful flowing lines which, whatever stylistic faults an expert might find, were obviously drawn by somebody with a flair for color, rhythm, clothes . . . and women.

"Women tell me they have rhythm," he said. "They are moving, dancing, doing ballet steps. I make them with thick thighs and long legs. I like that look, it's the Rio de Janeiro look. I hardly ever draw a man."

Miles was the only musician I've ever known who got applause for not playing . . . for walking around the stage in silence for as long as twelve bars between phrases. So I asked him: "Do you get involved with visual space too?"

"The guy who looks after my house in California, Mike, he calls me Chief. I say 'Mike, how do you like this?' He says, 'I liked it, Chief . . . just before you finished it.' So he thinks I spoiled it by making too much. I have to learn to stop. I know how to stop with music, but you have this problem of balance with paint and it's different."

There are abstractions with wide swatches of gold, copper, and metallic colors. Colors cake on canvas. Spare, almost skeletal shapes cavort on beige. There are occasional reminders of Arshile Gorky and Jackson Pollock. Series of color-ful squares are filled with circles. When the paintings are not signed, it is not always evident which end is up. And those thick-thighed, long-legged women from Rio show up everywhere all the time.

After entering his rock star period in the early 1970s, Miles was known for wearing colorful costumes. I asked him if his color instinct began with his clothes.

"Sometimes certain colors fit certain days," he said. "Like I'll want blue all over. But I might change my mind five times before a concert. I always decide at the last minute."

"Does music translate into color for you?"

"You mean do colors flash through my head when I play? You'd be surprised what flashes through my head."

He was chain-sipping iced tea. Central Park was spread out through the win-dow behind him. A business associate walked in and Davis said: "You should see a doctor." The man looked surprised and asked why. "You need a personality change." Miles Davis was also known as the "Prince of Darkness."

Although he kept referring to painting as his "hobby," the works exhibited in Munich were priced from $750. There was obviously still a good deal of ambivalence about his new activity: "Quincy Jones called me up and said 'Man, I want to buy one of your paintings.' I told him to call [his personal manager] Peter. But, hell, I'd give one to him. I'm always giving sketches away. If I had to make money from this, I'd starve. It's only my name. People say, 'Let's see what Miles is thinking about.'"

He looked down at the canvases on the floor and murmured, as though to himself: "Just doing this, could I make a living? Maybe so." Then the doubter turned into the confident pop star again: "Fortunately, I have something to fall back on. I make enough royalties so that I'll be ninety-five before I spend all the money and wear all my clothes."

"Do you approach a canvas like a musical composition, with some form in mind? Or do you improvise it like a solo as you go along?"

"The color. I get the color first. Then all the rest I improvise. Lines and circles. Maybe I'll want to wiggle the lines, maybe I'll draw a breast and an eye. I work from the subconscious, like music. It has to do something to me. I couldn't write a piece of music that doesn't make me tap my foot or make me feel something inside. Once the form is there, it's like an arrangement with openings for solos. It's a matter of balance. You can't have too much black. Like you can't have too much saxophone. Supposing there's a composition and the saxophone player can't get the style. You have to get another guy to fit in there. Like another color. Don't force it."

Miles went to Juilliard at the same time as Larry Rivers, one of our most respected and successful painters, who was a professional saxophone player and who still plays regularly. Larry and I used to play in a band together. I asked him about Miles's paintings.

"I haven't seen enough of them to be a good judge," he said. "But I keep wondering what I would think of the paintings if I didn't know who painted them. They're certainly not bad, they're not ugly. I just have trouble relating to them. When I hear Miles's records, I see him. I don't see him in his paintings. This may be a fault or a virtue. But I wonder if I'm only looking at them because they're by Miles."

Miles had problems moving from an improvised idiom to one where mistakes can be corrected. He compared it to acting: "If you're not careful you can lose it, lose the feel. I was doing a television commercial and had to say, 'The hottest ticket in town is ice-cold.' That's all I had to say. I said it over and over—ten, twenty times. And I lost it. That can happen when you keep redrafting something. You lose it."

The "Mike" mentioned above was Michael Elam, a young painter with a degree from New York University who was now traveling with Miles as general assistant and unofficial curator of his growing art collection. Miles had been asking Elam for details and confirmation about art history and technique throughout the interview:

"On the road, if it turns out I'm not going to get my price or there's some other problem with the gig, rather than argue with the promoter, Michael and I go to see what the young artists in town are up to. We bought some beautiful paintings from a Moroccan in Tours, in France. I think his name was Jamal. I like Europe. The music sounds better in Europe. I say, 'Michael, we'll spend $5,000. Let's go out and buy some paintings.'"

It may be that musicians start to paint because there is something about music that no longer satisfies them. Stylistic curiosity might very well wane after leading the way through bebop, modality, rock, and funk. Maybe you want peace and quiet for a change. Or you just want to look in a totally new place.

"It doesn't have anything to do with any of that," Miles said. "There's always music in my head. I hear music walking down the street. I hear it talking to you, now. Look, some of these people paint flowers and desks. They copy things. I can't copy. When I try it always ends up being something else.

"And once I start painting, I can't stop. I have to make myself stop a week before a concert or I'll never pick up the trumpet and practice. When I don't paint, I get nervous. But music and painting both turn me on. Why should I have to choose?"

MILES THE MOVIE STAR—*DINGO*

Interviewer: Mike Zwerin
International Herald Tribune, August 5, 1998

The third incarnation of Miles Davis began and ended with *Dingo*, his first and last starring role in a feature film.

The airplane carrying Billy Cross / Miles is grounded in the Australian out-back. The entire population, about seventy, of a mining camp 800 kilometers from Perth comes out to look at the trans-continental jet being repaired. To kill time, Cross takes out his trumpet and the band plays for the people. Ten-year-old John Anderson is transfixed by the music and the musicians. As they board, he runs to them. Cross, who lives in Paris, says to look him up if he ever gets there.

Fast cut to last week. In Paris to shoot *Dingo*, Miles Davis was lounging in a suite fit for an African king in the Concorde Lafayette Hotel. A hostess escorts you up to the VIP floor to open the elevator door with an electronic keycard. You wonder if you're locked out or he's locked in.

The royal hermit—a.k.a. "The Prince of Silence"—took his castle with him when he traveled. Custom-made clothes, bags from designer shops, and sound and image-reproducing devices were strewn about. Home was wherever he checked in. The Eiffel Tower was far below through the window, behind a gang-ster film with strings on a video monitor.

But first. Miles the musician. He has drummer problems: "Drummers are my pet peeve, maybe I'm hard on them. You always have to tell them what to play, what not to play. If a drummer has fifteen drums, he wants to bang on every one of them. Some drummers drop the tempo just so they can squeeze in their favorite fills. I might have my son play drums with me."

Rumor had it his son is reluctant. According to Miles's autobiography, their relationship was something less than ideal.

Miles the painter designed a logo for Hennessy cognac ("They're sponsor-ing a lot of jazz this year"). He was making big black, white, pink, and brown collages with pieces of copper, rusty nails, driftwood, and bamboo. Priced at

$70,000; "you can hang them if you have a house in the Hamptons." Further description (that hoarse whisper) was drowned out by the video. Following with something that sounded like "you following me?" filtered through.

He objected to the cliché roles offered black film actors. Pimps, for example. Which did not stop him from playing one in an episode of *Miami Vice*. It was hard to imagine him animated—he didn't have a band called "The Birth of the Cool" for nothing. He talked about Billy Cross:

"Twenty years pass and this kid comes to Paris. He plays trumpet now. He's been practicing every day. He's married with two kids. He wants to find out if he's good enough. I say, 'Don't ask me, you've got to find out that stuff yourself.' So I take him down to this club [filmed in the New Morning], tell the guy to let him sit in. I don't play trumpet anymore, I had a stroke."

An unbuttoned shirt hung to his hips. He was skin and bones. Dexter Gordon nicknamed him Wisp after a journalist described him as a "wispy trumpet player." There were scars. There had been accidents and operations. He slouched more than sitting, moved infrequently and with apparent difficulty. His face was younger than his body, thanks in part to his hair weave, although it appeared to be growing a pompadour. His skin was luminescent, like a photograph printed on metallic paper. Periodic burps ("pardon me") were tics more than bad manners. He said he did not remember his age.

"Am I sixty-four or sixty-five, Michael?" he asked Michael Elam, his aide-de-camp.

"You're sixty-four, Miles."

He said he got "shaky" in his $4-million house in California. (Whoa now. Check the tape. That's it; $4 million.) He just bought a new apartment on 57th Street.

"You like living in Manhattan? What about all the greed?"

"Where? Brooklyn?"

"Manhattan."

"What greed? It's always been like that. I don't know, really. I don't go out that much."

That night, the crew for the movie *Dingo* was dining in their canteen tent on the sidewalk near Metro St-Paul before shooting. The mixture of Australians and Frenchmen reflected the nature of the co-production. Director Rolf de Heer's last film was a "science fiction mystery thriller" called *Incident at Ravensgate*.

He described this one as a "human drama about the fulfillment of dreams and the avoidance of regret." Screenwriter Mark Rosenberg says he was inspired by the Guy de Maupassant story "Regret."

The young boy in the outback grows up to be a trapper of dingoes, wild dogs that kill sheep. Nicknamed Dingo, he plays trumpet with a country-and-western bush band called Dingo and the Dusters. He has a recurring dream in which Billy Cross keeps saying "come look me up in Paris." But he's stuck out there. Until a series of events forces him to make a decision to go.

Played by Colin Friels, Dingo tracks Billy Cross down. Neither bitter nor an addict, a gentleman, Cross is successful making electronic music. After Dingo shows up, he begins to play the trumpet again. Because of Michel Legrand, with whom he collaborated on the soundtrack, Miles plays over loose, walking 4/4 time again. Nice to hear.

De Heer goes to great lengths to make it clear that this is no jazz film, he is no aficionado: "It's not a genre film. Each one of us at some time in our lives wished we would have done something, or have had a dream we haven't executed. We say, 'I wonder what would have happened if I'd done that instead of this.' Do we regret not having done it? Dingo is lucky, he gets a chance to follow his instinct before it's too late."

Yaphet Koto was the first choice for the role. Then de Heer was on the point of signing Sammy Davis Jr. before the entertainer grew terminally ill. Until a friend came up with the idea, Miles Davis had never occurred to him. He was only vaguely familiar with his music. All he knew was his reputation, "which wasn't good." But a number of people were "keen on Miles, so I met him and decided to take the risk because I saw that if we could pull it off he'd burn the place up.

"He's a natural actor. Every day he gets better, he's faster, he learns more. He's easy to work with, he's intelligent and instinctive at the same time. He's on time, cooperative, and knows his lines. Nobody around here has ever seen that 'other' Miles, the 'nasty' Miles with the bad reputation."

He told his musicians: "Don't play what's there," he said. "Play what's not there." As a painter, he was beginning to learn that the work is often really finished before it is "finished."

Space plays a role in his acting too. De Heer describes him: "His sense of timing is phenomenal. You start to feed him his following line because he seems to have forgotten it. But then he comes out with it at just the right time and you're left with a mouthful of words you don't need."

P.S. The above was rewritten almost a decade later. Obviously, the movie did not live up to de Heer's blurbs. *Dingo* turned out to be something like one of the one hundred best completely unknown movies ever made. It's flawed, but not that bad, really. And it's a treat to look at Miles in color in Paris on the big screen.

ACKNOWLEDGMENTS

The bulk of these interviews were acquired from resourceful Miles Davis collectors, many of whom collect simply out of passion for the man and his music. They preserve for historians, biographers, critics, and Miles appreciators interviews and profiles that otherwise would be difficult to locate in their first incarnations in the transient pages of magazines, many now defunct with back issues rarer than one might suppose for publications that, in their heyday, enjoyed respectable circulations. Our thanks in this regard to Paul Bowe, Peter Losin (whose fantastic Web site we used as a resource over and over again), Terry Saundry, Rodman Marymor, Larry Crawford, James A. Chiarelli, Jan Lohmann, Amir Rahim, John Cottrell, and Enrico Merlin. We also thank for their assistance Da Capo Press, particularly Ben Schafer and Jonathan Crowe, and Robert L. Doerschuk.

For permissions granted to reprint interviews or publish original material, we thank: Chris Albertson; the Estate of Al Aronowitz (Al's children, Brett, Joel, and Myles); David Breskin (especially for his careful perusal of his piece and for correcting errors and omissions); Mary Bringle for agreeing to preserve her evening with Miles; Stephen Davis; Lorraine Feather (a gifted performer in her own right); Nat Hentoff; *Keyboard* magazine (and the ever-gracious Debbie Greenberg); Nick Kent; *Newsweek* (and Cynthia McKean); *The New York Times*; the Estate of Eric Nisenson and its executor, his sister-in-law Sally; KWMU-FM Radio; John Palcewski; Ben Sidran; Peter Watrous; Mike Zwerin; and all those whom we were unable to locate. *Miles on Miles* could never have existed without you.

For all those at Lawrence Hill Books, including Curt Matthews and everyone in the editorial production (with particular gratitude to Lisa Reardon), publicity, marketing, and sales departments, we appreciate your dedication to realizing this project. We must take a moment to acknowledge the astuteness, passion, constructive involvement, and overall excellence of Yuval Taylor, Senior Editor. Lawrence Hill is fortunate to employ Yuval; we trust his value will always be recognized and rewarded.

Editor Michael Dorr would also like to express his recognition of and thanks to Gerald Alper, Marie Baker, Judene Bennett, Marilyn Bloch, Sr. Mary Canice, Peter Connolly, Rosemary Dorr, the late Bea Friedland, Roberta Kramer, Sandra Claro Lavin, Jim Luttrel, Andrew Maishman, Richard Mason, Sr. Mary Matthews, Solange Mayers, Tom McManus, Howard Meyer, Jennifer Meyerson, the late Charles Neider, Trish (the "T" of N&Ts), the late David G. Walley, and Joanna Woolfolk. Particular acknowledgment must be paid to Sean Lavin, a brother and friend who has been there for me in all the right ways at all the right times for all the right reasons; the landscape would be exceedingly dull without him. And of course, my co-editor, the eclectic and multitalented Paul Maher Jr.—it's been a pleasure and privilege to work with him in a variety of capacities over the years.

PERMISSIONS

The editors gratefully acknowledge everyone who gave permission for material to appear in this book. They have made every reasonable effort to contact copyright holders. If an error or omission has been made, it can be brought to their attention at either paul_maherjr@yahoo.com or mkdorr95@cs.com.

"An Afternoon with Miles Davis," copyright ©1958, reprinted by permission of Nat Hentoff.

"*The* Miles Davis: A Semi-Affectionate Reminiscence," copyright © 1969, reprinted by permission of John Palcewski.

"Miles of Music," copyright © 1970, reprinted by permission of *Newsweek*.

"A National Treasure," copyright © 1970, 1996, reprinted by permission of the Estate of Al Aronowitz.

"Faded Blue Flowers," copyright © 1970, 1996, reprinted by permission of the Estate of Al Aronowitz.

"The Unmasking of Miles Davis," copyright © 1971, reprinted by permission of Chris Albertson.

"Miles," from *From Satchmo to Miles*, copyright © 1972, reprinted by permission of Lorraine Feather, executor of the Estate of Leonard Feather.

"My Ego Only Needs a Good Rhythm Section," copyright ©1973, reprinted by permission of Stephen Davis.

"At the Movies with Miles," copyright © 2008, printed by permission of Mary Bringle.

"Hangin' Out with Daffy Davis," preface from *'Round About Midnight*, copyright © 1996, reprinted by the Estate of Eric Nisenson.

"I Just Pick Up My Horn and Play," copyright © 1981, reprinted by permission of the *New York Times*.

"Searching for Miles: Theme and Variations on the Life of a Trumpeter," copyright © 1983, reprinted by permission of David Breskin.

"Miles Davis," from *Talking Jazz: An Oral History*, copyright © 1986, reprinted by permission of Ben Sidran.

"Lightening Up with the Prince of Darkness," from *The Dark Stuff*, copyright © 1986, 1994, reprinted by permission of Nick Kent.

"Miles Davis: The Picasso of Invisible Art," copyright © 1987, reprinted by permission of *Keyboard* Magazine.

"Miles Davis: Rebel Without a Pause," copyright © 1989, reprinted by permission of Peter Watrous.

"The Prince of Silence," copyright © 1998, reprinted by permission of Mike Zwerin.

"Miles the Painter: Colorful Flowing Lines," copyright © 1998, reprinted by permission of Mike Zwerin.

"Miles the Movie Star—*Dingo*," copyright © 1998, reprinted by permission of Mike Zwerin.

INDEX